NOT KNOWING
KNOWING
NOT KNOWING

Shmuel Erlich

NOT KNOWING
KNOWING
NOT KNOWING

Festschrift
celebrating the life and work of Shmuel Erlich

Edited by

Mira Erlich-Ginor

IPBOOKS.net
International Psychoanalytic Books

International Psychoanalytic Books (IPBooks),
30-27 33rd Street, #3R
Astoria, NY 11102
Online at: www.IPBooks.net

Interior book design by Maureen Cutajar, gopublished.com

ISBN: 978-0-9985323-2-5

Table of Contents

About the Editor and Contributors

Marilia Aisenstein is a Training Analyst of the Hellenic Psychoanalytical Society and the Paris Psychoanalytical Society. She has been president of the Paris Society and of the Paris Psychosomatic Institute, member of the editorial board of the "Revue Française de Psychanalyse", co-founder and editor of the" Revue Française de Psychosomatique." She has been chair of the IPA's International New Groups; the European representative to the IPA's Executive Committee. Presently she works in private practice and gives seminars in both the Hellenic and the Paris Societies and is the President of the Executive Board of the Paris Society's Psychoanalytical Clinic. She wrote chapters and books on psychosomatics and hypochondria and numerous (130) papers in French and International reviews. She is the recipient of the Maurice Bouvet prize in 1992.

Noga Badanes is a training analyst and faculty of the Israel Psychoanalytic Society. She works in private practice as a psychoanalyst. She has taught several clinical and theoretical seminars, both at the Institute of Israel Psychanalytic Society and Psychotherapy Programs at Tel-Aviv university. Was a member of the executive committee, admission committe and scientific committee. Teaches Freud, psychosexuality, and oedipus.

Hermann Beland studied Theology (protestant); Psychoanalyst (DPV, IPA, DGPT) in private praxis in Berlin; supervisor and training analyst German Psychoanalytic Association (DPV); leading positions DPV from 1984-92. Studies in prejudices; anti-Semitism; the role of projections in destructive outbreaks and wars; and in collective mourning. Co-organizer of group-conferences for national and international groups in conflicts; former member PCCA. Collected papers: *Die Angst vor Denken und Tun* (2008); *Unaushaltbarkeit* (2011).

Stefano Bolognini, psychiatrist and training analyst, has been national scientific secretary and then president of the Italian Psychoanalytic Society; member of the European Editorial Board of the IJP from 2002 to 2012; he has been IPA Board Representative and is currently the president of the International Psychoanalytical Association. Author of more than 200 psychoanalytic papers published in national and international journals. Published books: "Like Wind, like Wave", Other Press, New York, 2007; "*Il sogno 100 anni dopo*" (The Dream 100 Years after, Bollati Boringhieri, Turin 2000); "Psychoanalytic Empathy", Free Associations, London 2004 (also in Italian, Spanish, French, German and Brazilian-Portuguese editions); "Secret Passages. Theory and Technique of the Interpsychic Relationship", New Library Routledge, London 2010, published also in German, Italian, Spanish, Brazilian-Portuguese and Iranian-Farsi editions);"*Lo Zen e l'arte di non sapere cosa dire*" (Zen and the Art not to know what to say), Bollati Boringhieri, Turin, 2011.

Joshua Durban is a training and supervising child and adult psychoanalyst and faculty at the Israeli Psychoanalytic Society and Institute, Jerusalem. On the faculty of the Sackler School of Medicine, Tel-Aviv University, The Psychotherapy Program, the Post-Graduate Kleinian Studies and Early Mental States studies. Scientific Co-editor, with Merav Roth of the Hebrew edition of the collected works of Melanie Klein. Worked as an advisor to the Tel-Hashomer general hospital management in a project aimed at improving the physicians' well being and emotional contact with their patients. Initiated the first psychoanalytically informed course "On breaking bad news" at the Sackler School of Medicine, dealing with terminally ill patients and their families. Member of the IPA inter-committee for the prevention of child abuse. Works in private practice in Tel-Aviv with children, adolescents and adults and specializes in the psychoanalysis of ASD and psychotic children and adults.

Claudio L. Eizerik is Professor of Psychiatry (retired) at the Federal University of Rio Grande do Sul, Brazil. He is also Training and Supervising Analyst, Porto Alegre Psychoanalytic Society, former President of FEPAL and the IPA. He is an MD and PhD in Medicine, and is member of the faculty of the PhD Program in Psychiatry at the same university. He is the author of many papers, chapters and book, on the analytic training, the analytic practice, mainly on countertransference and the analytic field, the basis and practice of psychoanalytic psychotherapy, the process of ageing and the relations of psychoanalysis and culture. He was awarded the Sigourney award in 2011.

Shmuel Erlich is past-President of the Israel Psychoanalytic Society; Training and Supervising Analyst and Faculty member of the Israel Psychoanalytic Institute; Sigmund Freud Professor of Psychoanalysis (Emeritus) and former Director of the Freud Center at The Hebrew University of Jerusalem. Was for four terms European Regional Representative on the IPA Board. As Chair of the IPA Education Committee he researched and described the Three Models of psychoanalytic training, which are now the basis for evaluating psychoanalytic training. He has published on psychoanalytic and applied subjects, including: adolescent development and treatment; experiential factors influencing object relations; and psychoanalytic-systemic studies of group, organizational and social processes. Books: with Mira Erlich-Ginor and Hermann Beland: *Fed with Tears Poisoned with Milk*, the Nazareth Group Relations Conferences Germans and Israelis, the Past in the Present, Psychozial Verlag 2009; and The Couch in the Market Place, Psychoanalysis and Social Reality, Karnac2013.

Mira Erlich-Ginor is a training and supervising analyst in the Israel Psychoanalytic Society. She is engaged in differnt aspects of psychoanalytic education for almost two decades, in her society, in the EPF and IPA, she recieved the Psychoanalytic Education Today, IPA Award 2011. Mira is involved in Group Relations work – the application of psychoanalytic understanding to group, organizational and societal issues. Is a founding member and Past Chairperson OFEK, Israel. Founding member and secretary, PCCA: Partnership in Confronting Collective Atrocities She has initiated and participated in the "Nazareth Project": working with transgenerational transition of trauma in Israelis and Germans, She has written mainly on these two topics. She is Co-author with Shmuel Elich and Hermann Beland *Fed with Tears Poisoned with Milk*, the Nazareth Group Relations Conferences Germans and Israelis, the Past in the Present, Psychozial Verlag 2009. Mira is a Euro representative to the IPA Board.

Ludger M. Hermanns, Psychoanalyst and Group Analyst in private practice in Berlin. Member IPA/DPV. Specialist for Psychosomatic Medicine and Psychotherapy. Lecturer at *Karl Abraham Institute Berlin since 30 years.* 1983-2011 Psychosomatic Consultant in two Berlin hospitals. 1990 Foundation Member, now President of the *Archives for the History of Psychoanalysis.* Honorary Archivist of *DPV (German Psychoanalytic Association)* and of *Berlin Psychoanalytic Institute.* Since 2016 chair of *History Committee of IPA.* Co-editor of *Luzifer-Amor. Journal for the History of Psychoanalysis.* Editor/Co-editor of 20 books on the history of psychoanalysis, psychotherapy and psychosomatic medicine and author of 50 scientific articles: Including a 11 vol. series *Psychoanalyse in Selbstdarstellungen 1992-2017.* (Autobiographies of 62 internationally known psychoanalysts with German/ Austrian/Hungarian roots). Editions of the selected works of Ernst Simmel and Erich Simenauer. Latest articles about Jewish emigrants from Germany Max Levy-Suhl, Margarete Miriam Brandt and Salomea Kempner (2016).

Howard B. Levine, is a member of the Psychoanalytic Institute of New England, East (PINE), the Contemporary Freudian Society and the Newport (California) Psychoanalytic Institute. He is a former member of the Board of Directors of the IPA, on the editorial Board of the IJP and Psychoanalytic Inquiry and in private practice in Brookline, Massachusetts.

Irene Melnick Former President of the Israeli Psychoanalytic Society, and of the Training committee of IPS. Current Chair of the Scientific Committee of IPS. MA in Clinical Psychology at the Hebrew University of Jerusalem. Founder member of the Israeli Forum for Relational Psychoanalysis and Psychotherapy. Member of the IARPP. Training Analyst, works in private practice with new immigrants, Holocaust survivors, children of survivors, and victims of terror attacks. Teacher and group supervisor at the IPS

Marganit Ofer is a clinical psychologist and training psychoanalyst at the Israel Psychoanalytic Society. She teaches and supervises at the Center for Psychoanalytically Oriented Psychotherapy Studies (H.a.l.f.a.b.a.) and the Unit for Children at Risk devoted to the treatment of autistic children. Co-editor, with Robby Schonberger, of *The Meltzer Reader* (Hebrew). Was member of the scientific committee, member of education committee, chair of training in child analysis.

Merav Roth, PhD, is a clinical psychologist and a Training psychoanalyst at the Israeli Psychoanalytic Society. Chair of the Post-graduate Kleinian Studies and Chair of the Interdisciplinary Doctoral Program in Psychoanalysis – at the Psychotherapy Program, Sackler School of Medicine, Tel-Aviv University. Co-Editor – with Joshua Durban – of Melanie Klein – Selected writings Vol. B, Tel-Aviv: Book-Worm, 2013. Author of Reading the reader – a psychoanalytic perspective on reading literature, Jerusalem: Carmel, 2017.

Edward R. Shapiro, M.D. is the Former Medical Director/CEO of the Austen Riggs Center in Stockbridge, MA. A psychiatrist, psychoanalyst, family researcher, and organizational consultant, he is Clinical Professor of Psychiatry at Yale Child Study Center. Co-author (with A. Wesley Carr, Ph.D.) of *Lost in Familiar Places: Creating New Connections between the Individual and Society* (Yale, 1991), Dr. Shapiro is the editor of *The Inner World in the Outer World* (Yale, 1997). He has published over fifty articles and book chapters on human development, organizational and family functioning, and personality disorders. A Distinguished Life Fellow of the American Psychiatric Association, he is a Fellow of the A.K. Rice Institute and the American College of Psychoanalysis. He is on the Boards of the Center for Groups and Social Systems and the International Dialogue

Initiative, and on the Advisory Board of Partners Confronting Collective Atrocities.

Robby Schonberger is a clinical psychologist, training analyst and teacher in the psychoanalytic institute, Jerusalem. He also teaches in several psychotherapeutic programs in the Tel-Aviv district. He is the translator of Hanna Segal's book 'Klein', and scientific editor of the translations into Hebrew of books by John Steiner (in print), W.R. Bion (in print), and Donald Meltzer (in collaboration with Mrs. Marganit Ofer). He is also a poet and author of several poetry books.

Dorothee C. von Tippelskirch-Eissing, Dr. phil., Dipl. Psych., has studied theology, Jewish studies and psychology. She is working as a psychoanalyst in private practice in Berlin (Germany). She has been the Chairperson of the Karl-Abraham-Institute, Berlin Psychoanalytic Institute (BPI) and a Board member of the German Psychoanalytic Association (DPV). She is a Member of the International Psychoanalytic Association (IPA). Since 2015 she is the Chairperson of Partners in Confronting Collective Atrocities (PCCA).

Joseph Triest, PhD, Clinical psychologist and Supervisor, Training Analyst (IPS) and organizational consultant. President of the Israel Psychoanalytic Society. Teaches and supervises at the Israel Psychoanalytic Institute. Lecturer at Tel-Aviv University. Co-owner of the 'Triest-Sarig' Psychotherapy clinic. Member of OFEK, the Israel Association for the Study of Group and Organizational Processes; Co-Director and Faculty member in the Program in Organizational Consultation and Development: a Psychoanalytic-Systemic Approach (P.O.C.D).

Not to Know? To know? The Double Spiral

> *"In order to arrive at what you do not know*
> *You must go by a way which is the way of ignorance"*
> —T.S. Eliot (East Coker III, Four Quartets)

A "Festschrift" is an act of celebration, an act of love. The book is a party ("Fest"), contributions are gifts. Gifts to Shmuel Erlich on his 80th birthday, gifts to the professional community.

The book was planned both as a present and as an opportunity for the contributors to express friendship, gratitude and appreciation to a colleague, a teacher, a mentor and a leader in the psychoanalytic community. It became a bouquet of psychoanalytic flowers. The book was produced as a surprise, and I am grateful to all the contributors who kept the secret for many months.

For me personally, it is a way to celebrate years of partnership in creation: the creation of a family, of psychoanalytic thinking, of organizational building and of applying psychoanalytic learning to societal issues. From our work together in an adolescent unit in Eitanim Mental Hospital in the hills of Jerusalem, through bringing Group Relations methodology to Israel by establishing OFEK (Organization, Person, Group) as an Israeli organization, and later PCCA (Partners in Confronting Collective Atrocities) as an international organization, initiating and working for 25 years on the "German Israeli Project, the Past in the Present", and numerous less known initiatives, (many of these endeavors developed in partnership with engaged others).

On the making of the book

The book, probably every book that comes into being, is a small miracle. This was the miracle of synergy, of "working together" (*synergos*, συνεργός), through which the whole becomes greater than the sum of its parts.

The invitation to the contributors asked them to: "Write what interests you, what you are passionate about; if it touches on Shmuel's work – great; if not – good enough". This is what the 16 contributors did. They wrote for the book, or dedicated to it papers that they are passionate about. What emerged is a multi- dimensional image of Shmuel Erlich's work: his psychoanalytic passions are reflected in the various contributions, providing a panoramic view of psychoanalysis. This became clearer when the chapters that came in as isolated contributions converged into the categories that form the four sections of the book:

I. Shmuel Erlich, the private and public man.

II. Mainly Theory "*Among other qualities, Shmuel is a true Freudian, a reader who believes in metapsychology, a theory lover*", Marilia Aisenstein (Chapter 4).

III. From Theory to Practice Reflects Shmuel Erlich's many years in working with severely disturbed, psychotic patients in hospitals, and later in private practice. "*Shmuel Erlich is first and foremost a master clinician*", Edward Shapiro (Chapter 10).

IV. Psychoanalysis and Social Reality [Shmuel is a] "*....courageous man, proven in [his] founding and interpreting the German and Israeli group conferences on the Past in the Present, helping Germans to begin to mourn their inheritance of the Holocaust*". Hermann Beland (Chapter 3).

On the contributors

The book brings together some of Shmuel Erlich's past supervisees at the Israel Psychoanalytic Society and colleagues who worked with him in the psychoanalytic and Group Relations worlds. Ed Shapiro asked me a smilingly simple question: "Who are the contributors as a group, what do they represent?" Contemplating this question, it became clear to me that this is a group of "analysts on the boundary," a special position from which it is possible to look inside and outside, to push boundaries of familiar psychoanalysis with courage and originality. Most of the contributors inhabit more than one world and are comfortable moving between these worlds. They are distinguished by being leaders in their thinking and in their doing. From this perspective these are not just Shmuel Erlich's friends and supervisees, but representatives of what is so important to him: **to think and work from a position that is always both inside and outside.**

Shmuel Erlich has taught and supervised psychoanalysis for more than 30 years. The past supervisees who contributed to this book exemplify the ways in which good supervision offers both expertise and unique discovery.

> *"He was my supervisor in my psychoanalytic training, and although I have developed a somewhat different approach to clinical psychoanalysis throughout the years, he has been very influential in my thinking. I will always be grateful to him for giving me the fundamentals of psychoanalytic thinking together with the freedom to be myself"*. Irene Melnick (Chapter 12).

On the title:
Not Knowing – Knowing – Not Knowing

Imagine a double spiral, as in the structure of a DNA molecule. One spiral is 'Not Knowing,' the other is 'Knowing.' They co-exist and co-depend on one another so that one makes sense only in combination with the other (*"In order to arrive at what you do not know, You must go by a way which is the way of ignorance"* T.S.E).

This is my visualization of the oscillations between the two stances: Not Knowing – Knowing – Not Knowing: two modes of relating – to external reality (ontology) and to internal reality (epistemology) – forever present, though at a given moment either one can be in the foreground with the other in the background. The movement always starts from Not Knowing ... and returns there.

I have chosen this title for a book dedicated to Shmuel Erlich because the movement between not knowing and knowing is one of his major character-istics. Shmuel assumes that all is transient and at most, partly known. He sees the quest for 'knowing' as an illusion, and 'not knowing' not as a lack but as an important existential stance. It is Shmuel's Idiom – in the sense that it touches and reflects his most inner core. Recognizing this open space has helped him to become an appreciated teacher and mentor.

This title invaded my mind during a state of "reverie" in the middle of Shavasana – the moments of relaxation at the end of a Yoga practice. I know these moments as pregnant with untamed associations and I appreciate their creativity. The next day, retreating to critical thinking, my hesitations began: Is this the right title, can I come up with a "better", "cleverer", "truer" one? As I was sitting at my computer, ruminating, an email arrived that led to the feeling: "Yes, this is so right!" Noga Badanes sent her contribution (Chapter 14) that starts with the following quota-tion by S. Erlich: *"But now, my unknowing is perceived as valuable, as a guarantee for authenticity and subjective truthfulness. This unknowing protects me from futile repetitiveness that does not ask itself what it is attempting to say in each moment and each word... In my internal dia-logue with my own knowing and unknowing, I have touched my most internal, personal boundaries. In fact, I have touched the other inside me".* S. Erlich, 2001.

The idea of the double spiral resonates with Erlich's continuous re-search of the two modes of Being and Doing.

Overview of the book

The book as a whole gives a kaleidoscopic view both of psychoanalysis and of Shmuel Erlich's specific interests, keeping the tension between

Not Knowing – Knowing, most of the time implicit. The contributions present a breathtaking range of theoretical and clinical topics, tackling known concepts in a new light, pushing the familiar to new boundaries and introducing creative new ideas and applications of psychoanalytic understandings. A new light on known concepts is shed in Beland's chapter by his conclusion that the courage of the analyst is best understood as the toleration of separation anxiety; in Levine's suggestion that understanding psychosomatics from the perspective of unrepresented states will add to the understanding and treatment of these conditions; in Aisentsein's view of Primary Erotogenic Masochism as what helps us to "wait and hope, love and live", in Shapiro's necessity of the 'Third" when a dyad is in trouble; in Eizirik's take on psychoanalysis and culture and in Hermanns' asking about the choices of deported German analysts post WWII.

Pushing the familiar to new boundaries is exemplified in the chapters of Bolognini and Badanes, in which they give examples of work with countertransference in treating traumatized patients, and of Melnick's on the need of the analyst to own her dissociative states of mind.

There are suggestions of new concepts: on the development of a "Death Object" and its manifestations in terminally ill children and psychotic adolescents (Durban); the introduction of a new subject: the "iGroup" – a hybrid subject combining self and group (Triest); "Pervertization of Discourse" conceived of as a special state of mind that deceives and distorts meaning (Schonberger); the transformative power of reading literature through the development of an internal capacity to witness one's own trauma (Roth); and the notion of a "Multi-two-dimensional" organization as a way to understand the autistic experience (Ofer).

A new frontier in the application of psychoanalytic understanding to social phenomena is the "Nazareth Project", a project that brought together German and Israeli psychoanalysts to work on the residues of the Holocaust. The last two chapters (Erlich-Ginor, von Tippelskirch-Eissing) relate to this moving project.

The Book, chapter by chapter

Part I. Shmuel Erlich, by him – his autobiography, and about his work at the IPA

Chapter One is Shmuel Erlich's autobiography: *Migration and Homecoming, A Psychoanalytic Autobiography.*

Ludger Hermanns recently invited its contribution for the eleventh book of his remarkable: "Psychoanalyse in Selbstdarstellungen" ("Self-Portraits in Psychoanalysis"), published in April 2017 (Brandes & Apsel, Frankfurt am Main). The Self Portraits series brings together analysts who stayed during and after WWII in Germany, Austria and Switzerland with analysts who were forced to emigrate because they were Jewish. Shmuel, as a toddler, was forced to leave Germany.

Shmuel takes the reader through his becoming a person and an analyst in a candid and moving way. The biography starts with the history of his family in Poland and Germany; it takes us with him to the circumstances of escaping as a baby in December 1938 from Frankfurt am Main, a short while before it was too late. It invites us to experience life in Palestine – Eretz Israel, in its early, difficult years, before it became the State of Israel. These were formative years for the child and adolescent. The family left the harsh "promised land" for America – the "land of opportunities", providing Shmuel with opportunities to become a mature person and a professional. Later he returned to Israel to implement all he had learned as a psychologist and analyst; writing, developing his original ideas, and building and developing institutions in Israel and internationally.

Chapter Two, by Cláudio Laks Eizirik, *Shmuel Erlich and his many contributions to analytic training.*

C. Eizirik describes his meetings over the years with Shmuel and stresses Shmuel's outstanding contributions to the issue of analytic training at the IPA. He adds: "…But there are also some members, sometimes few, sometimes not so few, who have the feeling of US rather than the feeling of I, or the feeling of US AGAINST THEM, and these are the ones that allow each group to behave as a community or a work group. Shmuel was always one of this kind".

Part II. Mainly theory

Chapter Three, Hermann Beland, *The Courage of the Analyst.*

H. Beland starts with Freud's remark on dream distortion, which seems very important for any psychoanalytical philosophy of science: "*I think what enabled me to discover the cause of dream distortion was my moral courage*". The relationship of this remark to Plato's Laches, Spinoza's Ethics, Kant's fortitudo moralis, and Tillich's courage to be, is stressed. Following Bion, the analysis of the analyst's courage ends with the conclusion that *the courage of the analyst is identical to his toleration of separation anxiety.*

Chapter Four, Marilia Aisenstein, *Reflections on "Primary Erotogenic Masochism"*

M. Aisenstein argues that even if ignored or viewed in a negative way, "primary erotogenic masochism", described by Freud in 1924, is crucial and a "guardian of life". Masochism poses a question to psychoanalytic theory: if pleasure and displeasure can merge and coincide, then what becomes of the pleasure principle? She asks: Why should we not kill ourselves when our first disappointment strikes? Why do we love to suffer from love? Why? Because the intricacy of the two antagonistic drives is achieved on the basis and in function of a primary, erotogenic masochism, upon which the other forms of masochism—feminine, moral, and secondary—are propped up. She concludes that primary erotogenic masochism is what helps us to learn to wait and to hope. We need it to love and to live.

Chapter Five, Howard B. Levine, *Psychosomatics and Unrepresented States.*

For many American analysts, says Levine, the application of psychoanalytic thinking to the understanding and treatment of somatic conditions has been problematic and disappointing. For these conditions, the clinical assumptions of the archeological model of psychoanalysis that work so well for neurosis do not seem to suffice. In this chapter H. Levine reviews and restates the problem of psychosomatics from the perspective of unrepresented states and the transformational model of psychoanalysis, discussing the complexities of etiology, contemporary views of construction, myth making and *après coup* (*Nachträglichkeit*) and concludes with a brief clinical example.

Chapter Six, Joshua Durban, *Facing the Death-Object: Unconscious Phantasies of Relationships with Death.*

J. Durban describes the way death is perceived, encoded and represented in unconscious phantasy in both normal and pathological development . Durban claims that within the infant's psyche, a "Death-object" is gradually established, which is assembled from and composed of "death-equivalents".

These "death-equivalents" are proto-physiological and mental experiences that come as close to death as possible within life and thus are perceived, in unconscious phantasy, as linked with and projected into an object. The place and role of the Death-object is examined within the various experiences of deadness and murderousness, in terminally ill children and in adolescent psychosis. Clinical material from analysis with children demonstrates the point.

Chapter Seven, R. Schonberger, *Depleting Language and the Pervertization of Discourse – A Psychoanalytic Observation.*

In this chapter Schonberger tackles two main issues, in the light of several Bionian ideas: he discusses the phenomenon of depletion of words and of language in general and touches the kind of language that Bionian psychoanalysis strives to attain. In addition, Schonberger puts forward certain thoughts about what he calls: the "pervertization of discourse" a special state of mind, and a kind of action, deceiving and distorting meaning.

Chapter Eight, Joseph Triest, *Thoughts about a New Subject of Psychoanalysis: The 'iGroup'.*

J. Triest paints a portrait of a new contemporary subject that he has termed the "iGroup". It is a hybrid subject, a kind of "Centaur", half individual, half group, that owes its existence to the dialectic movement of 'unification and uniqueness'. This way of reflection creates the 'group-as-a-whole' as a 'subject-in-itself' – (a 'group third') – while simultaneously presenting the individual as a 'diffused subject' – a subject who inhabits parallel universes with permeable boundaries, which blurs the distinction between inner world and external reality, fantasy and fact, truth and lie – even the distinction between subject and object. Several theoretical and sociopolitical implications are discussed.

Chapter Nine, Merav Roth, *Literature's Keys "Before the Law" of Trauma.*

M. Roth describes the transformative potential embedded in reading literature and demonstrates a specific curative factor it offers: a development in the internal capacity to witness one's own traumatic personal history and experience. This is demonstrated through Otto Dov Kulka's book: Landscapes of the metropolis of death – a novel bearing Kulka's personal testimony about his experiences as a boy in Auschwitz. Through his self-witnessing journey Roth shows how reading literature supports the integration between two tendencies of the mind – the 'continuous doing' and the 'emergent being', thus promoting the ability to use the reflective, metaphoric internal witness.

Part III. From Theory to Practice

Chapter Ten, Edward R. Shapiro, *Hiding in the Dyad: What is a Manageable Frame?*

Even the best-trained clinicians can lose their way, says Shapiro. A notorious case reviewed here opens for examination the problems of treating severely traumatized and character disordered patients in a dyadic outpatient treatment. In a world where all established norms are up for question, holding a reliable framework for treatment is increasingly difficult. Shapiro asks what are the traps clinicians can get caught up in when they attempt to 'help' a patient? What is the "third" that can help stabilize a dyad in trouble?

Chapter Eleven, Stefano Bolognini, *From Consciousness to Awareness: the Lia's Case.*

Describing and conceptualizing work with a case of a traumatized patient, S. Bolognini explores the relations between the Ego and the Self in revisiting the traumatic area during analysis. Bolognini describes a condition of relative split between the cognitive Ego and the experiential Self, which, he claims, also corresponds to a partial psyche-soma split, where only the body remembers. Bolognini suggests the hypothesis that in order to stay constitutionally and functionally whole, or become so again, the patient requires, first and foremost, the support of an object capable of sharing the sensorial and emotional contents of the raw traumatic experience which the patient carries within him but has not integrated. Before we can attribute a meaning, we must be willing to hear it, to listen to it, to feel it.

Chapter Twelve, Irene Melnick, *Keeping in Mind: The Forgotten Patient.*

Disruptions in the mind of the analyst are frequently dissociated and revealed through enactments in the relationship between himself and the patient. Two vignettes describe these processes around the issue of forgetting the patient. Melnick asserts that these enactments are inevitable. The ability and willingness of the analyst to overcome his anxiety, guilt and shame, and to own his dissociative states of mind, are important for the progress in analytic treatment. The analyst's capacity to formulate his experience, promotes the patient's capacity to give words to his own unformulated experiences that have become dissociated. Once the experiences are being put into words, Melnick suggests, they can become integrated memories.

Chapter Thirteen, Noga Badanes, *On the edge: The psychoanalyst's countertransference experience.*

The mental activity of the analyst is examined. Badanes describes a specific psychological experience in which the analyst feels himself pushed to an unknowing emotional edge that is experienced as temporal psychosis. Badanes proposes that the ability of the analyst to sustain and tolerate this subjective, uncanny experience is perhaps the only way to connect to the unrepresented unconscious of the analysand. The analyst must rely upon his intuition, his capacity to reverie and to stand and bear his chaos and the frustration of not knowing until something takes shape and meaning.

Chapter Fourteen, Marganit Ofer, *Multi-Two Dimensional Thinking and the Absence of Nothing in Autistic Patients.*

M. Ofer discusses the absence of the concept of nothingness in autistic children. She suggests that autistic children exhibit what she calls a "multi-two-dimensional" organization, understanding and experience of the world. This amounts to an accumulation of two-dimensional understandings and experiences, an existence that is devoid of a psychic container. The conceptual model of 'existence without a psychic container' helps us understand experiences that lie beyond the familiar spectrum. Things are not projected into the other but rather regurgitated, shaken off. This understanding offers us a more profound familiarity with the autistic experience. A case demonstrates this conceptualization.

IV. Psychoanalysis and Social Reality

Chapter Fifteen, Cláudio Laks Eizirik, *Psychoanalysis and Culture.*

C.L. Eizirik discusses the relations of psychoanalysis with culture, departing from Freud's contributions, describing more recent insights both from analysts and non analysts (e.g. Zygmund Bauman), and suggests how psychoanalytic ideas can be helpful to understand individual and social human conflicts, and how to face them.

Chapter Sixteen, Ludger M. Hermanns, *The one-way road, an additional piece in the puzzle of German analysts post WWII.*

53 members of the German Psychoanalytical Society (DPG) were forced to leave Nazi Germany after 1933. Nearly all of them were Jews and some were persecuted as socialists and communists. L. Hermanns focuses on the question of why analysts who had to flee Germany did not return after the war. Hermanns continues to ask: Why should they? Why should they voluntarily return to a country that had expelled them,

and persecuted and murdered their relatives? "*One thing is for sure: One never returns, one always just goes away*" (Grinberg & Grinberg, 1990, p. 267). Hermanns elaborates about many of the well-known analysts and their fate.

The Germans Israelis Bind – The Nazareth Conferences

The two last chapters are dedicated to the "Nazareth Conferences". Chapter seventeen gives an overview of the project, its background, history, the conceptual framework of Group Relations, and the different modules of the work. M. Erlich-Ginor goes on to give vignettes of the work. The transformative power of the conferences is discussed.

Chapter eighteen builds on the description of the conferences and goes on to elaborate on the experience of a German participant.

Chapter Seventeen, Mira Erlich-Ginor, *Psychoanalytic Group Work with Transgenerational Residues of Historic Traumatization: The Case of the German-Israeli Conferences.*

Chapter Eighteen, Dorothee C. von Tippelskirch-Eissing, *Being German In a Conference "The Past in the Present".*

End on the way to the beginning: A lot of knowledge is embedded in the various chapters of this book. Testimony to the continuous struggle to decipher the enigma of the human mind, the human situation, the human social reality; a struggle to know that which was previously not known. 'Not knowing' and 'knowing' forever co-exist, equally valuable for our human and our professional existence. Shmuel Erlich is always occupied with questions of Being and Doing, Knowing and Not Knowing and the balance and interplay between them.

"What we call the beginning is often the end
And to make an end is to make a beginning.
The end is where we start from.

We shall not cease from exploration
And the end of all our exploring
Will be to arrive where we started
And know the place for the first time.
Through the unknown, unremembered gate"

T.S. Eliot (Little Gidding V, Four Quartets)

I. Shmuel Erlich
By him; On him

CHAPTER ONE

Migration and Homecoming:
A Psychoanalytic Autobiography[1]

H. Shmuel Erlich

To start, I would like to express my gratitude to Ludger Hermanns, who not only invited me to undertake this writing, but has patiently and consistently pursued me to do it and bring it to completion. It is an honor to join the row of outstanding colleagues he has assembled in these pages.

My personal feeling about this project is mixed, which is reflected in the amount of time it took me to get started. Writing an autobiographical account is a bitter-sweet undertaking: It is a reminder of one's advancing age, with the opportunity and obligation to review one's life before it is too late. At the same time, it is also a challenge that may lead to new insights and integration. I hope that undertaking this task will afford mostly the latter.

The word "migration" came to my mind as I began to write this account. This is certainly no accident: my life can be viewed as falling into several migratory periods that unquestionably proved decisive for all subsequent developments. It may provide a neat and ready way to categorize and describe the different periods and phases I went through in the course of my life so far. Beyond this, however, it also has another, deeper and no less meaningful significance: these migratory events and

---

[1] This Autobiography was originally written on Ludger M. Herrmanns request for his book series "Psychoanalyse in Selbstdarstellungen". Published in its eleventh volume in April 2017 in Frankfurt am Main, Shmuels birth place, at the Publisher Brandes & Apsel in the German translation of Dorothee Tippelskirch-Eissing and Christoph Eiss.

eras were occasions that stimulated inner processes which contributed a great deal to my makeup, my most poignant concerns, and my strengths and handicaps.

Early life in Germany – July 1937-December 1938 – Destruction and Escape

I have no conscious memories of this period except for the stories told by my family, yet it is in so many ways the decisive determinant and the matrix for all that followed. I was born in Frankfurt a/M to an orthodox Jewish family, the second and only son after my sister, nearly nine years older than me. My father owned a jewelry store and apparently travelled quite a bit on business in certain European countries in the period between the two World Wars. He was born in Proszowice, a small town near Krakow, Poland, and migrated to Germany as a very young man. He was the firstborn son, following two older sisters and preceding three younger siblings. My mother was born in Darmstadt, Germany, the first of six children in a family that migrated to Germany from what is now Belarus at the turn of the 20th century. My ancestral background was thus already heavily made up of migrations and the ethos of migrant families. Among other attributes, this ethos contained an important undercurrent of striving for success and for successfully adapting to the new environment. This was especially true of my maternal grandfather and his children, who boasted a high degree of absorption to the German environment and culture, yet without becoming assimilated. This absorption had little to do with the higher levels of German culture, since no one in my family had anything resembling a university education, and in fact all of my aunts and uncles had only fairly rudimentary formal education. But it had a great deal to do with adopting the German language, customs and everyday cultural aspects.

The family's religious background was deeply rooted in Jewish orthodoxy, in the form of what was then its contemporary, "modern" German-Jewish fashion. It consisted of adopting the German environment's outward manners of dress, speech and behavior, and at the same time adhering to the letter of Jewish religion in all aspects pertaining to holidays, observance of the Sabbath and dietary laws. It also meant that although they did not live in a ghetto, their social life was restricted to their Jewish friends and acquaintances. This life mode was embedded in and supported by the teachings of a renowned thinker and teacher of the previous era, Rabbi Samson Rafael Hirsch. He was summoned from his post as Chief Rabbi in Moravia to become the rabbi of the segregationist group that split from the main Frankfurt congregation, which had become reformed. This congregation, known as the "Israelite Religious Society" ("Israelitische Religions-Gesellschaft") or the *"Austritt Gemeinde"*, became very successful and influential under Hirsch's leadership, providing a model of leading a Jewish orthodox life and maintaining close contact with the general environment. Both my maternal grandfather and my parents were staunch members of this orthodox Frankfurt congregation, which practiced Judaism under the banner of *"Torah im Derech Eretz"* ["The Torah is maximized in partnership with worldly involvement"]. It was an orthodox Jewish answer and adaptation to the emancipation and liberalization that swept over European Jewish communities since the 19th century and was especially marked in Germany, where the Jewish Reform movement became dominant. This combined and complex identity was absorbed by me, and I will have more to say about the important place of religion and Judaism in my life.

The first landmark event in my life is undoubtedly *Kristallnacht*, November 9 1938. *Kristallnacht* saw our apartment in Uhlandstrasse 11 being ransacked, whatever could be broken was smashed and valuables robbed. My parents told me how the landlord and his son-in-law, who was an officer, stood in the doorway and tried to dissuade the attackers, but were pushed aside. My mother with my sister and me took shelter across the bridge in Sachsenhausen. My grandfather (I am referring always to my maternal grandfather, since I never knew my paternal one) and his family – my grandmother and their five unmarried children – left Germany in 1933, as did almost half of the German Jewish community, and chose to migrate to Palestine-Israel. My own immediate family stayed on in Germany, mostly because my father, who was completely enamored with the German culture and way of life, apparently refused to read the signs of warning on the wall until it was almost too late. He was rounded up and sent to the train station with many Polish Jews to be deported to Poland. Fortunately, he had some paper on him which quite miraculously allowed him to return home; otherwise we would not have seen him again. I still have the documents in which we (my mother and her two children, and my father separately) are ordered by the police to leave Germany within 24 hours. Although these documents are dated October 27 1938, we stayed on in semi-hiding until we left Germany on December 28 1938. Somehow we crossed the border into Switzerland where my father had a cousin, and after a short stay sailed from Trieste to Palestine-Israel, where we arrived on January 10 1939.

Childhood and Adolescence – the Creation of Israel – Dangers and Joys

I was brought up in Tel Aviv, at that time a fairly small but already vibrant town, with budding business, social and industrial enterprises. One of these was my grandfather's partnership in a carton producing firm. In his downtown office, which I used to frequent, I learned to type on a potable typewriter. Another enterprise was my father's involvement in the newly created Diamond Exchange, and I remember the small packets full of diamonds he would bring home and show me.

I grew up in a German speaking home and family. The family I had and knew for most of my childhood were all on my mother's side, my grandfather and grandmother and my aunts and uncles. In the Saturday family gatherings at my grandparents the language was practically entirely German, and when the adults spoke Hebrew it was poor and with a heavy German accent. This was typical of the vast majority of German Jews and the cause for much hilarity and joking at their expense. The Polish and Russian Jews were much quicker in mastering Hebrew, and were therefore also the cultural tone setters. I remember as a very small child accompanying my mother to a night course in which she tried to learn Hebrew. There was a movement to spread the use of Hebrew, and I remember that for a very short while my sister and I instituted a rule by which every time one of our parents would lapse into German they would have to pay a fine. I thus grew up speaking German with my family elders and speaking Hebrew with the rest of the world and, of course, at school. My mother taught me the Latin alphabet when I was four and I practiced reading the signs on stores, so in a way I could read German before Hebrew. I mention this because it is importantly connected with later events and developments.

The times were turbulent, full of dangers and hardship. My own first vivid memory is of white particles (I thought they were the kind of light-colored seeds popular in Israel as nuts to this day) showering from the ceiling, and my father grabbing me and running down a darkened and destroyed stairway (it was early afternoon and my father had just woken up from his *Schlafstunde*). What actually happened was that our house was directly hit by bombs dropped by Italian planes returning from a mission in Abyssinia (1941) and discarding the rest of their load over Tel Aviv. I distinctly remember a dead man in the street, dressed as a laborer, engulfed by flames, and the huge craters formed in the road.

The turbulence continued, as the struggle against the British Mandate intensified. I remember ducking into house entrances to escape bullets fired in the street. The all-around feeling was of grave danger and a life-and-death struggle. V-Day marked World War II coming to an end, and trickles of refugees and the stories of horrors began to arrive. Among these was my uncle, my father's youngest brother, who miraculously survived the camps. My paternal grandfather and all my father's siblings and their families and children were murdered together with other Polish Jews. I remember distinctly the summer evening when we were listening to the daily item on the radio, "*Who recognizes? Who knows?*", in which names of survivors were recited so their relatives would know they are alive and could contact them. I remember my father jumping up and crying: "Chune! It is Chune!" [the Yiddish version of his Hebrew name, *Chanan*] when my uncle's name suddenly came up. My uncle was in rehabilitation in Sweden as he was practically a skeleton, and eventually arrived and lived with us for a while. Two more nieces of my father had subsequently also arrived. As was common in those days, our small three-room apartment absorbed him as well as the others.

This period in Israel was marked by the stream of refugee survivors who were readily absorbed, and yet also regarded ambivalently by the generation of new Israeli Jews who prided themselves on their strength and courage and looked down upon these wretched diaspora Jews who "went like sheep to slaughter". It took many years for this ambivalence to be acknowledged and to change to some extent.

The schools I attended, both elementary and high school, belonged to the orthodox educational system, with morning prayers and much time devoted to Bible and Talmud studies, which I enjoyed and found fascinating. My high school teachers were truly outstanding, and to this day I owe a great deal to them. Many of them were German Jews with doctorates (sometimes even several!) from German universities. They were scholarly, utterly serious and knowledgeable. They represented a perspective that admired and cherished all forms of knowledge – science, philosophy, and Jewish studies. I was a very good student (I had won a scholarship for high school) and consciously felt that it was a great opportunity to be part of this environment and the excellence it fostered. There is no question in my mind that the foundation I received then and there proved immensely beneficial for my further development.

Parallel to the religious aspect of my education, which was intense and at the same time quite liberal, there was a deep involvement with Zionism. In spite of the hardships, the overall Zeitgeist was of great expectations, of the actualization of age-old dreams, of survival against all odds and triumphing over obstacles. Looking back, I think that one could already discern what are probably the two salient characteristics of the Israeli persona and culture: an omnipotent sense that there is nothing that cannot be fixed, resolved and overcome; and a somewhat paranoid and victimized attitude that the entire world is against us and no one is to be trusted. Although the times were objectively hard, I don't remember anyone ever complaining. The days were marked by struggle – against the British, against occasional Arab raids (bullets fired from Jaffa hit our Tel Aviv windows), against the world that stood in silence as our relatives were burned and slaughtered in Europe by Nazi Germany and its various allies. Politically, the country was deeply divided between admirers and staunch supports of communism and Soviet Russia, and those who opted for the West, for European and (much later) for American culture and economy. The UN decision of November 29 1947, to partition the land into a Jewish and Arab states, led to huge eruptions of joy and dancing in the streets, but immediately also to the invasion of seven neighboring Arab armies, as well as attacks by the local Arab population (later recognized as Palestinians). Guns, bullets and commando knives were what I collected as a boy.

Once again we were subjected to constant air raids that barely missed our house. The papers were full of attacks on buses and the convoys to the besieged Jerusalem, which had been conquered by the Jordanian Legion. People were being killed daily, among them an 18 years old first cousin of mine. He was the only child of an aunt and uncle on my mother's side, and the news of his death came on the eve of Passover, as we were preparing, as usual, to go to my grandfather for the family Seder. I still remember the heartbreaking cries and sobs of his mother as the festivity turned into sorrow and mourning. At about the same time, my sister, who had been an excellent student and a budding writer (her work was included in an anthology of Israeli writers) decided to give up a promising university career and join a Kibbutz, much to our parents' regret and sorrow. There she met and married her husband, and for a short while we found shelter there from the incessant air raids.

The War of Independence (1948-1949) continued and took its heavy toll, with many thousands killed and wounded and daily announcements of battles and bereavements. Waves of immigrants arrived and were absorbed by the fledgling state, leading to severe economic hardship. A strict rationing regime was instituted by the government, which made many products and foods scarce and limited, promoting a black market. My father's activity in the Diamond Exchange ground to a complete halt. In order to make a living, he reverted to watchmaking at home, assisted by his brother, as both of them came from a family of watchmakers and jewelers.

Life in America (1954-1971) – Immigrants in the Land of Opportunities

It was against this background of economic and general hardship that my parents decided to immigrate to the USA. It was a daring, courageous, yet perhaps even stupid decision on their part. They were already in their 50's, with no knowledge of the language and no real assets or special skills, yet the American dream exercised a very powerful attraction. We arrived in the US with no money, very few connections and a most uncertain outlook. I am not sure what made them take this rather hazardous step or what eventually sustained them. I believe, although it was hardly ever clearly stated, that they wished to provide me with a chance for a worldlier exposure they spend in the US must have been a very difficult period, far from family and friends. Their dream of rejoining the remainders of their Frankfurt community, who had settled in an area called Washington Heights in north Manhattan (humorously referred to as "*Frankfurt-am-Hudson*") succeeded only very partially, as they never really became part of this community or developed meaningful friendships. The three of us lived a fairly isolated and restricted life in our new American homeland.

My parents never became absorbed in the new environment. The differences between them became striking: although my father eventually opened a jewelry and gift store in the main street of Washington Heights, he never mastered the language and in fact reverted to reading the Jewish paper. My mother, on the other hand, taught herself English well enough to read TIME magazine. She became much more lively, assertive and full of initiative, and acted as the buyer for the store. This inequality between them, often the result of immigration, often made for strife in their relationship, which their social isolation did not help.

This migration was not without its tolls for me. As an adolescent (I was 16 when we left Israel) I was torn from my close group of friends, from my language and cultural background. Part of my reaction came in the form of rageful attacks against my father. I accused him of passivity and stupidity which nearly took our lives, because of his hesitation and belated action in leaving Germany. It was probably a displacement of my anger about being uprooted from my life in Israel, although I must say that I was a willing participant in this. Leaving Israel was considered a shameful act, tantamount to desertion. I remember being ashamed and apologetic when I informed my close friends about my impending departure, and my surprise at their response, which was one pf envy. At the same time, it also represented a rejection of the German part of my identity, which was now replaced by the newly adopted American one. But I owed much to this German part, which greatly helped me in mastering the English language; it would have been manifold more difficult if I had only Hebrew as my native tongue.

As a new immigrant and without financial resources I immediately started to work. I responded to a newspaper ad and got a job repairing cuckoo clocks in a firm that imported them from Germany. Working for a dollar-an-hour in a New York menial workshop along with Puerto Ricans and others of low socioeconomic standing, riding the sweaty subway in rush hours and feeling myself an infinitesimal particle in this bustling city of millions was a new and sobering experience. It taught me that only self-reliance can assure survival and perhaps lead to success, and that nothing in life comes easily. The last conclusion was probably an exaggeration, since I had a good deal going for me in terms of certain inner capacities, but I hardly knew or believed that at the time. But I was a diligent student of the American (more precisely, the New York) scene and culture, subscribing to and reading popular American magazines with short stories that often revolved around baseball players and other American cultural heroes, and moving on later to reading more sophisticated magazines, such as *The New Republic* and *Commentary*, two of the leading socio-political voices of the intelligentsia, with significant Jewish overtones and contributors.

I completed a year of high school and two years of college at Yeshiva University, at the same time graduating from its Hebrew Teachers College, which enabled me to teach in Jewish day schools. I loved world history, a subject in which I had received an excellent foundation in my Israeli high school, and thought I would major in it, but the prospect of becoming an academic in this area seemed unappealing and deterred me. At about this time, I discovered psychoanalysis by chance: it was through a book by Erich Fromm that spoke warmly and eloquently of the Sabbath, a synthesis which greatly appealed to me and opened up new horizons. When I told my father of my discovery of Erich Fromm it turned out that he knew him as a young boy in Frankfurt, which helped my feeling of familiarity. I switched my major to psychology and my academic base to the City College of New York, which had an outstanding psychology department. After two instructive years there I graduated and received my BA (1959) and enrolled in the direct doctoral (PhD) program in clinical psychology in New York University.

The NYU program was at that time one of the top three among many such programs in the US. In addition, it boasted a strong psychoanalytic perspective. I was fortunate to have outstanding teachers like Robert Holt (a renowned Freud scholar) and George Klein (a renowned psychoanalytic theoretician and researcher). My doctoral thesis stemmed from George Klein's research course and was awarded the distinction of "Best Dissertation," given for the first time by the New York Society of Clinical Psychologists. In it I examined, using the methodology of cognitive styles and controls that was prominent at the time, the factors responsible for the wide individual variations in susceptibility to a phenomenon called "delayed auditory feedback" (DAF). Given my budding psychoanalytic interest, I also studied the effects of traumatogenic contents under this experimentally induced phenomenon, which I explained in terms of the heavily overburdened ego-functions.

There was another passion, however, that at the time strongly paralleled my intellectual one: I developed a fine tenor voice and loved to sing. I took voice lessons for several years and sang operatic arias and Schubert Lieder. It fashioned a new bond with my mother, who had learned to play the piano in her youth in Germany, and could now accompany me. I was quite ambitious and seriously considered an operatic career. My teacher, a former Viennese professor, supported my ambition and for the last year of my study did not charge me, in exchange for our shared hope and desire for me to enter the auditions of the Metropolitan Opera. By that time, however, I was also deeply immersed in my clinical psychology studies and training. I felt literally torn as never before, and finally chose the psychology route, giving up my operatic ambitions for good.

My singing paid off in another respect: I obtained an annual position as cantor in a New York reform synagogue, which allowed us to get married. I had met my wife in a summer camp a couple of years earlier, and the engagement and marriage soon followed. We were both quite young and inexperienced, coming from similar Jewish orthodox backgrounds with strong Zionist leanings. Our first daughter was born in May 1965, at about the same time that I received my doctorate. It was a long and protracted birth in New York's Fifth Avenue Hospital, during which I was going out of my mind with worries and anxiety. At that time fathers were not allowed in delivery rooms and the nurses were not very communicative. The birth eventually came to a good end and we were blessed with a healthy daughter to whom we gave the middle name Joy, as an expression of our feeling. Two days after the delivery, my wife developed pains which were eventually diagnosed as osteomyelitis and required immediate surgery. She was not allowed to have contact with the baby for ten days, and I assumed some of the maternal duties and functions, such as bathing the newborn. Fortunately, we had engaged a nurse for the postnatal period and she gladly instructed and helped me. I still remember feeling deeply rewarded when my daughter gave me her first smile.

The NYU clinical psychology program included treating patients in the doctoral clinic under the supervision of psychoanalysts. Parallel to this, I also did a two-year internship in various Veterans Administration clinics and hospitals, where I experienced the personal and impersonal difficulties of working with psychotic, schizophrenic and other pathologies, as well as being part of the psychiatric team work. All of this, however, still felt unconvincing and insufficient. I strongly felt the need for better and more thorough grounding, and at the unequivocal recommendation of Bob Holt and George Klein I applied for a postdoctoral fellowship to the Austen Riggs Center in Stockbridge, Massachusetts. I drove up to Stockbridge, located in the Berkshire hills, on a snowy winter night, and spent the next day being interviewed by various staff persons, including Robert Knight, the medical director. I was unaware that he was already quite ill with cancer, and was surprised at what seemed like his occasionally drifting off into a quick sleep. Robert Knight would later read my case presentations and annotate them with his comments and corrections in red ink, until he died in May 1966, at the end of my first year at Riggs. I was accepted as a Postdoctoral Fellow, and my wife and I and our two-months old daughter left our Manhattan apartment and moved to Stockbridge in July 1965.

There is much to be said about our life in Stockbridge. It was an enchanted life in beautiful surroundings, with dramatically colorful foliage in autumn, heavy snow and ski in winter, and gorgeous lakes and country side in spring and summer, all imbued and colored by New England hospitality and cuisine. Against this WASP background we stood out in our Jewishness, since both my wife and I were committed to Kosher cuisine and Sabbath observance, in a community in which Jews were rather scarce, and those who were there were quite assimilated.

The six years (1965-1971) at Austen Riggs proved to be a decisive influence and a matrix for significant personal and professional growth and development. Clinically, it was a great learning experience. In this small, 42-bed open psychiatric hospital, every patient was in intensive, individual, psychoanalytic psychotherapy 4 times a week. Supervision was individual and per case, given by seasoned senior staff members, many of whom were training analysts. As Fellows, we took up roles in the Therapeutic Community and were immersed in the thinking and issues that pertained to it. There was an array of seminars given by outstanding teachers, in which one could struggle and achieve understanding of key concepts and issues in psychoanalysis, therapeutic community, clinical diagnosis, psychotherapy and the like. In short, it was a unique learning opportunity. Beyond this, there was a deep commitment to excellence and maintaining the highest professional and clinical standards, and a sense of being in a leadership position when compared to most other psychiatric and even psychoanalytic places. It should be remembered that at the time (late 1960s) psychoanalysis was at its apex in the US, and many chairs of departments of psychiatry and hospital directors were psychoanalysts. At the same time, psychoanalysis was formally restricted to medical practitioners, a situation that was about to change more than twenty years later.

When I arrived at Austen Riggs, the institute was in mourning over the untimely death of David Rappaport a year earlier. His spirit and the actual or symbolic presence of other well-known psychoanalytic personages permeated the atmosphere. One felt in the presence of an epochal, self-conscious and history-making institution. A deep acquaintance with Rappaport's writings, as well as Merton Gill, Roy Schafer and others, ushered me into the intricacies of the then prevailing ego psychology. In addition, there were seminars devoted to Freud's Chapter Seven of the Interpretation of Dreams, Fairbairn's and Guntrip's object relations approach, Bion's theory of groups, Talcott Parson's and Marshall Edelson's conceptualization of social systems, to mention but the most outstanding and memorable ones. At some point, Erik Erikson returned to Riggs from his stay at Harvard University, and the seminars we had with him were a pure delight. I developed a certain relationship with him, which was not close but had moments of closeness. He gave me the Swedish copy of his book, Insight and Responsibility, which had as its cover a picture in which I sit next to him in one of the seminars and look at him thoughtfully or admiringly, with the inscription: "To my guardian angel."

Although all this contributed much to my theoretical understanding and psychoanalytic thinking, my learning was in no way just theoretical. The patients I treated in four-times-a-week intensive psychotherapy presented an astounding array of human capabilities as well as pathologies. They varied from late adolescence to middle age, with diagnostic labels ranging from hysteria and depression to borderline and schizophrenia. The latter, of course, had to be capable of staying in this open hospital. Medication was used sparingly and was relatively primitive, given the state of psychiatric drugs in the 60s. There was nearly complete equality between psychologists and psychiatrists (except for performing medical functions) and an overall respectful attitude towards all ranks and specialists on staff.

I must mention another aspect of the hospital routine that was undoubtedly very anxiety provoking, but also a great stimulus for learning. Patients were admitted for an initial period of a month long intake and workup, at the end of which they would be presented by the therapist who did the workup and wrote it up, together with the reports of psychological testing, nursing, and community and activity staff. These rather long and elaborate presentations took place during lunch breaks, when one would eat, listen and read the report for the first time. At the end of the presentation, a staff discussion would take place, in which the patient's psychological makeup, dynamics, symptomatology, diagnosis and prognosis were discussed and evaluated and a course of treatment suggested (which might include the possibility of sending the patient back home or elsewhere). The staff discussion would always start with four speakers whose names were only announced when the presentation ended, and who would always speak in the same sequence: a first-year Fellow would start, followed by a second-year Fellow, a Junior Staff, and finally a Senior Staff member. I was thus often the first to start the discussion of a case I just heard, with someone like Erik Erikson, Margaret Brenman or another of my supervisors taking up the final discussion. Obviously those lunches were not remembered for the food one ate, but learning to think and to formulate extemporaneously and under pressure was one of the gifts I received.

As time went on, I became increasingly immersed in and drawn to psychoanalysis. At the time Riggs was affiliated with the Western New England Psychoanalytic Institute in New Haven. Some of the courses for the candidates were given at Riggs and I had the opportunity to participate in them. An opportunity and challenge presented itself in my third year, when I was invited to join the staff of a well-known New York hospital, along with the tempting offer to have fully subsidized psychoanalytic training at the New York Psychoanalytic Institute, the most prestigious and revered institute in the US. Aside from my reluctance to trade our life in Stockbridge for moving back to New York, there was a much more problematic issue: in my interviews it was made clear that while I would be gladly admitted and trained by the NY Institute, even including the clinical training (!), I would have to sign a slip of paper stating that I would only use my training for research purposes. At the time, the American Psychoanalytic Association, which was the sole provider of IPA psychoanalytic training in the US, accepted only medical doctors. Non-medical applicants were sometimes accepted as "research candidates" and were usually not admitted to the clinical courses. I was assured that this meant nothing, and that patients would be gladly referred to me. Nonetheless it evoked a strong reaction in me: Once again I would be the Jew and the outsider, tolerated and even respected, yet kept aloof and different. I declined the offer and for the first time felt highly motivated to enter analysis. This incident clearly stirred up all my difficulties around identity and belonging.

At Riggs it was customary and possible, and even financially subsidized, to be in analysis with a member of the senior staff. I chose to be in analysis with the recently arrived Leslie Farber, who came to Riggs from Washington DC, summoned by Otto Will, Riggs's new Medical Director and my supervisor. My analysis with Leslie Farber lasted only a year and a half, since at that point he decided to leave Riggs and move to New York City. Nonetheless, it was deeply significant in many ways. Leslie was a Training Analyst of the Washington Psychoanalytic Institute, yet he was quite unconventional: he did not use the couch (he offered to have a cot ready for me when I raised the point), and he put great stock in mutuality, which led him to talk a good deal about himself in response to some of my issues and associations. As Director of the Washington School of Psychiatry, he had invited Martin Buber to the US, and was deeply influenced and respectful of an existential approach. He was a gifted writer, had contributed to the intellectual magazine *Commentary* and published a couple of very interesting and innovative books. He was one of the wisest persons I ever met, and at the same time sober, totally unpretentious and with great personal integrity. The discovery that we had the same birthday date (July 11) was meaningful to both of us and signified the bond that formed between us. In the year-and-a-half of my analytic experience with him, possibly also because it was the first time I had a meaningful therapeutic experience, some real changes took place in me, the most remarkable being a gradual move away from my religious observance. Interestingly, Leslie was not at all happy with this, since he viewed internal religious feelings, struggle and conflict as valuable. Nonetheless, it marked the beginning of my distantiation from religion, at least in its outer manifestations of rules and observances, while maintaining an allegiance to the tradition and the sense of deep connection with the Jewish people and its history, couched in my childhood experiences as well as in my fairly encompassing education and knowledge of the biblical, Talmudic and historical sources of Judaism.

Another highly significant development was my exposure to Group Relations work, an area in which I eventually became very involved. As a member of the Therapeutic Community staff at Riggs I was sent to a Group Relations conference in New London, Connecticut in 1967. It was the first or second time that the persons of the Tavistock Institute of Human Relations who had developed this approach and methodology were invited to bring it to the US. I went to the Group Relations conference in New London, Connecticut not knowing what to expect, and I was deeply moved and thoroughly impressed by the experience. Although I had considerable experiences with group therapy and therapeutic community groups, I felt that for the first time that I understood what a "group" is and how it may be experienced and thought about. I followed this up the following year with a two-week Group Relations conference in Mount Holyoke, and determined to bring this approach to Israel when I return. I will have more to say about this later.

Return and Life in Israel (1971-present) – Personal and Institutional Building

The last year at Riggs was marked by my treating five very different and difficult patients and the institutional tensions and controversies that affected these treatments. The source and focus of the turmoil had to do with the changes introduced by Otto Will, the new Medical Director. Otto Will came to Riggs after a long and distinguished career at Chestnut Lodge in Washington DC, where he treated severe schizophrenic patients in a highly individual and devoted manner. Although he was an analyst, he professed a critical and even negative stance towards psychoanalysis, especially in its establishment and conservative political aspects. At Chestnut Lodge he was deeply influenced by Sullivan and Frieda Fromm-Reichmann, his analyst. He had little understanding of or use for the openness and therapeutic community approach of Riggs.

The senior staff at Riggs feared that he aimed to admit more severely regressed patients, which would have led to changing at least part of this open hospital into a closed ward. Indeed, Otto supervised my work with a particularly difficult schizophrenic patient who became severely catatonic immediately after his admission, and I learned a great deal from him in this work. He was convinced that a powerful link, or attachment, forms without words, simply by maintaining physical proximity and constancy. He was influenced in this by the work of an ethologist, John Paul Scott, who wrote about forming relationships with dogs and wolves, and he advised me to think of the patient as a wolf. That was actually quite easy, as the patient's face gradually became very gaunt, with fierce black eyes staring at me out of his speechless silence. He stayed in his room with the blinds closed and the air heavy with the smell of sweat, did not speak at all and was motorically severely inhibited and ambivalent (in Bleuler's sense). I would go to his room four times a week and simply sit there with him. After several months of this, he slowly began to emerge, together with me, from his room, very hesitantly increasing the scope of these "expeditions".

This meaningful therapeutic work took place against the background of the institutional tension around the issue of treating very regressed patients. As the patient improved and came out of his catatonic paralysis, a certain amount of flamboyant acting out emerged, some of it in the institution and some outside, in the local village. As I had predicted when I started this treatment out of awareness of the controversy that raged in the institution, the hospital found it intolerable and impossible to contain, and he was sent off to a state hospital with closed facilities.

Otto was absolutely right: Years later and after my return to Israel, when I was on leave from the army after the Yom Kippur war, the first phone call I received was from him, calling me from the US to make sure that I was all right.

Our family grew with the arrival of a second daughter in March 1967. The question where to raise our children, combined with the increasingly tense institutional atmosphere, made it clear that we would have to leave Riggs and our life in the Berkshires. By sheer coincidence, Hillel Klein, the medical director of a Jerusalem psychiatric hospital who was on sabbatical in New York, was invited to give a lecture at Riggs. After attending the diagnostic psychological testing seminar that I led, he offered me a position as chief psychologist in his hospital. After his return to Israel, he repeated his offer and suggested that in addition I would direct an adolescent unit to be established at the hospital. At the same time, Ze'ev Klein (unrelated) at the Hebrew University invited me to be a lecturer in the Clinical Psychology program he directed. The combination of a clinical with an academic position was definitely appealing and what I was interested in. We came to Israel for a month long visit (I had not been back for 16 years!) with our two daughters, after which we decided to make the move. I accepted both positions and undertook a new migration.

Our first year in Israel saw us living in a Jerusalem absorption center in makeshift conditions, while the house in which we purchased an apartment was slowly being built. There were numerous challenges and obstacles, such as getting used to the new bureaucratic practices (there were many), our daughters' adjustment to the different educational approach, and finding my professional and personal place. We were reunited with family I have not seen for 17 years, especially with my sister and her family with three sons. My sister and her family never strayed from their national-religious identity and outlook, which made it sometimes difficult to have open discussions. Yet we enjoyed spending Shabbat in their village home and the atmosphere of absolute peace and quiet engendered by their religious observance. At the same time, our own religious identity, already largely eroded before the move, became impossible to sustain and was rapidly abandoned in view of the political connotations attached to it in the Israeli social scene. The immediate choice point came up around having to decide what kind of school our children would attend, since the Israeli educational system separated religious from secular schools. We chose the latter, which immediately marked our position *vis-a-vis* my sister's family that was completely identified with the religious sphere, socially and politically. It may be regarded as a minor crisis, but it was a decisive step in terms of choice of identity, sociopolitical affiliation and family relationships. It definitely also reflected the atmosphere in Israel (to this day), in which religious and political affiliation have been welded together, with a sharp split and mutual exclusion between the religious-conservative and the secular-liberal stance. This split became increasingly pronounced and dominant following the 1967 War, when the religious political parties shifted from a middle-of-the-road to an ever stronger right-wing conservative political position.

I began my army service in 1973, shortly before the outbreak of the Yom Kippur War, in which I took an active part as a soldier, guarding a municipal installation in the Palestinian city of Ramallah. A few months earlier (February 1973) our third child arrived – a boy, and the first Israeli-born member of our family. After my release from the army, I served for many years (till 1991) in the Army Reserves in various professional roles and capacities, and for the last ten years supervising the psychologists responsible for officers' selection.

I applied to the Israel Psychoanalytic Institute in 1974 and was interviewed by Erich Gumbel Nomi Weiss. I was immediately accepted and even allowed to skip the first two years in which candidates only took courses, as I was told that I could probably teach some of these. I therefore started to take courses with some of the more advanced candidate years. This had the possible disadvantage of never having belonged to a particular "class" or candidate year, very much like my last year of high school in New York when I took courses with all the different grades. I was required, however, to be in analysis, which I actually very much welcomed. I felt and knew there was a great deal that was not touched in my previous analysis due to its premature termination. I started analysis with Eliezer Ilan, a German Jew who headed a renowned child and maternal clinic in Jerusalem, with whom I also had a working relationship in the university's clinical psychology program. I was used from my Riggs experience to be in analysis with a person with whom I shared a working relationship (and to treat patients in a community setting in which there were inevitably extra-therapeutic encounters) and did not find this to be an issue. I can certainly say this for myself, but I believe it was true for both of us, that this extra-analytic relationship never interfered or was a problem for either of us. I very much appreciated his wisdom and considerate, warm yet reserved handling of the analysis. The orientation was fairly heavily Freudian with a view towards object-relations, and I found this very helpful and liberating for me and my issues. But it also contributed to and served as an additional consolidation of my "home coming": his deeply German accented Hebrew felt like I was in my family again, and occasionally I could lapse into German associations and expressions and know that they were perfectly understood.

In 1977 I was invited to spend a sabbatical year at Yale University. On the way there we made a long camping journey through a number of European countries, and at some point we arrived in Frankfurt. It marked my first return to Germany and to Frankfurt after nearly 40 years. I was excited and emotional, but could not quite understand my feelings, which were a strange mixture of elation and sadness. I remember that the woman officer who examined my passport at the border crossing remarked that it was almost my birthday. It was confusing, yet in some way a homecoming. This homecoming continued: I found the house I in which I was born was born in Frankfurt and took my picture holding my four years old son in my arms, as I imagined my father carried me. But I also had an unpleasant experience. I knocked on the door opposite our apartment, which was closed, and when the man who opened it heard who I was and why I was there, I got the inevitable response, "But we knew nothing!" [Wir haben doch gar nichts gewusst!) I remember feeling a mixture of rage, disgust, pity and resignation. It was my first encounter with an actual German and with the poignant difficulty of dealing with German guilt feelings, but also with the rejection and hate it stirred up in me.

In July 1977 we arrived in New Haven, where I commenced my sabbatical year at Yale University and Yale Psychiatric Institute. It was my first return to the US after the move back to Israel and it definitely helped to convince me of my preference and choice to live in Israel. It was an important and richly rewarding year, in which I worked, mostly as supervisor, at Yale Psychiatric Institute, and took psychoanalytic courses at Yale Child Study Center. I made strong personal connections with some of the outstanding psychoanalysts in New Haven, such as Al Solnit, Sam Ritvo, Donald Cohen and Sidney Blatt.

Although as a family we enjoyed our stay in the US and the many advantages and pleasures that the American way of life offered, there were increasing tensions in the marriage, leading eventually (after our return to Israel) to its breakup and divorce. A few years later, a new relationship emerged which proved not only lasting and satisfying but a richly productive and inspiring partnership. We initiated and developed together many of the projects I have since been involved in, such as the founding and leading of OFEK (which Mira chaired for six years), as well as our involvement in various roles in the Israel Psychoanalytic Institute and Society, and generating and shaping together numerous ideas, publications and projects. Probably the most memorable and important one was the initiation and development of the German-Israeli Group Relations conferences, to which I will return later.

Mira and I were married in June 1983, and our daughter was born in May 1984. Our family expanded to include my three children, Mira's two sons from her former marriage, and our joint daughter. The household was always lively and full with the six children, their activities and relationships. It was very important and meaningful that all of them lived with us at one point or another. I was especially impressed with my son, who at the time of the divorce lived with his mother, but when the time of his Bar Mitzvah came near, announced to her his decision to come live with me, which took a good deal of courage. He and Mira's two sons were close in age, and we spent several anxious years when the three of them served overlapping periods in the army, a service that was further extended for all of them by becoming officers.

Hospital (1971-1985) – Developing Staff and Adolescents

In 1971 I took up my position as Chief Psychologist in *Eitanim*, a psychiatric hospital situated in the picturesque hills outside Jerusalem. I found a small psychology staff of 5 or 6 junior psychologists. By the time I left the hospital in 1984 it had increased to over 30. I initiated seminars on psychoanalytic concepts and psychodiagnostic testing for the psychology staff who worked in various parts of the hospital, and this also served the need for all to meet and come together. Several months after my arrival the new adolescent unit took shape. I became the first psychologist in Israel to head an in-service psychiatric unit, which the medical establishment fought, but Hillel Klein supported. Hillel and I wrote and published several papers together, including one on whether hospital democracy was possible, and another on the concept of a "family ego". Despite the fact that Hillel's personality made it sometime difficult to work with him, his leadership and support made it possible to establish innovative practices in the adolescent unit, which became a model for a psychodynamic therapeutic community. I was able to put into effect in a state hospital with limited resources some of the principles and the approach I had internalized at Riggs. The work with the psychology staff helped to raise their level and made the hospital a desired and reputable training place. In a way, there were certain similarities in helping these young professionals develop and grow and the treatment of the hospitalized adolescents. Indeed, I may have had both in mind when I published a paper describing the adolescent unit under the title, "Growth Opportunities in the Hospital."

University (1972-2005) – Freud in Academia

Parallel to the hospital work, I started to teach at the Hebrew University of Jerusalem in 1972, until my retirement in 2005. I taught and worked in the graduate (MA) program in Clinical Psychology and served as Chair of the Ethics Committee. Although for the most part I enjoyed and cherished my university affiliation, academic politics influenced and shaped many of the issues, such as admissions policy and academic rank. There was constant tension and strife between the academic psychologists and the clinical psychologists in the department. Nearly all the applicants for the MA program wanted the clinical course, which the academic-research faculty resented but had to tolerate. In turn, and since they had all the political power, they intervened in the admissions procedure, which included a personal interview in addition to academic achievements. The interview was declared to be subjective and unreliable, and the compromise was to allow it only as a negative factor, i.e., in order to weed out applicants whose personality was severely problematic and unsuited.

Another issue had to do with promotion and academic rank. The university policy was to rely almost entirely on the criterion of scientific publications, which were judged in terms of quantity and quality, contingent on the impact factor of the journals in which they were published. Controversies about this were university-wide, but it affected especially the clinicians, whose appointment was in the psychology department. Eventually a compromise evolved in the form of a parallel clinical track, limited to part-time employment and half the benefits, such as sabbatical leave. My academic advancement took place within this track. Beyond these inevitable academic politics, working with the aspiring young psychologists was mostly pleasurable and meaningful, and it was especially rewarding when I met quite a few of them many years later as candidates in the psychoanalytic institute.

The Freud Chair

The 1977 International Psychoanalytic Association held its Congress for the first time outside Europe and in Jerusalem. Martin Wangh led an initiative aimed at rectifying the break between Sigmund Freud and the Hebrew University. When Freud and Eitingon suggested in 1933 that a Chair in Psychoanalysis be established at the Hebrew University, the offer was rejected by the University Senate, which brought about Freud's estrangement from the University, in which he was on the Board of Trustees. Martin Wangh suggested that a Sigmund Freud Chair in Psychoanalysis be created and the university agreed. The chair was established in 1979, and somewhat later the Freud Center for Psychoanalytic Study and Research was added to it, with a library and administrative help. Joseph Sandler from London was appointed to be its first occupant. After four years Sandler returned to London, where he received the newly created Freud Memorial Professorship at University College London (UCL). He was followed in the Freud Chair at Hebrew University by several US analysts (Albert Solnit, Sidney Blatt and Bennett Simon) and one from Israel (Rafael Moses), all of whom served for only one academic year. It became clear that it would be nearly impossible to find an outstanding analyst from abroad who would meet the university standards for an academic professorship, and would undertake the move to Israel for a longer period. After the departure of Bennett Simon in 1992, I was asked to take over as Director of the Freud Center. In 1995, after an open search, I was elected to the Freud Chair and held both positions until my retirement from the university in 2005.

My activity as the Professor in the Freud Chair and Director of the Freud Center encompassed several areas: sponsoring and supervising doctoral dissertations and master's theses; teaching psychoanalytic courses that were open to the entire university; and promoting psychoanalysis within and outside the university. This last cause I pursued in several ways: First, by inviting prominent psychoanalysts from abroad for a brief stay, in which they would lecture to students and faculty as well as the psychoanalytic and professional community. Secondly, by organizing conferences under the auspices of the Freud Center, such as: "In the best Interest of the Child: Contemporary Perspectives" (November 1996) and "Freud at the Threshold of the 21st Century" (December 1999).

Group Relations

The third way in which the Freud Center under my directorship contributed to what may be termed applied psychoanalysis was to provide administrative and logistical support for Group Relations enterprises. As I mentioned earlier, I was determined to foster this approach in Israel, having been exposed to it at Riggs and gaining experience as staff in several conferences. It had to wait until 1984, when we finally formed a small group, together with Rafael Moses and Jona Rosenfeld, that aimed to pursue this goal. In the course of time several more joined us: Yigal Ginat, Rina Moses-Hroshovsky, Mira Erlich-Ginor and Avi Nutkewitch. We formed a non-profit organization, The Israel Association for the Study of Group and Organizational Processes (IASGOP), eventually changing its name to OFEK – Organization, Person, Group (the acronym works better in Hebrew, in which it also means "horizon"). With the help and close mentoring of Eric Miller, Director of the Tavistock Institute's Group Relations Program, we launched our first Israeli international conference in Arad in 1987. It was a historical landmark and the foundation of what grew to be a thriving, internationally prominent and recognized Group Relations enterprise. Eric Miller directed the first two international conferences, after which I took over and directed the next four.

I found in Group Relations theory and methodology a highly relevant and rich application of psychoanalysis. Couched in Bion's approach to groups and providing a unique confluence of psychoanalytic (mostly Kleinian) concepts with Open Systems theory, it is a powerful method that enables experiential learning about unconscious processes in oneself, in groups and in organizations.

A development stemming from our Group Relations experience was the launching in 1996 of a university based program in "Organizational Consultation and Development (OCD) – A Psychoanalytic and Open Systems Perspective". This two-year program, which encompassed theoretical courses, experiential events and supervised practice in consulting to organizations, was initially jointly sponsored by the Sigmund Freud and Martin Buber Centers at the Hebrew University, as well as the William Alanson White Psychoanalytic Institute in New York and OFEK. Notwithstanding certain changes over the years, it is still a thriving program.

The Freud Center under my leadership provided administrative support and a home base for these and various other enterprises. While I regarded such activities as a direct, important and meaningful application of psychoanalysis, and therefore a legitimate and laudable activity of the Freud Center, the committee overseeing the Center was less happy with it. Consisting mainly of members of the Psychology Department, I found little or no understanding in the committee of the importance that I attributed to these activities, which also earned money and helped replete the Center's budgetary deficit.

Germans and Israelis – The "Nazareth Conferences"

A further, most remarkable and rewarding enterprise that evolved from the Group Relations work was the series of conferences known in Germany as the "Nazareth Conferences" and in Israel as "Israelis-Germans

Conferences". In 1987, as the Freud Professor, Rafael Moses held a conference titled, "The Effects of the Holocaust on Those Not Directly Affected by it." Several German psychoanalysts participated for the first time in a conference which included mixed groups of Israelis and the German guests. The emotional impact on both sides was considerable, but due to the way the conference was designed and run it was difficult to work with it. Yet it clearly pointed to a need.

My second return to Germany took place in 1991. I met Horst Kaechele around a research project we were to co-direct. When he learned that Mira and I skied, he invited us to the Ulm Psychoanalytic Group's Ski Seminar in Austria, which we attended for three successive years. Our social interactions and personal experiences there left us with powerful impressions of the torturous and untouched residues of the Holocaust on the German colleagues. The war years were obliterated and missing from the case histories presented. At the social level, people would seek us out in order to talk in very personal and emotional ways. It was again a very ambivalent experience for me, which I later described in an open letter to *Psyche*: On one hand, a powerful sense of familiarity and being at home, as it were, and on the other, a constantly gnawing awareness of what this nation (though not these people) had done to my family and people, with every train ride a cruel reminder. Mira was more direct with her ambivalence and spent every evening in our room with a headache.

We came out of these experiences with a strong feeling that something needed to be done in order to allow both German and Israeli colleagues to work through their respective, yet so very different difficulties around the residues of the Holocaust, and the ways in which it affected their professional work and life. Our experience and involvement in Group Relations work quite naturally pointed us in this direction as the most suited avenue for the two groups to work on their respective issues. Yet it was not at all clear how GR methodology could be adapted to serve this end, since it was clear that an ordinary GR conference would not provide the suitable frame for this work. We enlisted our partners in OFEK, Rafael Moses and Jona Rosenfeld, who brought in our German psychoanalytic counterparts, Hermann Beland and Karin Lueders, both of whom immediately joined and subscribed to the project, and also undertook to attend GR conferences so as to gain experience with the method. But the major part of the task that still needed expert attention was the design of this special conference. This was accomplished with the help and leadership of Eric Miller, who, in a series of fax and written communications between London, Berlin and Jerusalem involving Hermann Beland, Rafael Moses and me, created the special design for these conferences.

Briefly described, the design adopted a number of elements from the usual GR conference, such as plenaries, small study groups, review and application groups, and a system event. The innovation had to do with the fact that to begin with, there were two identified nationality groups in this conference, unlike the usual GR conference, and in the way this was integrated into the structure of the conference and its events. It is noteworthy that Eric Miller declined to have a Large Group in the first three conferences which he directed. It was a measure of the enormous anxiety that all of us felt around the prospect of the coming together of Germans and Israeli-Jews. Our common fantasy was of an explosive, not to say murderous encounter.

The first scheduled conference in 1993 had to be cancelled due to the small number of registrants. We realized that this had to do with the fact that we had in effect performed an act of "selection", having restricted registration to psychoanalysts, which was another measure of our anxiety. We opened up the registration, and the first conference took place in Nazareth in 1994 with 33 Germans and 13 Israelis. To the opening German question, "Why are there so few Israelis here?" the Israeli-Jewish response was, "There would have been more if you had not killed so many". After this dramatic and difficult beginning the work continued productively. After another conference in Nazareth there was one in Bad Segeberg, Germany, which was followed by the untimely deaths of Eric Miller and Rafael Moses. It is remarkable that when I first raised the idea that the next conference should take place in Germany, it was criticized and rejected because no Israelis would come to Germany. I argued that if this work has meaning, this should not be the case. There were preparatory meetings of the Israeli conference members in which the issue was presented and discussed. The Israeli members eventually decided that if they were to attend a further conference it would only be if it took place in Germany. Indeed, the number of Israelis in Bad Segeberg was the highest of any conference.

The next three conferences took place in Cyprus, with a gradual process of becoming ever more open and inclusive – to Diaspora Jews, Others, and eventually to Palestinians. One of the subsequent developments was the initiative of the staff, after the first Cyprus conference, to incorporate itself into an organization that would be dedicated to this work. It was in part also related to my having retired at that point from the university and the loss of the backing of the Freud Center. We founded a non-profit organization registered in Germany, under the title: "Partners in Confronting Collective Atrocities" (PCCA). This organization has successfully conducted a number of Group Relations conferences in Cyprus and Europe, as well as events at IPA Congresses. The focus eventually shifted to atrocities in Europe in a series of three conferences which I directed and took place in Poland.

My engagement in Group Relations work has been an absorbing, instructive and most satisfying part of my career and work life. It is indeed striking and informative that this work always took place alongside my engagement in psychoanalysis without conflict or competition. Although many or most analysts do not share this dual commitment, and some may even view it suspiciously, as if it detracts from a psychoanalytic identity and immersion in psychoanalysis, I have found it to be a source of enrichment for my psychoanalytic understanding and work. At this point I must return to my course in psychoanalysis.

Psychoanalytic Institutional Activity

I qualified in 1983 from the Israel Psychoanalytic Institute (later the Max Eitingon Israel Institute of Psychoanalysis) and a year later presented a theoretical paper and became a Full Member. My involvement and commitment to the Institute, the Society and to psychoanalysis became a central and leading component of my life and identity. I started to teach at the Institute when I was still a candidate, and continued to do so without interruption up to the present. I served on various committees, and in

1993 was elected Chair of the Education & Training committee. I set out to make major revisions in the training program: a defined core curriculum (there was none); semester long, weekly courses (it had been bi-weekly); re-structuring the Education Committee into sub-committees responsible for specific areas (till then the committee met and worked as a whole, and its major time consuming occupation was to read and evaluate the final case presentations of candidates); taking the evaluation of these graduation papers out of the Education Committee and assigning it to ad hoc Reading Committees; and abolishing the vote on admitting candidates to the Society, which had been anxiety producing. The general underlying principle was drawing a clearer boundary between the Society and the Institute and making the Education Committee more functional. These structural changes have persisted to the present.

In 1998 I was elected President of the Israel Psychoanalytic Society and served from 1999 to 2002. In this role too I initiated several structural changes. The Society, which numbered about 40 members when I was a candidate, began to expand and grow at an increasingly rapid pace (it now stands at over 250). This increase brought about a shift from a small, family-like group to a more formal organization which necessitated organizational change and adaptation.

In terms of the dynamics, there were a number of difficulties the Society was struggling with. The major and most troubling one was the proliferation within the Society of different psychoanalytic schools and factions that totally rejected and disqualified each other. The 80s and 90s saw the rapid growth of Self Psychology in Israel. The views advanced and practiced by this group, which had many adherents among both members and candidates, were anathema to those of a more traditional or classical point of view, in particular the Kleinian approach, which has also begun to flourish. Ego Psychology, which had been the dominant perspective in the 50s, 60s and 70s, came into universal disrepute, and object relations, in one form or another, gained ascendance. These developments obviously paralleled what was happening in the psychoanalytic world. In the Israeli Society they bred mutual rejection, paranoid distrust and growing paralysis, as everything was becoming politically tainted and personally tinged. Against this background of suspicion and disqualification, for example, I was unable to bring the supervisors together when I chaired the Education Committee. It also became virtually impossible to review the progression and evaluation of candidates, a difficulty that persists to the present, despite some minor improvements.

A further development that took place against the backdrop of these controversies was the debate about the appointment of Training Analysts. After a 13-year long debate and controversy, a compromise solution was reached. Appointment of TA by an attempt to establish merit was completely abandoned, and instead, the IPA's basic administrative requirements plus a self-declaration of conducting a minimum of three analyses since qualification were accepted as sufficient. The self-declaration is sent to the membership, and if no objections are raised, goes into effect after 30 days. This procedure worked smoothly enough, and resulted in the Israel Psychoanalytic Society having the highest rate of Training Analysts in Europe (and probably anywhere) at about 60% (!) of the membership. At the same time, however, the actual percentage drops to the more familiar rate of 20-24% when only those who are actually engaged in training functions (analysis and supervision of candidates) are considered. In effect, the burden of evaluation and appointment has shifted to the candidates, and there is a striking parallel between the inability to assess candidates and training analysts.

Another difficult issue I faced during my presidency was the establishment of a new psychoanalytic institute in Tel Aviv. This controversial development came about with the direct assistance and leadership of a few members of the Israel Psychoanalytic Society and people from abroad, who helped a group of disgruntled psychotherapists, many of whom had been rejected several times by our Admissions Committee, to start a psychoanalytic institute and declare themselves psychoanalysts. I and many others in the Society were not opposed to the creation of an additional psychoanalytic institute in Israel, thus breaking the hegemony of the Israel Psychoanalytic Society and Institute. I did object, however, to the manner in which this was done. Rather than create a Study Group under the auspices of the IPA, which would develop under close supervision and support, they confronted us with a self-declaratory act and a *fait accompli.* Many in our Society, however, did not see or appreciate this difference, probably because they did not share my international perspective and experience and felt no allegiance to the IPA. Furthermore, for quite a few it was a new and welcome source of additional income, since the candidates of the new institute needed training analysts and supervisors from the Israel Psychoanalytic Society. In the course of time, however, many of these people withdrew their active support and participation in the Tel Aviv Institute of Contemporary Psychoanalysis. I brought the matter to open debate in our General Assembly, but refrained from putting it to a vote out of fear of losing such a vote and causing an open split in the Society.

My participation in the EPF Council during the presidency of David Tuckett proved to be an entry into the international sphere. The innovations introduced by Tuckett included the creation of Working Parties in four areas: Theory, Education, Clinical and Interface. As chair of the latter I assembled a group from various European societies to conduct a research project in the area of interface. We interviewed analysts and candidates representing different psychoanalytic developmental stages (candidate, junior analyst and training analyst) in 13 societies, using a semi-structured interview, about the participation of analysts in four extra-analytic activities: academia, psychotherapy, media and politics, art and culture. The results were striking: when directly asked about the need for interface, there was nearly unanimous agreement about its positive value. But when inquired about the various areas separately, a great deal of anxiety and ambivalence emerged about these activities and the persons engaging in them. We interpreted these findings as reflecting uncertainty, anxiety and ambivalence about the psychoanalytic identity. We presented our findings in the EPF conference in Sorrento, but regrettably never published them.

In 2003 the IPA established its new Board of Representatives and I was elected as a European Representative, and served on the Board until 2015 (with a hiatus 2007-2011). I served on several committees, but the most important was undoubtedly that of Chair of the IPA Education Committee, to which I was appointed by IPA President Claudio Eizirik and continued under Charles Hanly. I played an instrumental role in obtaining the Board's approval for the historic recognition of the three models of training – Eitingon, French and Uruguayan. It was the culmination of a process that had started under Daniel Widlocher in 2003 and was completed in 2007. In the Education Committee we drafted six criteria for defining each of the three models, which served as their defining rules. I believe this process was needed and important in many ways in order to introduce greater clarity and order in the perennial controversies about the frequency of analysis in the training. Our aim was to shift the focus from frequency to the fundamental conceptualizations characterizing each model, out of respect for the model's internal consistency. I have no doubt that this is not the end of this development. It is a dynamic process that will continue and hopefully come to an eventual resolution and recognition of the advantages and disadvantages of each model, and perhaps to an eventual integration.

More recently, I was appointed by Stefano Bolognini to Chair the newly created Institutional Issues Task Force. This too represents an important dynamic shift for the IPA. For the first time it was recognized (and approved by the Board) that group dynamics and organizational processes play an important role in psychoanalytic institutions and societies.

Psychoanalysis – A Love Affair

I have focused a good deal on my activities in the institutional and organizational aspects of psychoanalysis. This probably reflects my respect for these processes and dynamics, and my interest and growing expertise in them over the years. It would be quite misleading, however, if I have created the impression that this represents my major or exclusive activity and the source of my professional fulfilment. My engagement in psychoanalytic treatment and practice has been uninterruptedly the central focus of my work life since qualifying, and indeed has increased over the years and become almost exclusively my daily routine and engagement, complementing my institute teaching and supervision of candidates.

Psychoanalysis, in both its clinical application and contribution to theoretical exploration, has been an unending source of gratification for me. It is the best, even if the most time consuming, way to help those who can be helped by it. Beyond this, it is for me an indispensable way of understanding human behavior and all its complexity on both the individual and group and organizational levels. I do not mean to deny or minimize the moments and periods of difficulty and frustration, of doubt and exasperation. These are the inevitable parts of what the engagement with psychoanalysis, which is after all engaging with everything that is human, brings with it. Psychoanalysis is indeed an impossible profession, not only because of such difficulties, but because it is so difficult to objectify and hence to justify, defend and teach.

One of the discoveries I have made is that although psychoanalysts subscribe to the notion of an unconscious, and perhaps even to a dynamic unconscious, we are, like everyone else, quite incapable of absolving ourselves of the great stock we place in our consciousness, in our words, thoughts and interpretations. It is quite common to encounter in psychoanalytic discourse a conviction, as if something or other is actually known, or an appeal to "what we all know", belying the unknown and unknowable that forms the most essential and greater part of our mind. This is understandable, after all, because psychoanalysts, as all human beings, need to hold on to something reliable and real, and like everyone, find it hard to tolerate the 'not knowing' that psychoanalysis requires. This tension is what makes our profession so impossible. It becomes especially obvious and burdensome when we are called upon to assume the mantle of 'the experts'.

I owe much to the excellent early psychoanalytic education I received. My roots in ego psychology have been both instructive and helpful. I was then gradually influenced by the work of Winnicott and others, cherishing the place and role of experience and mutuality in the creation of subjectivity. I introduced my institute class to Melanie Klein, who has since then gained in centrality and influence in Israel. Although I studied Freud's writings under Robert Holt, it was only much later, when as Freud Professor of Psychoanalysis I offered a year's course in the development of Freud's thought at the university and at the Institute, that I came to increasingly appreciate and understand the ingeniousness of his thinking. Teaching Freud's papers has become one of my central activities and commitments. I have been asked to conduct an ongoing Freud Seminar that is open to all members of the Society and has been going on for the last fifteen years. I also teach Freud's seminal metapsychological papers to our candidates. I and others have greatly enjoyed this delving deeper into Freud's papers and it has been a major gratifying experience.

An expression of my appreciation of and learning from psychoanalytic thinking has been my writings, and I cannot complete this review without alluding to some of their themes, since they reflect my various interests and the diverse areas of my exploration and work.

The first group of papers, published mostly in the *Psychoanalytic Study of the Child*, revolved around adolescence and its themes: suicide, denial, fantasy and reality, boundaries and limitations, and termination.

The second group concerns the development of my theory of the experiential modalities of *being* and *doing*, which unknowingly parallels Winnicott's concept but also differs from it. Briefly stated, my thesis is that all experience is the product of the dual (rather than single) processing by two contiguous, parallel modalities that continuously process our internal and external sensations, perceptions and thoughts. The differences between these modalities stem from the different ways in which the relationship of subject and object is experienced: in the *being* modality they are experienced as fused, united and merged, whereas in the *doing* modality they are experienced as separate and autonomous. This gives rise to a variety of fundamentally different experiences as well as psychic functions that are not readily distinguishable, especially when the concepts enabling such fine distinctions are missing. An illustration of this is the experience of loneliness, which is entirely different in the two modalities. To my mind, this work, which originally stemmed from re-reading Freud's *On Narcissism*, has not received the attention it deserves, since it is capable of explaining some of the major controversies in psychoanalytic theorizing, such as conflict and deficit theories.

The third group deals with organizational and group dynamics viewed from a combined psychoanalytic and systemic or Group Relations theory and perspective. They include subjects like ego and self in the group, the identity of the psychoanalyst, the elusive meaning of the organizational subject. Another group deals with the issues of discourse with the enemy, the mind of the terrorist, and the invasion of analytic space by communal trauma. More recently I focused on envy in groups and organizations, including psychoanalytic institutes and societies, and on revisiting the concept of trauma which has lost much of its specificity and analytic grounding. It is interesting to note that these three areas of my work overlap to a considerable degree. They form the foundation of my book, *"The Couch in the Marketplace: Psychoanalysis and Social Reality"*.

Another book that was published together with Mira Erlich-Ginor and Hermann Beland, *"Fed with Tears, Poisoned with Milk,"* describes the initiating and learning associated with the first three "Nazareth" Conferences: Germans and Israelis, the Past in the Present.

I think it is fairly obvious that what I am concerned with and shapes my thinking and activity is, on one hand, the attempt to explore the inner world and its psychical functioning, and on the other, the way it interacts with external reality, especially in its social aspect. I believe this combination, or attempted integration, is what psychoanalysis is all about. In this sense, and to my mind, psychoanalysis extends much farther than its therapeutic application and endeavor. As Freud believed and taught, these different areas represent the combined realms of human experience, politics and behavior that can only be fathomed with the help of psychoanalysis, and I hope I have contributed in some small measure to this precious undertaking.

Homecoming

I have described in some detail the journey of migratory moves that defined and shaped my life. Can I say anything about homecoming? I think I can, although it may still be a process in the making.

In the first place, there is a certain homecoming that has to do with the German language. The work in the German-Israeli conferences is one aspect of it, but there have been others. I was invited many times to Germany to lecture, conduct seminars and supervision and consult to psychoanalytic institutes. Since I never learned or acquired the German language in any formal sense, I am always hesitant and reticent about using the language. I write my papers in English (as I do this one) and they are then translated by generous colleagues. But even reading them out loud to the audience has been a problem. I remember the first time I did it in front of an audience of 1200 persons and felt I was nearly on suicide mission. What is remarkable, however, is that with time and repeated practice this has become increasingly easier and even pleasurable. My basic childish German, spoken with my parents, has gradually improved, and although it is still a far cry from my command of Hebrew and English it feels increasingly free. The greatest compliment I have received several times was to be told that my accent was perfect and if anything, I have a Hessen accent. In a sense, it is a certain homecoming and renewed connection with my parents and especially my mother.

A significant milestone in this connection took place in 2015, when the German Psychoanalytic Association (DPV) elected me as its Honorary Member (*Ehrenmitglied*). It was a moving experience of the closing of a circle, especially as it took place in Bad Homburg, near my birth place in Frankfurt. In connection with the meeting's theme of responsibility, I spoke of "Integrity and reciprocity in psychoanalysis – who is responsible for what?" under the motto: "Few are guilty, but all are responsible", taken from Rabbi Abraham Joshua Heschel. The address was warmly received and referred to many times, but it was especially moving to the German colleagues that I spoke German.

Perhaps symbolically, a similar homecoming was also marked in Israel. Three months after I received the honorary membership of the DPV, I was honored with a Recognition Award for a Lifetime Contribution by the Israel Psychotherapy Association, as an acknowledgement of my contributions to the profession in Israel. For me it was a welcome and important confirmation of my conscious motivation, when I left the US to return to Israel, to contribute from what I had so generously been given there and to help the mental health field in general and clinical psychology in particular to develop and grow. But it also underlines the fact that my return to Israel, despite or together with all the tensions and life threatening situations it sometime involves, has been truly a homecoming. There is no question in my mind that, for better or worse, this is my home and where the bulk and substance of my roots are. I find life in Israel more challenging, but also more pleasurable and rewarding, in terms of the immediacy of people and experience, than any other place I know.

Another homecoming that also took place in 2015 had to do with discovering and joining my father's roots in Poland. When Mira and I were in Krakow for a conference, a Polish colleague insisted on taking us to Proszowice, my father's birthplace, which is only half an hour from Krakow. The visit there developed unexpectedly to a meeting with the Mayor and others in his office. The first discovery was a picture of Jewish young men, in which I immediately recognized my uncle Chanan, or Chune Erlich, as he was named in the inscription under the picture and as we knew him. But it then continued to an even more startling discovery. A picture hanging on the wall in the corridor was unexpectedly brought in by a journalist, one of the Polish participants in the meeting. It was a picture of the first City Council of Proszowice in 1919, when Poland was freed. In it, standing proudly with his beard and kipa, was my grandfather, Kalman Erlich, whom I never knew, except for the single picture we had of him. It was a totally unexpected discovery, since no one has ever mentioned his being on the City Council, and an emotional reconnection with my father's roots and with my ancestor, who was murdered in the Death Camp of Belzec, together with hundreds of thousands of Polish Jews.

A close friend and colleague once remarked that I tend not to work with my American identity. On reflection, I find some truth in this. Unquestionably, I am more comfortably at home with the Jewish, Israeli and even German parts of my identity. And yet, there is an undeniable American part as well. To begin again with language, although it is an adopted one, English has been the most comfortable way to express myself in writing. But it goes much deeper than that. I have internalized certain American values and attitudes, such as the positive value of competition, as long as it is fairly conducted, in promoting progress. Another value is the belief in the essential equality of all human beings, a notion which is sometimes under attack in Israel, where the Jewish identity of being "The Chosen" people often prevails. Probably playing down my American identity has to do with the fact that it was imposed on me by migration and associated with the traumatic uprooting in my adolescence.

Finally and above all, my identity as a psychoanalyst is the thread that weaves together all the other fragments and parts. It enables me to ask myself questions about my identity and the ways it has been shaped and constructed by these different life events and circumstances. In terms of my daily life and work, it is the foremost one, and the source of the great satisfaction, next to the pleasure and satisfaction from family, children, and our so far 11 grandchildren.

Jerusalem, August 2, 2016

CHAPTER TWO

Shmuel Erlich and his many contributions to analytic training

Cláudio Laks Eizirik

My first meeting with Shmuel Erlich was in 1999, at Arden House, near New York, where Bob Michels had organized a conference on the relation of psychoanalysis and the university, for the Committee on Psychoanalysis and Society, that I chaired at that point. Among the papers presented and discussed by so many distinguished professors, both analysts and non analysts, I was impressed by the clarity, objectivity and intelligence that Shmuel showed in his interventions. But most important for me was the opportunity to talk quietly with him, to exchange life and professional experiences, family histories, and even Jewish jokes. I liked him from the beginning of our relationship. His blue eyes, his frank smile, the warmth and interest he showed for people, all of these traits gave me the feeling that I was in touch with someone somehow familiar, a man one could trust.

Among so many wonderful Shmuel´s achievements that deserve celebration, in this Festschrift, I will focus mainly in his decisive participation in the evolution of psychoanalytic training. As one of his most talented analysts, Shmuel had a central role in the evolution of Israel Psychoanalytic Society, and is one of the most admired and skilled training and supervising analysts of his country, but he is also well known for his many papers on psychoanalytic issues, chapters in books and books (my favorite one is "Fed with tears, poisoned with milk"), by his continuous presence in the international psychoanalytic community and by his special talent to work with people, both individually and in groups.

As we all know, along the decades, issues connected to training were at the core of many decisive progresses, as well as controversial shifts, conflicts, splits, threats to the unity and functioning of societies, regional federations and the IPA.

Otto Kernberg and Robert Tyson (2011), describing the efforts of their administration (1997-2001) concerning psychoanalytic education, mentioned that over many years they had been concerned by what seemed to them a certain stagnation in psychoanalytic institutes, a failure to develop new methods of education, and the predominance of rigid hierarchical systems resulting in a nonfunctional distribution of authority centered in the training analysis system. One of the new ways of conducting analyses approved in their term was concentrated analysis. This led, according to them, to a general discussion of alternative models of psychoanalytic education, such as the French and the Uruguayan models, neither of which fit within the predominant Eitingon model of training prevalent throughout most psychoanalytic societies.

This proposal intensified and gave a sense of urgency to the concern of their administration with the problem of psychoanalytic standards, alternative models of analytic education, and general innovation of psychoanalytic education. It was to prove one of the most difficult, long-term concerns for their and the succeeding administrations, and a resolution would only be achieved many years later. They consider that the struggle to modify and to improve traditional educational procedures exemplifies the intense individual psychological and organizational opposition to change within the IPA.

Daniel Widlocher (2011, p. 512-3) reported, in a candid way, what happened next, in his administration (2001-2005). In his words: " Had the moment come to clearly call into question the apparent unity of the training rules? The decision that was taken at my request did not answer the concern about changing the written rules, but it did address the issue of acknowledging that a certain ´hypocrisy´ existed inside the IPA. By recognizing some variability in the rules, we acknowledged a reality, and therefore the possibility of discussing it instead of hiding it under the carpet. It had to be made possible to talk frankly in the IPA about this issue. Otto Kernberg had opened the discussion about the training functions, showing how controversial it was to bind these functions to the unique status of the training analyst. The issue of the frequency of sessions was more delicate and touched the heart of our practice…"

And he continues : " I began to have private encounters with many members of our Association, with the aim of exploring this issue. I was struck by the gap that existed between the silent uneasiness of interviewed groups and the much more open attitude of colleagues seen on an individual basis. This or that colleague, who had the reputation being quite attached to maintaining the rules of the setting, would admit in private that a greater openness was necessary…I had to decide that we should talk about it, and then we should consult together collectively. Here, I came up against a resistance that made me feel this ambivalence: the opponents to change never wanted to be exposed to votes but held up any decision and took refuge in guerrilla fighting behind the line. This strengthened my conviction that drastic measures had to be taken and that therefore a greater flexibility of methods should be acknowledged and, hence, tolerated…So finally the principle of flexibility was accepted, with the reservation that we would have to discuss individually the choices that this one or that one made."

During all this controversial period, I was a member of the Board, in different capacities, and so was Shmuel, as European representative since 2003. My initial impression on him , now that we were sharing this and other difficult issues and situations, was not only confirmed, but I was able to observe more closely his way of behaving and to expressing himself. Sometimes we shared ideas and positions, sometimes we were in opposing fields, but what struck me was his objectivity, the clarity with which he expressed his ideas, his sense of humor and perhaps more than anything, his integrity and decency.

As it happens in all human groups, there are some members who bring to the group mainly their own agenda, open or hidden, and these are the ones who more strongly contribute to the formation of the different basic assumptions described by Bion. But there are also some members, sometimes few, sometimes not so few, who have the feeling of US rather than the feeling of I, or the feeling of US AGAINST THEM, and these are the ones that allow each group to behave as a community or a work group. Shmuel was always one of this kind.

And so I arrived at a turning point in my relation with Shmuel and I dare to say to a turning point in the history of discussions on analytic training. There is a moving novel by a Spanish writer, Javier Cercas (2012), called Anatomy of a Moment, in which he describes a specific moment in recent Spanish history, and shows how and why each character behaved at that specific situation.

It happened in July, 2005, in Rio, a few days before I became the President of IPA. One of the most difficult tasks for anyone who begins a new administration is to select the right person to perform this or that task. With the help of the other officers, I was selecting and appointing the chairs and members of different committees, but the most delicate and difficult choice, considering the state of affairs just described by Widlocher was precisely the Education Committee. As it is usual in these moments, I was receiving suggestions of several possible choices for this decisive position. Then, during a Board meeting, I saw clearly that only someone with Shmuel 's integrity, ability to listen and to organize, intelligence and academic profile could chair the Education Committee in such a delicate and tense moment.

I still can remember our conversation during the break of one of the last Board meetings under Widlocher presidency. After some brief introductory remarks, concerning the difficult situation we were living, I invited him . He looked at me with surprise, and remained silent for a moment. Then he said that I was taking a very risky attitude, since I did not know him enough, and that I should think better about inviting him. I answered that what I knew about him was enough for me, and that I trusted him. From this point on, I am not sure about what precisely happened next, but it seems to me that he asked for some time, possibly consulted with Mira and other colleagues, but in the next day or so, he accepted the challenge.

If there is one decision I never regretted during my term , this was it. With the help of the other members of the Education Committee (Fernando Weissman, Sander Abend, Aloysio d´Abreu, Marie-France Dispaux and Daniel Jacobs), and with the full support of the Executive Committee, Shmuel produced an impressive amount of information about the already identified three models of training, organized it in a coherent and scholarly description of each and all main aspects of each model and in one year we were prepared for discussing and eventually approving three historic decisions.

In order to write this contribution I went back to my files, after many years without consulting them about this specific issue. The Minutes of a meeting of the Board of Representatives, held at the Maritim Berlin Hotel, on Saturday 28, July 2006, show that three motions were approved unanimously. The first was to adopt the policy that those constituent Organizations which have training models "clearly based" on the Eitingon, French and Uruguayan models, will be regarded as meeting the IPA´s minimum standards and criteria for qualification and admission to IPA membership. This was a significant departure from the previous policy which only accepted the Eitingon model. The second was to consider the question of frequency as constituting one aspect of the coherence of training models, rather then the significant determinant of standards. The third was to adopt the policy of requiring some kind of oversight or regulatory role to be exercised by the IPA. The next steps would be for the IPA to consider how its various procedures on training issues should be modified to reflect these changes of policy by the Board. It took some time to complete these procedural steps, but the main thing was achieved at that meeting.

Reading the minutes, it is worthwhile to mention that at a specific point when criticism and doubts where raised about the issue of frequency, " Dr. Erlich suggested revisions to his Committee´s report. So that paragraph VI, 5, would be amended as follows…". What I want to point out is something beyond the content, but rather to the way Shmuel behaved at the meeting, always ready to listen , to understand the other side of the issue, and to look for a solution that could be acceptable.

In this specific meeting something really unexpected happened: the three motions were approved unanimously, in sharp contrast with the difficult discussions we were having so far, and that of course would continue, as ever. My memory, if we think in the anatomy of a moment, and this is not written in any minutes or reports, makes me think that there was a synergy among Shmuel, Piers Pendred, Monica Armesto and myself, in the way we planned, presented and chaired this meeting, with so many breaks, small groups discussions and clarifications, amendments, that the whole Board were behaving as a real work group. A feeling of US prevailed.

In my own report on my administration (Eizirik, 2011), I considered the main concerns that were voiced during these discussions. On the one hand, some Board members felt that we were living as if we were blind to the reality existing in our psychoanalytic community, that is, the fact that we already had several training models. Others, however, felt that any change would mean a loss in quality and potentially open the gate to all kinds of second class and uncontrolled training.

Looking back now, what we eventually achieved has an aura of "mission impossible" because of the heated debates, occasional harsh exchanges during and between Board meetings, and the warnings that any substantial change would run the risk of splitting the IPA. In my view, the outcome shows something that Shmuel taught us, in different contexts and historic situations- that human groups, even psychoanalytic ones, may sometimes be able to achieve rational goals and to move forward. From a personal perspective, I feel that this was one of the riskiest issues we faced in the last years in our association, and it produced moments of great anxiety and fear in many of us, including myself, hand-in-hand with the sense that we had a historic task to accomplish and that we could not give up our responsibility.

While I write about those facts from 10 years ago, it occurs to me that analytic training remains as one of the main and perhaps the most difficult issue for our psychoanalytic community. Continuous challenges, different perspectives and analytic traditions still struggle to find out a way of keeping the unity into the IPA despite the diversity of its component societies and regions. It is my hope that past but also recent achievements may be helpful in order to stimulate more rational, flexible and realistic ways of keeping our community working and developing in creative ways.

In the following years, Shmuel was extremely active, and always effective in the next steps concerning the procedural adaptations, amendments and Board approval, as well as considering and performing the oversight functions specified by the Board.

During those four years (2005-2009) we worked in close collaboration, and as far as I can remember, without any conflict or disagreement. It was always a pleasure to meet Shmuel and Mira socially, and to work with both of them.

From then on, naturally, our lives followed different paths, as I was no longer active as a main player in the IPA community. But at any meeting, at any event, when we see each other, an immediate smile, a tight hug and a friendly kiss renew our mutual affection. At these meetings, he tells me about his current activities, and his eyes shine and his smile widens when he describes what he is doing in this or that area, but analytic training is always a special interest. As I write this paragraph, it occurs to me that Shmuel , at these and other moments, seem to be enjoying what he does, often jointly with Mira, with the pleasure of a child who discovers and expands his explorations of the infinite world.

And now, my dear friend, Mira surprises us all with this incredible news: Shmuel will be 80 years old ! I see you in my memory in so many different moments: at Arden House ; at your apartment in Tel Aviv, talking with both of you with Marisa ; celebrating your birthday in Berlin, in that unforgettable IPA congress where you moved lots of colleagues with your new activity called Being in Berlin; at the Peking University, you and Mira sitting on the floor of that huge auditorium while I tried to make myself understood talking about psychoanalysis and culture to hundreds of Chinese students and teachers ; at a sad dinner in Chicago, with losses in my mind, ; at the Boston congress ; exchanging news by email during threatening or moving or happy moments…

In this celebration, in this Festshrift, I must say that I feel happy to count among your many friends, that I feel honored to have taken part on your incredible amount of achievements, that I feel grateful for the unique opportunity of learning from you how to be a great professor, a tireless fighter for the noble causes you devote your life, that I feel admiration for your love and partnership with Mira and your family, and that I feel deeply moved for being celebrating the many lives of a true MENTSH.

References

Cercas, J. (2012) *Anatomia de um instante*, São Paulo, Globo.

Eizirik, C.L. The IPA administration from 2005 to 2009. In Loewenberg, P. and Thompson, N. (2011) *100 Years of the IPA*, London, Karnac.

Erlich, H.S., Erlich-Ginor, M., Beland, H.(2009) *Fed with tears, poisoned with milk*.Giessen:Psychosozial-Verlag.

Kernberg, O. and Tyson, R. The IPA administration from 1997 to 2001. Ibid.

Widlocher, D. The IPA administration from 2001 to 2005. Ibid.

Minutes of a meeting of the Board of Representatives, Berlin 2006. Maritim Berlin Hotel, Saturday, 28 and Sunday 29 July 2006.

II. Mainly Theory

CHAPTER THREE

The Courage of the Analyst

Hermann Beland

This essay is dedicated to Shmuel Erlich, friend and courageous man, proven while staying modest as an especially courageous analyst in founding and interpreting the German and Israeli group conferences on the Past in the Present, helping Germans to begin to mourn their heritage of the Holocaust.

1. From the History of Courage

Beginning with Plato, running throughout the centuries are attempts to understand courageous acts. A particular high point in the thinking about courage as a stance in life and about thinking and acting may be Paul Tillich's book "The Courage to Be", published in 1952. In its four introductory chapters, Tillich presents the four forms of courage in the history of the Western world: courage and bravery (Plato + Thomas Aquinas), courage and wisdom (the Stoics), courage and self-affirmation (Spinoza), and courage and life (Nietzsche). At the beginning of "The Courage to Be", Tillich points out the first unsuccessful discussion of courage in Plato's dialog "Laches", which Socrates ends with: "Then, Nicias, we have not discovered what courage is." The Athenian general Nicias (whose name is connected with the Nicias Peace, the last peace treaty between Athens and Sparta before the Spartans finally defeated Athens), in his argument with Laches, also an Athenian general, had defined courage as the *knowledge of that which inspires fear or confidence in war.* The difference between the generals had arisen out of these two Athenian fathers and generals' search for instructors in courage and bravery for their adolescent sons. Earlier, the generals had tried to view Laches' definition of courage – *steadfastness in battle* – as the essential courageous achievement, but speaking against this was that a courageous person must also be able to courageously flee, if he cannot otherwise save his life. The knowledge of what must be feared (courage as flight) and of what must be dared (courage in battle) sounds satisfactory and comprehensively right, but unfortunately, when clearly viewed, this knowledge ultimately means *having to know everything*, which, as Socrates notes, does not exist and cannot exist. The unconscious group capacity, Bion's basic assumption of fight/flight, is well contained in the rejected definition, however.

Figuring in Plato's dialog *Laches* is the consideration whether courage is not the most decisive life competence among the four life competences most highly esteemed in Antiquity and the Middle Ages, the essential arête, the decisive virtue, *the courage for life as achievement*, which should be viewed as more basic than wisdom, justice, and prudence.

In the history of philosophy and the history of ethics since Plato, there has been a dispute between the primacy of *knowledge* or the primacy of *will* in courage, between ontological theory as the decisive orienting knowledge that enables one to practice bravery (Thomas Aquinas, Paul Tillich) and courage as self-affirmation (Spinoza) in the existential sense of "*do everything you do with your whole heart; do with your whole heart everything*" (cf. the "heart" root of the word for courage: "coraggio" in Italian and "courage" in French and English).

Thus, since ancient times, a dispute has existed on this issue between the two basic philosophical dispositions, the primacy of categories of action or of being, perhaps an unavoidable dispute among philosophers, like that between Kierkegaard and Hegel and between Kant and Heidegger, because existential decisions cannot be derived from ontological conditions. This historical dispute is also reflected in the various accentuations that lie behind the various approaches to psychoanalytic technique (know-how technique versus container-contained technique).

I think the expression »the courage of the analyst« belongs to the Spinoza tradition in a special way. So I would like to add a few words about this humane philosopher, whose life also lends him credibility. One sees clearly that Paul Tillich, like people in the 18th century, regarded Spinoza and his humanism as very impressive, precise, and benignly thinking and his person as more likeable than that of any other philosopher. Leibniz, Lessing, Mendelssohn, Goethe, and Schleiermacher all loved this man, while theologians of all directions – Catholics, Protestants, Orthodox Jews, and pious Muslims – hated him as a false teacher. In the 18th century, it could still be dangerous to publicly esteem Spinoza. Even in the years of Goethe's youth, a person shown to be a Spinozist had to expect to be religiously and societally defamed. In 1656, the Amsterdam synagogue was the first to damn and exclude Spinoza. In 1759, Laurence Sterne made this bizarre excommunication public in *Tristram Shandy*, thereby proving the development of tolerance in the Enlightenment. But Sterne's character Parson Yorick then dies by revenge in his struggle against hypocrisy and arrogated dignity.

The central term in Spinoza is self-affirmation. "The endeavour, wherewith everything endeavours to persist in its own being, is nothing else but the actual essence of the thing in question." (The Ethics III, Proposition VI). The word "persist", in turn, recalls General Laches' first attempt to determine the meaning of "courage" as "steadfastness". The soul's striving to preserve itself (conatus animae) means the same thing as its courage to achieve (ipsius agenda potentiam) and the potency with which it affirms and posits itself (affirmat sive ponit – Ethics III, 56). The knowledge expressed in the self-affirmation of one's own being is mediated by reason, that capacity of the soul to have accurate ideas. Rightly and correctly acting is acting in accordance with reason's guidance, and that in turn should mean the same thing as affirming one's own being.

In psychological terms, one could equate this self-affirmation with the positive narcissism that, from birth on, tries to succeed in each action, to do it properly, and thereby to affirm oneself (the achievement of accomplishment, self-respect). Psychoanalytically, the opposite of the power to accomplish is helplessness and its normal consequence, depression (cf. Edward Bibring 1953).

Spinoza splits courage and self-affirmation into two terms, fortitudo and animositas. In Tillich's translation, animositas is courage in the sense of a total act of the person. "Animositas I understand namely the desire (cupiditas)," writes Spinoza, "with which everyone strives to preserve his being solely in accordance with the dictates of reason." (Ethics, III, 59) What follows from this is typical of Spinoza's understanding of self-affirmation as well as of reason: a specific quality contained in animositas is generositas, the desire with which everyone strives to foster his fellow humans and to bond with them in friendship. For Spinoza, love for others is thus contained in self-affirmation. It is even the same as self-affirmation.

We cannot conclude this brief description of Spinoza's equating courage with self-affirmation without mentioning the grounding of self-affirmation in the divine self-affirmation, an idea for which Spinoza's thinking is famous (deus sive natura). If the soul views itself *sub specie aeternitatis*, from the standpoint of a form of eternity (Ethics V, proposition 30), then it sees its own self-affirmation, like that of all beings and things, as part of the divine and it sees its self-love and its love of neighbor as part of the divine self-love and, in amor intellectualis, finds its happiness as part of the divine happiness.

The main problem of self-affirmation is first solved in divine participation: *because negative affects can be overcome only by positive affects, amor intellectualis overcomes hate and fear in the feeling of happiness.* "The courage to be is possible because it is participation in the self-affirmation of Being itself," Tillich summarizes at the conclusion of his chapter on Spinoza (Tillich 1952, 22).

At the end of his *Ethics*, Spinoza asked himself why almost all people do not follow his path, and he answered: because it is difficult. For "…all things excellent are as difficult as they are rare." (Ethics V, 42) Tillich regards this information as both melancholy and resigned. But in my view, Spinoza's writings, also in this passage of The Ethics, do sound neither melancholy nor resigned.

2. The Courage of the Analyst, First Approximation

I now return to the courage of the analyst. It ought to be involved with the most important aspect of our stance and work, i.e., overcoming anxiety, first and above all in the analytic session, in overcoming the anxiety of both the analyst and the patient. It should also be involved in overcoming pain in the analytic session and in dealing with analytic inability, the defeat of not understanding. Analysts have always been modest people, which is why they speak with their field's understatement about the analyst's *tolerance of anxiety* and about the analyst's *tolerance of pain* when they try to specify more closely the analyst's courage. We think we know, after all, that all these central analytical professional tolerances derive from the infant's toleration of frustration, as Bion understood it, which draws its life-preserving power from the nursing mother's understanding (rêverie), but which can break down if the baby is not understood. In the worst case, the breakdown of the baby's tolerance of frustration because it is not understood, can lead to psychosis.

With the courage of the analyst (as of the patient), we thus seem to find ourselves in a primary anthropological issue.

We are all equal before the demands of frustration tolerance, nicely democratically equal, as guaranteed in the constitutions of democratic states: there is no difference between men and women in being courageous. If we as analysts have met the demands of frustration tolerance in our work, then we have been courageous. We have stout-heartedly faced the danger originating in the patient, have not allowed ourselves to be intimidated by his ban on thinking, have painfully tolerated injuries and our own errors without taking retribution, and, after not understanding for a long time, we have understood and communicated a primary matter. As in Bion's beautiful definition of transference interpretation, we have communicated to the patient the analyst's working hypotheses that he has formed of the models and hypotheses that the patient has formed of the analyst. (Bion 1963, p. 17)

What was courageous about that, we may ask?

Was it perhaps the stoutheartedness?

What does courage feel like, what does it look like, when it is psychoanalytic?

Is there perhaps something special about the dangers to the analyst that his courage must correspond to?

Are there perhaps differences after all for male analysts in distinction from female analysts?

What about the courage in the face of analytic groups?

What about the courage in the face of the neighboring sciences and in the face of society as a whole and its current tendencies?

Does the courage of the analyst apply to his dealings with the unconscious in all realms, i.e., to his dealings with his own unconscious, with the traumatically altered, split unconscious of the patient, with the unconscious fate of a candidate, which has become his or her organized character, with the unconscious of the group of colleagues, with the unconscious of his own society, with the unconscious in psychoses, with the unconscious in malignant societal prejudices, in religious wars, in war per se?

3. Freud's Moral Courage

At the end of his short, two-and-a-half page essay "Popper-Lynkeus and the Theory of the Dream", Freud wrote, "I think what enabled me to discover the *cause of dream distortion* was my moral courage." (Freud 1923f, S.E.19, 263)

This sentence was the starting point of our theme. It is extremely interesting in terms of the history of knowledge and the history of science. By means of Freud's a self-knowledge as researcher, which probably came from his self-analysis, it explains why he and not some other great discoverer of the laws of human thinking solved the "deepest and most difficult problem of dream life" (Freud), the riddle of dream distortion. It was a moral courage, the fortitudo moralis, as Kant had termed this central competence of the human mind.

I do not know whether Freud took his term from Kant. If so, then in the epistemological sense. But I don't know when this term actually originated. The ancient Greeks, the Romans, and the Scholastic theologians of the Middle Ages probably didn't know the term, but indeed the matter (one need think only of Sophocles' Antigone). Perhaps the term begins with Luther (decisions of conscience, pecca fortiter!). The clearest definition that I found in Kant clearly relates to the social danger to a researcher whose research results disturb the moral sleep of humanity. Kant once wrote:

Finally, belonging *also to courage that is purely moral is* the resolution to dare something that duty commands, even at the danger of others' ridicule. – *To this belongs* a higher degree of courage, because *love of honor* is the constant companion of virtue, and he who is otherwise adequately composed against *violence* but seldom feels equal to *ridicule* if one refuses him this claim to honor by laughing in scorn." (Kant 1968, Vol. 10, p. 589, fn 2, trans. here Mitch Cohen)

Here one would like to say someone is speaking from experience.

At any rate, everything started from this point, Freud's moral courage as the paradigm of the revolutionary new science: dream *interpretation* as the royal road to the unconscious, the recognition of the repression of the most brutal and sexually ruthless desires of childhood and of the denial of the traumata of relationship, the discovery of these wishes themselves, the recognition of the primary process of unconscious thinking, the comprehension of neurosis, psychosis, and normality, Freud's insight into inhibition, symptom, and anxiety, into transference and the art of treatment, into id, ego, and superego. But what did Freud mean by moral courage? And why did he hide this central discovery of his self-analysis in the *Zeitschrift des Vereines Allgemeine Nährpflicht*, where hardly anyone would find it?

In 1909, Freud had inserted a remark into Chapter VI of the "Interpretation of Dreams" that answers both questions for the moment:

Since I may be allowed to term *the tracing of dream distortion to censorship as the core of my view of the dream*, here I insert the last part of that story "Dreaming like Waking" by [Josef-Popper] Lynkeus (Vienna, 2nd edition, 1900) in which I rediscover the main character of my teaching. (Freud 1900a, S.E. 5, 309 – trans. here Mitch Cohen)

After this remark, Freud quoted the story of the man who had the capacity to think while dreaming as well as while awake, which is traced to the moral clarity of his nature, his goodness, his justness, his love of truth, because of which, without any conflict within himself, he required no distortion, because he required no repression. He was at peace with his conscience. In 1914, Freud took up this thread in his *History of the Psychoanalytic Movement*. He commented on how he had been shaken by Josef Popper. Independently from Freud, Popper had discovered the most original and significant part of Freud's dream theory, "tracing dream distortion to an inner conflict, a kind of inner dishonesty" (Freud 1914d, S.E. 14, p. 19).

In 1932, finally, in "My Contact with Josef-Popper-Lynkeus", Freud raised a monument to his veneration of this benign humanitarian, the friend of Ernst Mach. Ten years after Popper's death, "overcome by the encounter with his wisdom", Freud wrote:

> …if science tells us that such a person, wholly without malice or falseness and lacking all repressions, does not exist or is not viable, then it could still be guessed that, to the degree that an approach to this ideal state is possible, it had found its realization in Popper's own person. (Freud 1932, S.E. 22, 224 – trans. here Mitch Cohen)[1]

So Freud owed to his moral courage an anthropological discovery of revolutionary significance, the discovery of the repression of the cruel

---

[1] At the end of his "Anthropology from a pragmatic point of view", Kant spoke of the current necessity to dissemble and spun out a fantasy contradicting this necessity that fits precisely with Freud's discussion of Popper-Lynkeus. "It could well be that creatures possessing reason existed on some other planet that could do no other than to think aloud, that is, *when awake as when dreaming*; whether in society or alone, they could not have a thought that they did not simultaneously utter. … If they were not all as pure as angels, then it cannot be imagined how they get along with each other, the one having only a little respect for the other, and how they endure each other." (loc. cit. 688) Kant did not expect a change in structural dishonesty through the voluntary agreement of the individual, but only "through progressive organization of the citizens of the world in and toward the species as a system, i.e., cosmopolitically associated" (loc. cit. 690).

and the raw sexual wishes of childhood in himself, and thereupon in all people, mortally dangerous and destructive, oedipally organized, becoming present in dreaming and in symptoms, *but distorted*. What did Freud need his courage for? He referred to the new discovery of the threefold nature of the modern human and to the discovery of a second, the unconscious logic of the primary process that Matte Blanco (symmetrical and asymmetrical thinking) and Bion (theory of thinking) further illuminated in their different ways. The threefold nature of the human being consisted of

1.   his pleasure-seeking, criminal unconscious nature, the id,
2.   his moral nature, the superego, and
3.   his prudent nature, the ego.

Freud's courage to seek and speak the truth was moral courage, because he had to acknowledge his own unconscious sexual ruthlessness and meanness and had to learn to tolerate them before he could historicize them as repressed wishes. He had to naturalize them: there are unavoidable laws of development that dictate these wishes, laws valid for every person and all of humanity.

Beyond that, it was his moral courage, because he had to come into conflict with society's moral narcissism, with societal hypocrisy, and he had to overcome his social anxiety, his at least in unconscious and paranoid fear of being socially ostracized or lynched if he carried out his research to the end. No one before him had endured this socio-moral anxiety and overcome the resulting inhibition of research and discovered the unconscious as the true psyche.

Freud's courage was thus moral in three ways:

1.   in relation to himself, against his superego anxiety and against his social anxiety;
2.   in relation to society and its moral and religious illusions (sexuality of the child, sexuality of the woman, ubiquitous repression, the neuroses, psychopathologies and psychoses of humanity, the development of culture as oedipal development of religion, etc.); and

3.   especially in relation to the illusions of science and scientists, in particular the illusions in academic developmental psychology, in biological anthropology, in psychiatry, and in sociology.

Freud reported in The History of the Psychoanalytic Movement "that, at the end of the 1890s and the beginning of the 20th century, he was completely isolated for years." He accepted without hesitation economic disadvantages for the sake of his research. I mention both aspects, isolation and economic disadvantages, because they definitely could occur again in the future of analytic courage.

4. The Courage of the Analyst, Second Approximation

I'll now leap to the present and speak about the courage of the analyst today, about a theory of this courage, and about the five fields of his courage. They are:

a)   the courage in self-knowledge;
b)   the courage of abstinence;
c)   the courage to interpret transference;
d)   the courage to speak publicly in one's own and other groups and to interpret groups;
e)   the courage to publish scientific writings.

In support, I'll repeat the famous lines from Freud's May 1916 letter to Lou Andreas Salome, which Bion has placed in the center of attention:

"I know that I have artificially blinded myself at my work in order to concentrate all the light on the one dark passage: on connection, harmony, nobility and all you [Lou] call the symbolic. I refrain, frightened by the experience of such a demand; each expectation carries with it the danger to see the expected recognition as distorted, though perhaps beautified." (Freud 1960, letter of May 25, 1916, p. 327/28; quoted in translation by Wilfred Bion 1970)

Bion later pointed out that the most difficult part of the analytic stance is the solitude that must be chosen to fulfill the task. He said abstinence was the overcoming of an animal legacy: the herd animal mentality. We would prefer to be together and not feel cut off from the source of life that the patient becomes for us in decisive moments. We don't want to spoil things between the patient and us with a necessary interpretation. And we don't want to see him as so cruel that he must be feared. "At no time must either analyst or analysand lose the sense of isolation within the intimate relationship of analysis." (Bion 1963, 15)

In every session, the analyst must tolerate his own separation anxiety if he is to be able to serve his patient's psychic integration and assumption of responsibility. Actually, he must be prepared for the feeling of dying. Behind Freud's renunciation of connection, harmony, nobility, and the symbolic stands his tolerance of separation anxiety, as much as it stands behind Bion's translation of Freud's renunciation as No Memory, No Desire, Not Knowing while analyzing. Tolerant of separation, separated from securing knowledge, "the piercing shaft of darkness can be directed on the dark features of the analytic situation" until a gestalt emerges, the unknown of this session. (Bion's paraphrasing of the above description by Freud, Bion 1970, 57)

I therefore suspect that *the courage of the analyst is identical to his toleration of separation anxiety*. The fear of pains and cruelties is also only one of the separation anxieties.

In the psychic realm of toleration of separation anxiety, both patient and analyst and both analyst and his group discover the analytic possibilities of knowledge that are adequate to disturbances of thought and to psychological growth. In methodological uncertainty of not knowing, the analyst concentrates on the disturbed conditions of thought in the psychically disturbed person, in the empirically supported hope that truth can be found and will heal. Practically, this means that, in the material of the session, the analyst attends to those aspects that, no matter how familiar they are, are unknown to him and to the patient. This uncomfortable/frightening state of not knowing should be endured without grasping for facts or logic until a pattern emerges that integrates the patient's scattered disconnections and can be formulated as the hypothesis that the patient posits about the analyst, the transference hypothesis (cf. Bion 1970, p. 124). The working hypotheses of the inter- pretations enable the patient to learn about the convictions that unconsciously guide him. This self-knowledge gradually frees him from the iron grip of the structural positing, the unconscious false convictions derived from traumatic fears. The patient's self-knowledge increases his toleration of anxiety and his endurance of unhappiness about his earlier errors, the destruction they wrought, and his limited life. They enable the patient's new self-affirmation, his courage to live. If the psychoana- lyst owes these desired results to his overcoming of his separation anxiety, i.e., to his separation courage, then his self-affirmation as ana- lyst can grow with each working day.

Looking back on the history of psychoanalysis, we can note that the great discoveries about the unconscious have been made by men and women who endured more anxiety than others and who, despite anxiety, continued to conduct research. Freud had to endure moral paranoid anxiety; Melanie Klein had to endure depressive anxiety; and Bion had to endure the fear of going insane, the worst form of separation anxiety. Bion then placed separation anxiety at the center of all developmental problems. He is the great psychologist of psychotic communication and was therefore the discoverer of the basic processes of normal thinking. All three were thus especially courageous in their analytic work and have thereby gained their function as role models and our gratitude.

References

Bibring, E. (1953). The mechanism of Depression. In: Greenacre (Ed.) (1953): *Affective Disorders*. Int. Univ. Press, New York).

Bion, W. R. (1967). A Theory of thinking. In: W. R. Bion, *Second Thoughts*, 110-119. Karnac, London.

Bion, W. R. (1963). *Elements of Psychoanalysis*. Maresfield Reprints, London

Bion W. R. (1970). *Attention and Interpretation*. Tavistock Publications, London Sydney Toronto Wellington.

Freud, S. (1900a). *Die Traumdeutung*. S.E.,. 4-5. GESAMMELTE

WERKE: II/III, i-701. Imago Publishing Co., Ltd., London

Freud, S. (1923f). Joseph Popper-Lynkeus und die Theorie des Traumes. S.E., 19: 285.

Freud, S. (1914d). Zur Geschichte der psychoanalytischen Bewegung. S.E.,14: 1.

Freud, S. (1932c). Meine Berührung mit Joseph Popper-Lynkeus. S.E., 22: 217.

Freud, S. (1960). *Briefe 1873 – 1939*. Zweite, erweiterte Auflage. Ausgewählt und herausgegeben von Ernst und Lucie Freud. Fischer, Frankfurt am Main 1968.

Kant, E. (1968 [1798]). Anthropologie in pragmatischer Hinsicht. *Kant Werke Vol. 10*, ed. W. Weischedel. Wiss. Buchgesellschaft, Darmstadt.

Matte Blanco, I. (1975). *The Unconscious as Infinite Sets. An essay in Bi-Logic*. Duckworth, London.

Platon: *Sämtliche Dialoge, Bd. 1, Laches und Euthyphron*. Herausgegeben, Vorwort und Einleitung zur Gesamtausgabe von Otto Apelt. Felix Meiner, Hamburg 1988.

Spinoza, B. de (1980³ [1677]).: *Ethica. Opera: lat. u. dt. = Werke /Spinoza. Bd. 2 Tractatus de intellectus emendatione. Ethica*. Hg. von Konrad Blumenstock. Wiss. Buchges., Darmstadt.

Sterne, L. (1967 [1759-67]).*The Life and Opinions of Tristram Shandy, Gentleman*. Penguin Books, Harmondsworth.

Tillich, P. (1952). *The Courage to Be*. Yale University Press, New Haven, Connecticut.

Reflections on
"primary erotogenic masochism"

Marilia Aisenstein

FOR SHMUEL:

Shmuel's friendship is meaningful for me. We first met long ago in London at a council meeting. During this meeting we expressed opposite views. Afterwards we talked together and became friends. Through the years since that we have shared many administrative and scientific meetings and friendly encounters.

> *But we also share a passionate interest in Freud's oeuvre.*

> *Among other qualities Shmuel is a true Freudian, a reader who believes in metapsychology, a theory lover.*

> *That is why I have chosen to offer him some reflexions on a topic which is important to me although little known in analytic literature. Even if ignored or vied in a negative way "primary erotogenic masochism" described by Freud in 1924 is to my mind crucial and "guardian of life".*

Masochism is enigmatic and its very existence poses a question to psychoanalytic theory that Freud himself would qualify as essential: if pleasure and displeasure can merge and coincide, then what becomes of the pleasure principle?

Here lies the economic problem of masochism, and the crucial text of 1924 will conceptualize it by displacing the question of the strange relationship between pleasure and pain onto a radical re-examination of the entirety of psychoanalytic theory outlined until then.

It may seem rather unthinkable that Freud—who was working on the theme of sexuality, which masochism is a part of, which he had evoked since the Three Essays on Sexuality (1905)—discovered only in 1924 that defining the pleasure principle from the economic point of view renders masochism unintelligible.

If one had to state the problem more simply, one might effectively become astonished that, strictly compared to discharge, pleasure is opposed to displeasure or tension, retention, and excitation. What was thus denied was that there is pleasure in the tension of excitation.

Rereading "Instincts and Their Vicissitudes" of 1915 after the fact clearly shows that nothing before 1920 succeeds in throwing light on masochism as a clinical fact. One must wait for the conception of a "Beyond the Pleasure Principle" for "the problem" of masochism to be finally posed in a heuristic manner.

Enigma comes from the Greek enigma, which implies firstly the idea of detour. The meaning "obscure" or "mysterious" is a later semantic shift. For this kind of enigma, the necessary detour passes through a revision of the first theory of the drives, which enables us to consider self-destructiveness. The second drive opposition brings together in the form of libido the sexual drives and the drives of conservation in the face of the death drive—unbinding movement such as it is defined in the Outline of 1938.

The second drive theory brings with it the conception of the second topic, which is richer and more complicated than the preceding one, but above all it lays out certain problems differently: If the pleasure principle—until then considered as the guardian of psychic life—merges with displeasure, then displeasure can become life's objective. And Freud will have to ask himself what then is the guardian of our psychic life. The answer is held in the eleven pages of the article of 1924 and it must pass through the recognition of an erogenic, original masochism whose existence until then had been denied.

From that point on, it is the latter which becomes the guardian which vouchsafes life because it is the witness and the remnant of the alloy of the two drives: libido, on the one hand, and the death drive, on the other. Thus is born the fundamental notion of drive intricacy.

If to the opposition between sexuality and conservation is substituted the harnessing of the drive libido and the death drive, then we must conceive of a libido which is an impassioned binding, like Freud defines it in the Outline, to which is opposed, in order to avoid a coalescence a principle of unbinding which permits the long way, waiting, and therefor desire. The notion of human desire involves expectation and consecutivly time .

Now, waiting is unthinkable if we do not imagine a masochist cathexis of displeasure or a masochistic dimension of existence which allows for the cathexis of the hallucination of pleasure.

Why should we not kill ourselves when we our first disappointment strikes? Why do we love to suffer from love? Why? . . . Because the intricacy of the two antagonist drives is achieved on the basis and in function of a primary, erotogenic masochism, upon which the other forms of masochism—feminine, moral, and secondary—are propped up; secondary masochism being the reversal of sadism on the person proper, which Freud had described in 1915 as the only form of "masochism."

For the study of a variety of illustrations of masochism and its enigmas, I refer you to two very different writers. The first, Gilles Deleuze, made a fundamental contribution by having shown that masochism is neither the antonym nor the compliment of sadism, and how the entity "sadomasochism," invented by Krafft-Ebing, poses some very complex problems. There is no reversal but rather a dual, paradoxical creation. The sadist partner of the masochist is an integral part of the masochistic scenario and, further, he has been trained in his task, he accepts its rules and thus cannot be thought of as merely a perverse sadist.

I cannot go here into all the points Deleuze makes concerning Freud, and so I must content myself by saying that he does ask some very problematic questions.

The other writer is Benno Rosenberg, who authored a remarkable monograph and many other fascinating articles. His main thesis is based on the hypothesis of an originary masochism binding destructiveness which, when projected, becomes sadism. This way of conceiving masochism enables us to avoid the pitfall of a genetic vision. He likewise sees primary projection as the foundation of later mechanisms of negation. An introjected sadism becomes a self-directed sadism which engenders guilt. Differentiating moral masochism from guilty feelings is at the bottom of the dynamic between the ego and the superego.

As the guardian of life (to use Rosenberg's expression), masochism is not mere masochism in that it primarily binds destructiveness to it; it can also constitute secondarily an "attempt at healing." This explains the vices of perverse masochism in a "cold psychosis" (Jean and Evelyne Kestembergs' concept), in which self-destructive and self-mutilating behavior may, by their very excess, be seen as palliative in relation to the failure of the initial masochistic nucleus.

A theory as original as the constitution of the psyche founded on an originary masochistic nucleus which organizes the satisfaction–hallucination of desire and temporality cannot fail to shed light on the two drive drifts into somatosis and a perverse acting out. Should we conclude that these two outcomes are a challenge to what Benno Rosenberg called the "masochistic dimension of existence"?

Basing ourselves on the clinical recognition of this "masochistic dimension," we can once again see as valid the concept of the death drive: the primary ego is created out of an initial narcissism thanks to a redirecting of a part of the death drive thus captured in order to act on behalf of the libido against the attacks of the death drive. It is a matter of making use of the very essence of the death drive and its specificity while fundamentally reversing its aims. The redirection thus takes on an existential value and is at the basis of the binding value of negation. I agree entirely with Benno Rosenberg in conceptualizing the necessity of the masochistic dimension of existence in addition to the necessity of what we call the death drive.

For what is the extraordinarily robustness of the human psyche made of, that robustness which drives us to resist the most horrible suffering, our own sadism as well as another's? How is it that we are able to accept a life with suffering? How can we tolerate suffering if it is not intrinsically bound to the libido and, thus, eroticized?

My own position follows the theory of the Psychosomatic School of Paris. Working with extreme cases of patients suffering from painful, disabling and even deadly somatic disorders has led me to advance the hypothesis of how the failure of masochism as an existential dimension of the psyche and the guardian of life, is founded on the failure of primary, erotogenic masochism. Primary masochism was described by Freud in 1924, it is considered primary for it does not follows a first state as secondary masochism which is defined by the reversal of sadism on one's own person . It is a state, very similar to primary narcissism , in which the death drive is still directed against one's own self, but bound by the libido and linked to the latter.That is what Freud describes, after 1920 as "fusion "of drives.

Secondary masochism comes additionally to primary masochism as to reinforce it. What I call "failure of primary masochism" would be the consequence of a lack of the fusion of instincts.

If the great psychosomaticians of the first generation, in particular Pierre Marty, did not often speak of masochism, it is because, describing a new clinical practice defined by a semiotic void, narcissism and masochism were only expressed in the negative.

In fact, from 1914, in "Narcissism: an Introduction," and through the theory of the drives, Freud had evoked somatic disorders and described the narcissistic backward surge necessary for the processes of healing to begin. A withdrawal of the narcissistic libido from the objects and the external world ,and a masochistic cathexis into the suffering body merges here but are often absent among somatic patients referred to psychoanalysts. I refer here to chapter two of the 1914 article, (SE 14, p. 67-102, pages 82-83) were Freud explains the necessary withdrawal of the libido into the body when there is illness :

"We should then say : the sick man withdraws his libidinal cathexes back into his own ego, and sends them out again when he recovers… The way in which a lover's feelings, however strong, are banished by bodily ailments, and suddenly replaced by complete indifference, has been exploited by comic writers to an appropriate extent." writes Freud.

This withdrawal of the libido and masochistic cathexis are generally absent in our patients who do not abandon their external interests and refuse regression.

In general classic medical therapy alone does not suffice if they are to be treated. Further sometimes missing from these unusual clinical pictures is anxiety which, like pain, is counter-cathected, negated, or anesthetized?

Now, masochism is the eroticized cathexis of suffering whose paradigm is physical pain since its reference is the model of the body.

Pain and the Pleasure Principal

Pain as such is difficult to conceive of and little exploited in psychoanalytic theory. A recent number of the Revue française de psychosomatique [French Review of Psychosomatics] rises to this challenge.

I think it important that since Freud, and after the watershed year of 1920, there existed a displacement of the "enigma" of masochism onto the "enigma of pain." From this moment on, when Freud accepted that his strictly economic conception of the pleasure principle fails in the face of masochism, he revised the pleasure principle by carrying out a rehabilitation of excitation. The tension of excitation, while painful, contains some pleasure in it. Whence the subversive idea that the masochistic pleasure of pain becomes—after the economic problem of masochism and in the second theory of the drives—the very model of pleasure. Curiously, in 1905, in the Three Essays, Freud approached this vision which he himself then abandoned. It is thus that Freud relinquishes the term "enigmatic" in order to accept the paradox of masochism as such. What remains enigmatic is pain that always shows the double valence of pleasure and its beyond.

We ought to recall here that Sigmund Freud himself, a specialist of psychic and moral pain, began his career by studying an anaesthetic, cocaine. The anaesthesia that Freud evokes in Draft G constitutes a protection against what is unbearable in the drive, "the anaesthesia is the cause of the melancholia" (S.E. I, p. 203), he writes to Fliess, thereby emphasizing the paradox tied from the start to pain, or to its negative, anaesthesia.

Those three pages were extracted from a paper never published in English but in French under the Title: "Douloureuse Enigme, Enigme de la Douleur." Primary erotogenic masochism is what helps us to learn to wait and to hope. We need it to love and to live.

Dear Shmuel I wish you to still have sufficient hope and will face with pleasure the next twenty years.

Marilia Aisenstein,
Paris, September 2016

References

Deleuze, D. (1972). *Presentation de Sacher Masoch*, Paris Edition de Minuit

Freud, S. (1899). Letter to Fliess, Draft G, S.E., 1: 203. London: Hogarth

Freud, S. (1905). Three Essays on the Theory of Sexuality. S.E., 7: 123-303. London: Hogarth

Freud, S. (1914)., On Narcissism, an Introduction. S.E., 14: 67-105. London: Hogarth

Freud, S. (1915). Instincts and their Vicissitudes. S.E., 14: 109-141. London: Hogarth

Freud, S. (1920). Beyond the Pleasure Principal. S.E., 18: 1-65. London: Hogarth

Freud, S. (1924). The economic problem of Masochism. S.E., 19: 155-176. London: Hogarth

Freud, S. (1938). An Outline of Psychoanalysis. S.E., 23: 139-209. London: Hogarth

Rosenberg, B.(1999). *Masochisme Mortifere et Masochisme Gardien de la Vie*, Paris Ed PUF

CHAPTER FIVE

Psychosomatics and Unrepresented States
Howard B. Levine, MD

For Shmuel with love and appreciation

In his 1937 paper, *Constructions in Analysis*, Freud restated his metaphor of *analyst as archaeologist*. In speaking of "the psychical object whose early history the analyst is seeking to recover" (p. 260), he proposed that like the ruins of Pompeii or the contents of the tomb of King Tut:

"All of the essentials are preserved; *even things that seem completely forgotten are present somehow and somewhere, and have merely been buried and made inaccessible to the subject. Indeed, it may, as we know, be doubted whether any psychical structure can really be the victim of total destruction.* It depends only upon analytic technique whether we shall succeed in bringing what is concealed completely to light." (p. 260, italics added).

Like the ego psychology and conflict theory that I grew up with, this quote from Freud seems to hold the tacit assumption that all experience, internal and external, is psychically represented, even if unrecoverable ("buried and made inaccessible") or too deeply defended against ("concealed") to ever become conscious. Similarly, one usual reading of Kleinian theory implies that because the object is an inborn component of the drive and all internal experience is organized and stored as 'unconscious phantasy' – i.e., *somewhere in the mind* – then both drive and internal experience are by definition *psychic* and *represented*.

These assumptions, which presume that a basic neurotic structure lies at the root of psychosomatic illness, and the implications for setting and technique that follow, have been intimately connected, especially in the US, to the disappointing and problematic history of attempts at analytic treatment of psychosomatic disease. Hypotheses of Ferenczi (1926) and Alexander (1950) about organ neuroses, primary symbolism and the presumed psychogenic origin of the classical psychosomatic illnesses – or the ways in which they were interpreted or applied – often led to grave difficulties and resulted in disillusionment concerning the efficacy of analysis in these situations. Among the most significant difficulties were the assumptions that psychosomatic illnesses would:

- be found to have an underlying pre-existing, symbolic, conflictual, unconscious basis and meaning.
- be linked to a pre-determined, unconscious, specific and therefore discoverable constellation of emotions, such as hostile-aggressive or dependent security-seeking feelings.[1]
- be amenable to analytic exploration, interpretation, and treatment by a relatively silent analyst in a *decoding* or *uncovering* process analogous to the analysis of dreams and Oedipal neuroses.

One complicating factor that these early efforts may have failed to take sufficiently into account was something pointed out by Green (1997), who, following Winnicott and Bion, argued that psychosomatic, borderline and other non-neurotic patients are dependent on affective communication and *"seem to need a sharing of their experience,* which does not mean collusion with it, *in a non-intrusive exchange which gives them a feeling of existence,* in which sufficient space can be formed, albeit manufactured space, for their silent self, and where the defensive meaning of their state can be acquired without there being a compression of their inner world." (pp.200-201, italics added). Note his emphasis on psychic space being *manufactured*, with meaning being *created*

---

[1] This opened up the potential to search for and expect to discover a kind of one-to-one correspondence or informal "universal symbolism" associated with each category of disorder. Thus, asthma, for example, was often spoken of as "the body's expression of the stifled cry and tears of the infant for the mother" (Peter Knapp, personal communication, 1974).

('acquired') rather than *found* ('uncovered'). Too often in the past, mistaken assumptions about the need for abstinence and neutrality to deal with an underlying neurotic, albeit primitive, structure for psychosomatic symptoms led to a too silent and affectively disengaged analyst and an increasingly frantic, clamorous and somatically regressed patient.

Further confusion arose from the failure to appreciate that rather than having a psychically organized and ideationally saturated aetiology to begin with, "bodily symptoms can become secondarily linked with fantasies and affects and, therefore, appear [only retroactively] to give a somatic disease symbolic meaning" (Taylor 2010, p. 183). There were other problems as well,[2] but none perhaps were as significant as *the clinical assumption that the classical setting and rules of technique that were appropriate for and suited to the analytic treatment of neurosis could be equally applied to the analysis of psychosomatic disease.* Here, experience too often revealed that a silent analyst, or an expectation that psychosomatic patients could use the setting and analytic object relationship to maintain their capacity to think reflectively, free associate, work symbolically or emotionally regulate themselves often proved disastrous. Consequently, by the 1970s and 1980s, psychosomatics had become relatively marginalized and neglected in the U.S. in our psychoanalytic training programs and as a subject of analytic study.

But what if analysts approached the problem from a different set of theoretical assumptions with a different set of implications for listening stance and technique? Would that lead to a different understanding of psychosomatic conditions and a different, more successful set of analytic outcomes? What if we turned to a theory whose origins are implicit but undeveloped in the work of Freud, one that allowed for psychic deficits and absences, as well as psychic presences and conflicts?

Such a theory would take note of Freud's (1899) early observation that we may not have memories *from* childhood, but only memories

---

[2] See, for example, Rappaport de Aisemberg's (2010) description of "the concept of mixed neuroses" in which "there coexists in the same subject a psychoneurotic organization and a somatic one, with a deficit in the psychic linkage [between the two.]" (p. 115).

about childhood that are assembled and completed in a present moment, in a specific context and with a specific unconscious purpose or his (Freud 1915b) insistence that drives were 'frontier concepts' – (exemplars of *pre- or proto-psychic registrations of somatic turbulence*); of Bion's (1962) assertion that the emotions were beta elements and therefore not yet psychic and the data of psychic reality were discernible not by empirical observation of sense data, but only by an ego function called *intuition* (Bion 1970)?

These and other contemporary developments, such as the shift in emphasis in the psychoanalytic cure from the exclusive search for hidden or disguised psychic *contents* to the development and strengthening of the *capacities* to contain, create and think thoughts, have changed our thinking about analytic process and technique. Hartke (2013) noted the shift in the goals of contemporary analysis, which he suggested now aims "primarily at the expansion of the mental container, instead of the predominant work on unconscious contents" (p. 132); Ferro (2015) stated that: "the purpose of analysis is to work not so much on insight, the overcoming of splits, repression, or historical reconstruction, as on the development of the instruments for thinking" (p. 512); and Botella (2014) argued that the true object of study for psychoanalysis is not remembering, but what lies behind, generates, and forms the memory and makes it capable of reorganizing psychic life. Nosek (2015) summarized this more contemporary view of the work of analysis in the following terms:

"We do not capture knowledge but expand our expressive repertoire. As when climbing, we broaden our field of vision and also see what we do not know further away. We do not fill in gaps, we gain height. We create new stories and successively reinterpret old accounts. If we do not do this, we tend to become paralyzed in the security of dogmatic narratives." [p. 527]

What each of these authors implies is the need for a metapsychology that offers analysts what I have called a *two track theory of psychoanalysis* (Levine 2010), *transformational* as well as classically *archeological*.

Following the implications of Bion's (1970) distinction between the domains of **O** and **K** and the many 'post-modern' implications present in the thinking of Freud,[3] my reading (e.g., Levine 2012, Levine, Reed and Scarfone 2013) of the work of Andre Green and the Paris Psychosomatic School allows that experience in the pre-verbal periods and acute and chronic traumatic disruptions of psychic organization can produce areas of psychic void, de-cathexis or discontinuities in psychic organization and functioning. What Green (2005) called ' tears in the fabric of the psyche' and Marty (1967, 1968) described as *progressive disorganization, operational thinking, essential depression*, etc. These in turn lead to or are associated with weakness, loss or failures of representation that clinically manifest themselves as psychic deadness and 'desertification' and/or economic overload phenomena: panic attacks, impulsive discharges, affect storms, structural failures of the capacity for thought and other symptoms associated with massive homeostatic imbalances and breakdowns, including somatic and psychosomatic illness.

The challenge that this presents to analysts involves a choice regarding their basic theoretical assumptions. Putting the matter in the terms used by Freud (1937) in his Constructions paper, the question that each of us must decide is this: Is everything that happens – i.e., all experience, internal and external, all 'psychical objects' and 'psychical structures' – inscribed or preserved and therefore "present somehow and somewhere… merely … buried"? If so, is this "somewhere" *always* psychic – i.e., in and of the mind? Freud's assertion, especially the 'somehow and somewhere,' requires a very careful reading, especially in the light of our contemporary recognition that "the Unconscious" may refer to far more than that which is repressed.[4]

---

[3] See Levine 2016b for a fuller explication.

[4] That recognition, by the way, is one that was first offered by Freud himself in his 1915a paper on **The Unconscious**. There, he noted that some unconscious instinctual impulses are "highly organized, free from self-contradiction" (p. 190), relatively indistinguishable in structure from those which are conscious or pre-conscious and yet "they are unconscious and incapable of becoming conscious." (pp. 190-1). He continued: "*qualitatively* they belong to the system *Pcs.* but *factually* to the *Ucs.*" (p. 191,

In the Constructions paper, it is not clear from the context in which Freud used the term, *psychical object,* whether he was referring literally to a psychical *object* (as in internal object or target of cathexis) or to a psychic *content* (as in phantasy, representation, idea, perception, memory, wish, etc.). It is also unclear how heavily he is leaning here upon the use of the word, *psychic.* Is he saying that once something is or becomes psychic then its traces always remain? But is there a 'before' to the 'after' of 'becoming psychic'? Is Freud leaving open the question of whether or not there may be *non-psychic forms of inscription or registration of experience*? In his Outline (Freud 1938) he talks of the psychic "in forms unknown to us" (p. 145).

This is the question of the *pre-psychic* or *proto-psychic* that I have raised in previous writings (e.g., Levine 2012, Levine, Reed and Scarfone 2013). Do the theories we hold allow for experience that is inscribed, but not yet *psychically* represented? If so, how do we understand such inscriptions and speak about their impact? What kinds of theories are available to us to do so? Do we hold a theory that assumes that all registrations or inscriptions of drive derivatives and perceptions are psychic in some sense and so there is no 'frontier' in need of crossing? Or do we believe that some registrations or inscriptions are pre- or proto-psychic, not yet organized, and a theory of frontier crossing is necessary?" And if the latter is so, does this imply different implications for analytic listening stance and technique?

Green (2010) raised similar questions in his extended response to Marty:

"How is the primitive material of the mind whose transformation gives birth to representation conceived, and how can this hypothetical material be used in psychoanalytic practice?" (p.1).

Can one "postulate *the hypothesis of the prepsychic* as a somatic sphere that is, or is not, capable of becoming psychic" [?] That is the question." (p. 2).

---

original italics).He later maintained this distinction when he introduced the structural theory (Freud 1923, p.24).

Green's conjecture of a "somatic sphere" is reminiscent of Bion (1993), who imagined a dialogue between *Psyche* and *Soma* in which each possessed a different language: the language of the body and the language of the mind. Thus, Bion counterposed pain or *"figments of digestion"* to anxiety and other mental states or *"figments of imagination."* (Bion 1993 III: 433–434)

Lest we go too far afield or get lost in the disturbing irony of Bion's 'imaginative conjecture,' which condenses wit, word play and biological speculation with psychoanalytic theory and experience, let me simply remind you of how often we have heard analysts and therapists say things like "the body always remembers" or "even if it is not psychic, the pre-verbal trauma is always inscribed."

Following the logic of the argument that I am putting forward, a model for the treatment of psychosomatic conditions could derive from an understanding of the *unstructured unconscious* and non-neurotic (unrepresented) states, instead of or in addition to the *dynamic* or *repressed unconscious* and neurosis (See also Levine 2012). What are the clinical manifestations and implications of this alternative view?

At times of emotional crisis, the discourse of patients who are at the mercy of the unrepresented may become disorganized and demonstrate a failure of meaning at a fundamental level (Green 2005). It is for this reason that carefully following these patients' associations and then interpreting unconscious phantasies or defenses may prove insufficient for the analytic task at hand.[5] Instead, or in addition, *the analyst may have to rely upon intuition and act[6]* (spontaneously and often unconsciously) so as to help the patient create words with which to form associations, imbue those words with consistent symbolic meaning and link those associations to other narrative fragments. At such moments,

---

[5] See also Bion's (1970) argument that the subject of psychoanalytic inquiry is not of the senses"

[6] By "action," I mean not only physical acts, but also – and more often – acts of spontaneous, intuitive, internal emotional resonance and/or expression (feeling or imagining what the patient may not yet clearly feel or know) that effect and reflect psychic figurability (*figurabilite´*) (forming an image that structures or conveys something implicit or imminent but not yet represented in the patient's or analyst's psyche).

the goal of the analyst's intervention is aimed more at facilitating psychic functioning than recovering a lost memory or de-coding a repressed symbolic element.[7]

Thus, in my work (Levine 2010, 2011, 2012; Levine, Reed and Scarfone 2013), I have emphasized the importance of:

- helping patients to recognize and name affect states;
- constructing plausible sequences of cause-and-effect narratives of emotional interaction and reality in the here-and-now of the analytic relationship; and
- building presumptive thoughts and strengthening the patient's capacity to think them.

In doing so, I have argued for a kind of analytic action that may appear to an outside observer as intuitive rather than deductive, anticipatory rather than reactive; and inspired rather than fully grounded in the patient's manifest associations.

While spontaneous 'internal acts' may be preferable to motor acts, sometimes the latter are inevitable and necessary to actualize or call attention to some aspect of a newly emerging Experience.[8] Often, these "actions" (frequently classified as 'enactments') are the external markers of an act of figurability (Botella and Botella 2005) through which the unrepresented acquires specific ideational form. Cassorla (2013) has described how the unwinding of a temporary stalemate may begin with and even require an unconscious, jointly created enactment, which not only gives form to something nascent, not yet or only weakly represented, but also calls attention to its emergent existence.

In retrospect, the action that I am trying to describe may be seen as a reflection of and response to unconscious communication from the

---

[7] The process that I am trying to describe, which should be recognizable to practicing analysts, is analogous to that of weaving a patch to repair the unity of a torn fabric or, sometimes more aptly, first operating the tool and die press so as to create the tools that are necessary for the repair!

[8] Think of Botella's (Botella and Botella 2005) spontaneous and unplanned outburst of "Grrr! Grrr! The wolf!"

patient. Sometimes, the communication is a mute, unconscious, covert plea for help in the transformational processing of raw sensory disturbance that we call containment (Bion 1962, 1970) or acts of figurability (Botella and Botella 2005). While to an outside observer these may seem prosaic, supportive or cognitive, they are, in fact, intersubjective, transformational and come from a deep analytic sensibility, as the analyst's actions contribute as catalyst, co-constructor or alter ego to the patient's on-going strengthening of representations and formation of psychic structure.[9]

What I am proposing is that the analyst must not only use his or her subjectivity as a source of data about the patient and the analytic situation, but must expect that in addition to helping patients discover and explore their dynamic unconscious – that is, helping them search for something that is hidden, but discernible by the effects it has on what *is* available to consciousness – the analyst may also be faced with the challenge of helping patients *create* that dynamic unconscious. The latter occurs as the analyst initiates or catalyzes processes that strengthen and/or integrate patients' abilities to think by helping give form to something that was previously weakly or un-represented. Thus, analysts must expect to find themselves unconsciously participating in dialogical and interactive processes, which have the effect of offering patients – or helping them to create or approximate – something that may not yet have achieved sufficient 'presence' in a figured form. It is only after figuration has taken place that there may be anything that can then be repressed and subsequently 'uncovered' or 'de-coded.'

Prior to being strengthened or created this 'something' may make its presence known via vague or eruptive states of emotional turbulence, impulsive action, somatic illnesses or difficulties in thinking and psychic regulatory processes, including those that Marty called *operational thinking* and *progressive disorganization,* but it may be 'invisible' or only weakly discernible *as content*, unless or until it's trace is strengthened or

---

[9] It remains an open question as to whether the dividing line between this kind of transformative action and more traditional descriptions of countertransference are very difficult to discern or do not in fact exist!

transformed into being (achieves representation) by an intersubjective process of construction or co-construction.

The potential plasticity of the forms it may assume once it is transformed implies that its eventual figuration may be highly influenced by the unique subjectivities of each member of the dyad and the unique, moment-to-moment conditions of their relationship. Consequently, in practice, it may be very difficult and sometimes impossible to answer the question, 'Whose construction is it?' The questions of to whom the final content of the representation 'belongs ' or how to distinguish a truly intersubjective act of figurability from the imposition of an analyst's countertransference need or the expression of a patient's transference compliance remain complex, enigmatic and perhaps can never be resolved. And in the case of severely traumatized patients and/or those with primitive personality disorders, the unintended imposition of an 'analytic false self' that nevertheless offers structure and facilitates the patient's capacity to think, defer action and regulate affects may be the best or only – outcome possible (Donnet 2010).

Elsewhere (Levine 2016b), I have described how in analysis, the 'shadow of the object,' in the form of some aspect of the analyst's subjectivity, inevitably falls in some degree upon what we might call the 'micro-constructions of everyday analytic engagement,' giving the resulting ideational content a personalized 'flavor' of each distinct analytic dyad and moment. The resulting narrative description is an emerging truth (Levine 2016a) that functions in the cure as a construction in the same dynamic sense that Freud described in 1937.

References

Aisenstein, M. Rappoport de Aisemberg, E. (2010). *Psychosomatics Today: A Psychoanalytic Perspective.* London: Karnac Books, 2010, pp. 181-200.

Alexander, F. (1950). *Psychosomatic Medicine.* New York: Norton.

Bion, W.R. (1962). *Learning From Experience.* London: Heinemann.

Bion, W.R. (1970). *Attention and Interpretation.* London: Heinemann.

Bion, W.R. (1993). *Memoir of the Future.* London: Karnac.

Botella, C. and Botella, S. (2005). *The Work of Psychic Figurability*. London: Routledge.

Botella, C. (2014). On remembering: The notion of memory without recollection. *Int. J. Psychoanal.*, 95:911-936.

Cassorla, R. (2013). Reflections On Non-Dreams-For-Two, Enactment And The Analyst's Implicit Alpha-Function. In: Levine, H and Brown, L., eds., *Growth and Turbulence in the Container/Contained*. Hove, England and New York: Brunner-Routledge, 2013.

Donnet, J.-L. (2010). Personal communication.

Ferenczi, S. (1926). *Final Contributions to the Problems and Methods of Psycho-Analysis*. London: Karnac Books, 1994.

Ferro, A. (2015). A response that raises many questions. *Psychoanal. Inquiry*, 35:512-525.

Freud, S. (1899). Screen Memories. S.E., 3: 299-322. London: Hogarth

Freud, S. (1915a). The Unconscious. S.E., 14: 159-215. London Hogarth

Freud, S. (1915b). Instincts and their Vicissitudes. S .E., 14: 109-140. London:

Hogarth

Freud, S. (1923). The Ego and the Id. S.E., 19: 1-66. London: Hogarth

Freud, S. (1937). Constructions in analysis. S.E., 23:255-269. London: Hogarth

Freud,S. (1938). An Outline of Psycho-Analysis. S.E., 23: 141-208. London: Hogarth

Green, A. (1997). *On Private Madness*. London: Karnac.

Green, A. (2005). *Key Ideas for a Contemporary Psychoanalysis* London and New York: Routledge, 2005, pp. 212-226.

Green, A. (2010). Thoughts on the Paris School of Psychosomatics. In: Aisenstein and Rappoport de Aisemberg, eds. *Psychosomatics Today. A Psychoanalytic Perspective*. London: Karnac, 2010, pp. 1-46.

Hartke, R. (2013). Psychological turbulence in the analytic situation. In *Growth and Turbulence in the Container/Contained. Bion's Continuing Legacy*, ed. H. B. Levine & L. J. Brown. New York: Routledge, pp. 131-148.

Levine, H. B. (2010). Creating analysts, creating analytic patients. IJPA 91: 1385-1404.

Levine, H. B. (2011). (2011). Construction then and now. In: *On Freud's Constructions in Analysis.* Edited by S. Lewkowicz, T. Bokanowski with G. Pragier. London: Karnac, pp. 87-100.

Levine, H.B. (2012). The colourless canvas: Representation, therapeutic action and the creation of mind. IJPA 93: 607-629.

Levine, H.B., Reed, G and Scarfone, D., eds., (2013). *Unrepresented States and the Creation of Meaning.* London: Karnac/IPA.

Levine, H.B. (2016a). Psychoanalysis and the problem of truth. *Psychoanalytic Quarterly* 85:391-410.

Levine, H.B. (2016b). The Fundamental Epistemological Situation. Psychic Reality and the Limitations of Classical Theory. Given as the 2016 Abraham Lecture, Berlin, Germany.

Marty, P. (1967). Regression et instinct du mort: Hypothese a propos de l'observation psychosomatique. *Revue Française de Psychanalysis* 31:1113-1133.

Marty, P. (1968). A major process of somatization: The progressive disorganization. *International Journal of Psychoanalysis* 49:246-249.

Nosek, L. (2015). Variations on a theme by Antonino Ferro: alphabetizing the emotions. *Psychoanal. Inquiry*, 35:526-554.

Rappaport de Aisemberg (2010). Psychosomatic conditions in contemporary psychoanalysis. In: *Psychosomatics Today: A Psychoanalytic Perspective*. London: Karnac Books, 2010, pp. 111-130.

Taylor, G. (2010). Symbolism, symbolization and trauma in psychosomatic theory. In: *Psychosomatics Today: A Psychoanalytic Perspective.* Edited by Marilia Aisenstein and Elsa Rappoport de Aisemberg. London: Karnac Books, 2010, pp. 181-200.

CHAPTER SIX

Facing the Death-Object: Unconscious Phantasies of Relationships with Death[1]

Joshua Durban

One of the many things I've learnt from Prof. Shmuel Erlich during my years of supervision with him was the importance of psychoanalyzing various levels of human experience. The analyst should observe and interpret the constant interplay between a level where subject and internal object are clearly defined, able to maintain a sense of separateness and interact with one another (the mode of *doing*), and the level of being merged or fused with the object (the mode of *being*). I found this to be particularly relevant to my work with children on the autistic spectrum and with psychotic children and adolescents. In those patients there is both an inflation of the 'doing' mode, albeit assuming pathological forms, as well as a collapse into an overwhelming phantasy of being fully merged and non-differentiated from the object so as to avoid psychic pain and nameless dread. This inflation of doing and deflation of being serves as a defense against the predominant early anxieties. These 'anxieties-of-being' arise out of the child's fragile experience of not having a well-defined, bounded and on-going existence in time and space. Such anxieties dealing with annihilation and death bring to the fore the question of whether and how death is experienced in the psyche. I shall try to deal with some aspects of this

---

[1] An earlier version of this paper was first presented in the Annual DPV conference, Bad-Homburg 2010 and later included in the book Nissen, B. (Ed). 2012. Wendepunkte: Zur Theorie und Klinik psychoanalytischer Veranderungsprozesse. Psychosozial Verlag.

question in the following chapter. I am very grateful to Shmuel Erlich for his years of guidance, inspiration and support.

In the last part of Marcel Proust's monumental study of being and time "In Search of Lost Time" (1981), called "Time Regained", he reaches the final part of his self-analysis. Proust finally addresses the subject of transience and death as well as the inevitable mental pain they evoke. He discusses the interplay between memory, time, mortality and immortality and tries to comfort himself with the idea that internalization, memory and his literary life's work, will all go on and thus provide some kind of solace. Proust describes the internal presence of death and his relationship with it thus:

> *"The idea of death took up permanent residence within me in the way that love sometimes does. Not that I loved death, I abhorred it. But after a preliminary stage in which, no doubt, I thought about it from time to time as one does about a woman with whom one is not yet in love, its image adhered now to the most profound layer of my mind, so completely that I could not give my attention to anything without that thing first traversing the idea of death, and even if no object occupied my attention and I remained in a state of complete repose, the idea of death still kept me company as faithfully as the idea of my self"* (p. 523).

I wish to highlight and discuss some ideas regarding this topic which we all do our best to avoid: our internal, unconscious relationship with death. I will describe the way death is perceived, encoded and represented in unconscious phantasy, in both normal and pathological development. I wish to suggest that within the infant's psyche, a 'Death-object' is gradually constructed. It is assembled from and composed of sensory-perceptual as well as object-related experiences, which I call "death-equivalents". These "death-equivalents" are subjectively perceived proto-physiological and mental experiences which come as close to death as possible within life. They are first equated with the body and then, in unconscious phantasy linked with and projected into an object. This object is in turn endowed with death-like qualities and annihilating characteristics. Thus the death-object is a component of and sometimes even antedates the bad-object and the murderous archaic superego. It is an internal unconscious attempt to deal with death and to form various pacts and relations with it. The aim is to ward off death anxiety and earlier anxieties-of-being which cause nameless dread and the experience of losing shape (Durban, 2014). The personified Death-object turns the intolerable and formless into a tolerable form.

The idea of transience emphasizes the linear progression and passage of time with its inherent implications of change and mortality. However, in the internal world it is instantly met by death denial: the unconscious phantasy of stopping the flow of time so as to avoid death. This is exemplified in the ideas of timelessness, of circular or oscillating time (Meltzer, 1976), of eternity and immortality. Culture, religion and the continuity of trans-personal and cultural survival embody our attempts to enact the internal phantasy of "symbolic immortality" (Lifton, 1983) namely, the often creative denial of transience, and therefore of death, and the attempts to transcend it (Roth, 2017). This might be expressed through the belief in God, science, art, family, children, a national group and one's life-work which will all continue to exist after our death. However, our unconscious phantasies regarding death itself remain deeply hidden although they determine to a large extent our relation to life, to time and to the way we face the certainty of our own death and that of others.

As Proust describes, one can form an intense relationship with death in very much the same fashion one can do so with a person.[2]

Death and Childhood

From early infancy on, every individual needs to cope with two unsolved

---

[2] Proust's internal relationship with death, as well as his unconscious attempts to ward it off are evident not only in the content of his writings, but also in his style (seemingly endless sentences which undermine linear time) and in the way he wrote using obsessive alterations and corrections and last minute additions which went on even as his books were already in press.

riddles: the riddle of one's birth and that of one's death.[3] Children, as young as 2-3 years old, usually go through a phase of a wide interest not only in sex and in the riddle of their creation (expressed in the unconscious phantasy of the primal scene), but also in death of others (what might be called the phantasy of 'the final scene') as well as in their own death. This is an inevitable part of their early Oedipal phantasies and of the accompanying castration anxieties which lean on some budding early perception of the possibility of physical damage, loss and of not-being. Moreover, children speak about death, are afraid of it , are intrigued by it and even drawn to it. Death occupies their imagination and their internal world often without their ever having encountered it directly. In their drawings we may find early attempts to represent it as a dark background or as a blank, white space which cannot be filled. Gradually, this background assumes in the course of their development different shapes and figures, menacing or idealized. In the infant's internal world love and death often intertwine. One such case is the primal scene phantasy, where children are convinced that father is most probably killing mother during intercourse or that they cause one another bodily harm. For the young child death is associated with a multitude of emotions: curiosity, fear, arousal, guilt, loss of love, bodily mutilation, greed, envy, exclusion, loneliness and dangerous threats from the father or the mother. Children form their own developmental theories regarding death. Like any other theory in the mind it is composed of instincts, desires and needs, affects, objects and relationships with these objects. All these form the internal script or narrative which we call unconscious phantasy: "They are the mental representation of those somatic events in the body that comprise the instincts, and are physical sensations interpreted as relationships with objects that cause those sensations"(Bott Spillius et al., 2011, p. 3). According to Kleinian psychoanalysis this is the basic unit, the psychic molecule or atom which forms the mind (Isaacs, 1952; Steiner, 2003). Furthermore, most of our bodily experiences, including the pre-natal ones, are inscribed in unconscious phantasy (Durban, 2011). These experiences often under-

---

[3] Rabbi Abraham Ibn Ezra, the famous Jewish sage and mathematician said: "Life is a riddle which death solves."

go some form of personification or animation. Accordingly, each child has his own personal death. Very often, though, when these theories or questions regarding death are presented to the parents or other adults, their shocked reactions manifested in quasi-religious or mystical explanations such as "all those who die go to heaven" create in the child a mixture of denial, paranoia and secret pacts with this frightening death. A 4 years old girl confided in me while bursting into tears, that she couldn't stand the eyes of her deceased grandmother and of her dead dog following her every where from heaven. "Maybe it is best if I die too and go to heaven so that I can join Nana and Doggie watching people doing bad things all day."

Freud and Death

Freud (1915, 1916, and 1917) pointed out the unconscious link between transience and mourning. The acceptance of transience and with it the reality of death arouses anxiety and grief but may also lead to a deeper appreciation of life, beauty and love. Our denial of death embodied in our striving for immortality, in our manic omnipotence and in the attempt "to eliminate death from life" (Freud, 1915, p. 289), often leads to a shallowness of experience, to frustration, melancholia and often than not to cruelty, war and cultural madness (Freud, 1915, 1916). Each group, nation and culture has its own typical relationship with death stemming from unconscious phantasies about it. As is the case with the individual, the group's unconscious relationship with death will determine, eventually, its relationship with and attitude towards the value of life.

It is interesting to note that in Freud's paper "On Transience" (1916), he frequently uses words such as "extinction", "doom", "vanish", "decay", "nothing", "destruction", "loss", "temporal limitation", "crumble to dust", "decease" and "mourning", but not even once does he mention death as such. Immortality, however, and striving for the eternal as expressed in our love of nature and in art, is mentioned abundantly without any disguise. It is as if death lurks in the shadows, present but invisible throughout the paper, thus reflecting our own death- denial. In spite of Freud's ground-breaking contributions, not much has changed regarding this denial. I often wonder whether Freud's preoccupation with the death instinct towards the end of his life, a concept which apart from Kleinian theory and practice has remained like a bone stuck in psychoanalysis's throat (Lazar & Erlich, 1996; Lazar, 1997), was perhaps his stubborn way of reminding us that death is here, in us, ever-present and that we must acknowledge its presence in our psyche and explore it within our internal world.

Death in modern western society is still insulated, isolated, medicalized and nominated as the arch-enemy, as an 'illness'. The fight against it is carried out covering a wide spectrum ranging from new life-prolonging medical innovations and genetic manipulations, through the developmental prolongation of infancy and adolescence well into the late 20's and culminating in the anti-aging craze. Meanwhile, it seems that death certainly does not remain unoccupied and it manifests itself not only through the reality of transience, but also, as Freud has pointed out, through human cruelty, endless wars, new diseases, destructiveness and aggression. The more we try to push it away and repress it the more evident it becomes- on the intrapersonal, interpersonal, social and cultural levels.

A similar interplay between acknowledgement, splitting and denial characterizes the psychoanalytic approach to death (Sekoff,1999; Willock, 2007). Razinsky (2010), traces the origins of this oversight or, occasionally, active rejection to "Freud's formulations—both surreptitious and explicit— that death cannot be represented in the unconscious and that death anxiety is secondary to other issues (1920, 1923). These tendencies, both implicit and explicit, have continued to resonate throughout the vast majority of analytic literature. It is claimed, however, that one exception to this overall trend is the death drive theory, which supposedly places death at the center of the analytic perspective". However, by introducing the concept of the death drive Freud paradoxically contributed to the removal of death itself from the discourse since we are dealing now with a drive, an internal force which is silent, invisible and non-representable and un-mentalizable. Moreover, the concept of the death drive itself have been wildly attacked and debunked on the grounds that it is unscientific.

But could it be that we perhaps, after all, try and deal with death in our internal world? If we accept the psychoanalytic claim that every conceivable experience regarding survival is inscribed in the internal world as a narrative regarding an object, what is the object of death? If life, security,, continuity, creativity. sanity, authenticitiy, love and relationship are represented by the primary good breast (Klein,1957), could it be that death is also part of the bad , persecutory, annihilating breast? These questions are inevitable unless, of course, we resort to the argument that there is something which we know to exist, and which presents itself as a fact, but cannot be represented.

Some further theoretical considerations regarding the internal inscription of death

Before proceeding to the clinical examples, I would like to go back to some crucial theoretical milestones which have contributed to our understanding of the psychoanalytic significance of death. Death, as well as the death drive, is usually described psychoanalytically in three distinct ways: 1. as something which is invisible, unknown, an uncanny background: 2. as a process or a force such as the death drive (Freud, 1919, 1920) or a destructive force within (Klein, 1946) and 3. As something which undergoes personification and animation by being projected into objects (as in paranoid-schizoid anxieties and phantasies), and as populating the archaic superego (Klein, 1946, 1948, 1957). Melanie Klein claimed that death and fear of death are present in the mental phenomena from the beginning of life, following the anxiety of birth. Klein disagrees with Freud's view that 'the unconscious seems to contain nothing that could give any content to our concept of the annihilation of life', because "if we assume the existence of a death instinct, *we must also assume that in the deepest layers of the mind there is a response to this instinct in the form of fear of annihilation of life".[4]*

---

[4] The centrality of a primary fear of death is described superbly by Money-Kyrle (1955);"The old analytic argument against the existence of a basic fear of death rests, implicitly if not explicitly, on the discovery that what is consciously thought to be a fear of death often turns out to cover other unconscious fears, such as the fear of castration. *But it is now fairly generally agreed that there are fears more basic than the fear of castration or loss of love (Freud), or even the loss of all capacity for pleasure....There is, for instance, the terror of disintegration. It may not be easy to be sure-still less to convince the*

Joan Riviere (1936) relates to this issue and writes:" I am not suggesting that there is any such 'kind of knowledge' in the child, but I think there is reason to suppose that a child experiences *feelings*[5] of the kind, just as any adult can *feel* 'like death', and in a state of great anxiety often does." (p. 278). She then goes on to describe what might be some of the earliest "death equivalents" which arise in situations of frustration vis-a–vis the breast: " The child is overwhelmed by choking and suffocating; its eyes are blinded with tears, its ears deafened, its throat sore; its bowels gripe, its evacuations burn it. The aggressive anxiety–reaction is far too strong a weapon in the hands of such a weak ego; it has become uncontrollable and is threatening to destroy its owner.....The end-result of aggression directed outward…is again to produce the worst danger-situation possible, the closest proximity to death " (p. 279-280).

Klein goes on to describe how this fear of death and death anxiety are projected into the object. Thus the primitive superego would be constituted (partly) by cruel and dangerous figures (internalized devouring mother and father), that become the representatives of the death instinct.

Bell (2007) describes three overlapping models in contemporary Kleinian thinking which conceptualize the death-drive and its functioning in purely psychological terms. The first model "focuses on a drive that *aims*

---

doubters- *that such anxiety attacks express the fear of dying. But there are other pointers, of a more general kind, which are perhaps easier to follow. Why, if there is no fear of death, are nearly all religions so concerned with immortality? Why, in our ambitions, are we so passionately anxious for something of ourselves, a work of art, a scientific contribution, a business, or just our good name, to be accepted and to survive? Why, not only for our pleasure but for our peace of mind, do we need children who should create grandchildren, and so on? Why, in short, do we strive for immortality- or at least for immortality by proxy? Or how better can we describe those moments of deep despondency, which no one altogether escapes, than as a feeling that there is no joy in fighting an enemy who must ultimately defeat us- no joy in living if death or destruction must surely overtake us and all our works, those offshoots of ourselves we try to save?....We may not be able to from an idea of our own annihilation, but in common with other animals we are certainly predisposed to anxiety at threats of it"* (pp. 288-289).

[5] Klein herself referred to pre-verbal emotions and phantasies which are revived within the transference as "memories in feeling" (1957, p. 180).

at destroying life and all that is identified with living, most particularly thought, and the capacity to perceive…it is provoked into action by such factors as the presence of goodness that is separate from the self, awareness of limitation or obstruction. The pleasure it brings is an instantaneous pure pleasure in destruction. The phenomenology of this activity tends to be *violent, noisy…and is thus more manifest.* Model 2 emphasizes annihilation of self and object. *"It operates as a continuous tendency or disposition,* which becomes manifest as *a seductive lure into mindlessness.* One might say *it is active in pursuit of a deadening passivity".* The third model describes death as similarly quite. It deadens and prevents development *but* it aims not at annihilation but more at *"maintaining a particular kind of paralysis, needing the object to stay alive in order that it can continue to be treated in this way. The pleasure derived has a sadistic character."* It is interesting to see how Bell's descriptions of the death drive, like Klein's descriptions of the bad breast filled with destructiveness and annihilation, or Money-Kyrle's description of death the enemy, Rosenfeld's destructive narcissism or Bion's hostile and murderous no-existence object, often endow it with almost human-like traits: it has a cognition, an intention or a motivation and it seeks an object- the living subject. These traits are indeed characteristic of the unconscious phantasy of the death-object.

The psychoanalytic study of early anxieties has presented us with a vast material regarding what might be described as unthinkable, pre-symbolic 'anxieties of being': the dread of disintegration, loss of shape, psychic deadness and psychic numbing, loss of the mind, being drained of vitality, leaking out, loss of dimensionality, etc. All these earliest anxieties are directly or indirectly linked to the threatening possibility of death. So how, then, is this death dealt with within the psyche?

Furthermore, the terrors of the dismemberment, disintegration, and decay of the body after death have all been frequently represented in ritual, myth, legend, art, and religious belief throughout the ages. So, too, has the wished-for triumph over these inevitable processes (Gottlieb, 2007). We are all familiar with various artistic images of death such as death the reaper, the dance of death and the mask of death. Also familiar is the projection of death into individuals, groups and religions and the attempt 'to get rid of death by death' namely- the annihilation of the other as a projected container of death.

An altogether different approach to death is the Zen-Buddhist one, which bluntly confronts death-denial.

Zen Buddhism advises its practitioners, especially the monks, to take the reverse attitude to denial, namely: an open-eyed confrontation with mortality and death. This is done in order to free the person from the sufferings of denial and from the agonies of the illusions and delusions caused by clinging to desires.[6] The acceptance of death leads to a deep appreciation of life because of its impermanence and to the shedding of false hopes and attitudes stemming from omnipotent narcissism. Monks' descriptions of their thoughts and feelings during death-meditation resemble those which are enhanced and acted out in some mental pathologies and are also often mentioned as central by people who face death or are dying[7]: 1. Fear of bodily pain and disintegration. 2. Mental pain, fear and anguish caused by loss of a sense of time and mind. 3. Loss of the significant loving relationship with others. 4. A prevailing sense of unimportance which threatens healthy narcissism and omnipotence. 5. Fear of having no identity. 6. As a consequence of all this- loss of meaning, loss of thought and loss of purpose. All of the above are quite accessible experiences which are present from the beginning of life and which partly compose our "death equivalents".

In order to really contemplate death and accept transience one must work through paranoid and depressive anxieties which lead to the true acceptance of reality namely: the acceptance of helplessness, finiteness, dependence and separateness. Thus the acceptance of transience, imply-

---

[6] The following lines are taken from a very ancient text instructing monks towards enlightenment through death-meditation:"The monk contemplates that dead body which has been dead for 1, 2 days up to 6,7 days, pecked by crows and vultures, eaten by wolves and jackals, burnt by fire, buried in the ground and subject to decay, festering and decaying…a skeleton of bluish color, fettered, rotten and eaten more than half with bones connected…without skin, with flesh and blood removed, only connected by sinews… having seen this he compares it with his own body: now my body will be like this, subject to that law.." (Majjhima Nikaya, Bhiksu Thich Minh Chau,1991).

[7] When I was working in a children's hospice for terminally ill children, they would often express and seek to discuss those themes with the therapists.

ing the irreversibility of death, is a major psychological achievement although quite elusive- once it's there and it's already gone. It is therefore a life's work to try and come to terms with death. In other words- alongside the work of mourning (Trauerarbeit) and general working through of anxieties (Durcharbeit) there might be an unconscious work of death (Todsarbeit). It is here that the Death-object makes its appearance.

Early anxieties and death-equivalents

The death-object serves as a creative, internal unconscious attempt to represent death and to form various pacts and relationships with this object. The death object stems from the infant's inherent unconscious awareness of death. It is gradually assembled from birth, and possibly even earlier, from accumulating "death-equivalents" which are subjectively perceived life-threatening experiences which deal with disruptions in the sense of continuity of being and of relating to the object. These "death-equivalents" are first proto-physiological in nature and are immediately equated with the body-as-an-object (or 'the mother-body') and then projected into other objects. Early on, these "death equivalents" resemble more "death equations" in the sense that they are symbolic equivalents as described by Klein (1930) and Segal (1957), characteristic of psychotic thinking. They are initially somatic, concrete, pre-symbolic and split-off. In the course of development the "death equivalents" become better linked with an object, internalized and assimilated into complex affective and cognitive systems.

I have borrowed the term "death equivalents" from the American psychiatrist R. J. Lifton who first described them in his ground-breaking book "The broken connection" (1983) which discusses men's problematic relationship with death. Lifton focuses on the idea of the symbolic continuity of life and writes:"We require symbolization of that continuity, imaginative forms of transcending death, in order to be able to confront the fact that we die. The sense of immortality is by no means mere denial of death…it is our need for a symbolic relationship toward that which has gone on before, and that which we know will go on after… and in that sense the symbolization of immortality is an appro-

priate expression of our biological and historical connectedness". (p. 17)
Lifton traces the developmental origins of the need to symbolize death
and thus come to terms with it from the moment of birth. He writes:"
Earliest emotions having to do with separation, stasis and disintegra-
tion- as opposed to connection, movement and integrity-serve as 'death
equivalents."[8] (p. 12)

Psychoanalytic literature is suffused with references to feelings and
phantasies regarding death, annihilation, psychic and object deadness
etc. These descriptions are often associated with a psychic loss of the
object and the coverage or containment it provides for the evolving self.

The "death-equivalents" encompass a wide range of affective-somatic
experiences, which are inscribed and encoded in the psyche from internal and external sources in the course of development. To mention just a
few- intra-uterine stress and traumas, the trauma of birth, extreme
physical discomfort, pain and hunger[9] (Klein, 1957), difficulties in
breathing, sleep, lack or loss of love (Freud, 1917, 1923), frustration,
internal destructiveness , excessive splitting, disintegration and failure in
transformation (Klein, 1946, 1948; Bion, 1970), bodily distress and
illness, over-exposure to death of others and life-threatening situations,
aging and old age (Jaques, 1965;Junkers, 2006), death of parents with the
ensuing loss of the illusion of infinite potential for development
(Brearley, 2005), insufferable mental pain concerning object-loss or
premature separation (Tustin, 1972, 1981, 1987, 1990, 1994), states of
discontinuity, disintegration of identity (De Masi,2004), disorientation,
lack of bodily control and holding or containing (Winnicott, 1962),
extreme forms of mental isolation, non-feeling or emotionlessness (Green,
1986;Ogden, 1995;Eigen,1996), non-relation and meaninglessness

---

[8] Lifton has told me in a private conversation that the idea of the "death equivalents" has
struck him upon his entrance, at the end of WW2, to the Nazi death camps as part of
the U.S liberating army. The sight of the camp survivors alongside the idea of annihilating of an entire ethnic group aroused in him a sense of witnessing and experiencing
near-death while still being alive.

[9] "For hunger, which rouses the fear of starvation-possibly even all physical and mental
pain-is felt as the threat of death" (Klein, 1957, p. 201). Furthermore, hunger is often felt
by the infant as an attacking object within.

(Heidegger, 1962). By their being threats to our survival, these death-equivalents are the closest we get to death while still being alive and are therefore associated with it.

While death in the psyche is usually described in terms of a silent background or as an uncanny deadly/passive presence (as in the case of the death-drive or in its personification, for instance, as a "dead mother"), the death-object is usually personified and animated as a result of the projection of the death-equivalents with their life-threatening properties into objects with which relationships are formed: paranoid, Oedipal, idealized, sado-masochistic or merged. In this way the unthinkable, unspeakable experience is turned into some kind of a relationship with an object within an internal narrative, albeit with death itself. In other words it might be said that the death-object alleviates nameless dread. However, the death object acquires obsessive, repetitive and compulsive traits which simultaneously enact the inertia of death while trying to control and master it.

Pacts and relationships with death

The death-object is connected either to the fear of dying (physically or mentally) or to the wish to die, which Dante described so chillingly in his Inferno "Now help, Death, help" (Dante, 11:120)[10]. We all form secret pacts and agreements with this death-object in order to control it and, paradoxically, not die. Death is dreaded and is incontrollable and we have to convince it somehow to keep us alive, even at the cost of losing all our psychological vital life-signs.

The death-object carries many functions and plays different roles, not necessarily all bad. As will be demonstrated later on, the death object can also evoke loyalty, passion and even addiction. It is sometimes, indeed, the tyrannical, idealized, persecuting and murderous bad-object or superego (Rosenfeld, 1987) with which we are locked in a pathological organization (Steiner, 1993) resulting in murderous mourning (Durban, 2016). The individual, in an attempt to ward off the internal experience of death and

---

[10] Sometimes also translated as "Now come, death, quickly come".

psychic trauma, may project and create death externally, may identify with it and thus become dominated by destruction and murderousness. This is the mechanism of "killing death by death" typical of murderous mourning. In addition, in this special kind of mourning, there is an inversion of life and death and so death becomes an all-powerful figure which is idealized and seen as a protector against suffering. This might lead not only to murder but also to psychic deadness and actual suicide. Mental pain is perceived in unconscious phantasy as an emptying-out of parts of the self, which the lost object was felt to hold and contain, or as an attack by an object which suffocates, tears-apart, burns and drowns. Sometimes there are dominant experiences of losing one's center, falling to pieces, being cut and mutilated, melting and losing one's orientation and shape (Winnicott, 1962).

Every "death equivalent" is related to some form of loss and therefore to mourning or to the inability to mourn. In early states of mourning, where there is still insufficient mentalization and symbolization and loss is experienced as a 'nameless grief', the mourner tries to deny its loss through massive projective identification, which creates an undifferentiated mixture of self and object and of life and death. This leads to the phantasy that if one lets the object die, one will die with it. In one patient's words "it is either murder or suicide".

Bion discusses the idea of nothingness and representation or lack of it in the psyche and writes:" The patient feels the pain of an absence of fulfillment of his desires. The absent fulfillment is experienced as a' no-thing'. The emotion aroused by the 'no-thing' is felt as indistinguishable from the 'no-thing'....'Non-existence' immediately becomes an object that is immensely hostile and filled with murderous envy towards the quality or function of 'existence' wherever it is to be found" (1970, pp.19-20).

These no-feelings or no-emotions, as is the case with severe Autism, may sometimes indicate the lethal internal taking-over of this "No-thing" or "non-existence" object, or what I call "the death-object". In autism , where the earliest anxieties of being are prevalent and the infant feels he's dissolving, liquefying, freezing, burning, being in bits, falling without stop and losing orientation, the death object is often a solid, hard autistic object to which the child clings desperately so as to gain some shape and control.

There is a constant interaction between the "death equivalents", the ability to create a personified death-object, projection and introjection. When projection prevails we often encounter patients who enact sadistic, death-like murderous situations so as to get rid of the internal, tyrannical death-object which threatens to annihilate the vulnerable living parts of the personality.

When there is a failed attempt at creating a death-object which could be projected or, simultaneously, serve as a container for the "death equivalents", death resides within the psyche and becomes identified with parts of it or with bodily functions. Betty Joseph describes in her classic paper "Addiction to Near-Death (1982), an intricate malignant, sado-masochistic, addictive and highly self-destructive relationship with death which a certain group of patients feel unable to resist: "It seems to be like a constant pull towards despair and near-death, so that the patient is fascinated and unconsciously excited by the whole process" (p. 456). She suggests an important insight as to what could be the possible causes for this type of death-addiction:"My impression is that these patients as infants, because of their pathology, have not just turned away from frustrations or jealousies or envies into a withdrawn state, nor have they been able to rage and yell at their objects. I think they have withdrawn into a secret world of violence, where part of the self has been turned against another part, parts of the body being identified with parts of the offending object, and that violence has been highly sexualized, masturbatory in nature, and often physically expressed" (p.455).

Sometimes the death object is depicted as a savior- a God of cessation and Nirvana or of sleep-like release and salvation, which offers a handy solution to the pain and suffering of living and to the painful reality of transience and of mortality. Anthropology makes use of the cultural differentiation between a 'good death' and a 'bad death'. "In general, a good death represents a cultural ideal, which enacts a symbolic victory over death. It reinforces the core values of the community and the sense that life is worth living. A bad death does the opposite. It leaves the survivors feeling alone, cut off, in despair, and helpless in the face of death conceived as nothingness and without meaning" (Abramovitch, 2000, p. 256). In the internal world, however, such a distinction is not that clear since death might assume a positive meaning precisely because of its potential to obliterate psychic pain and suffering. Freud in his paper "The Theme of the Three Caskets" (1922), writes:" psychoanalysis will tell us that in dreams dumbness is a common representation of death" (p. 294) He goes on and adds silence, hiding and not being found as other unmistakable symbols of death in dreams.[11] I would describe them as "death equivalents". To go back to death as the savior, Albert Einstein quipped, along similar lines that "The fear of death is the most unjustified of all fears, for there's no risk of accident for someone who's dead." However, this sleep of death or false Nirvana, unlike true Nirvana or enlightenment, necessitates the use of extremely destructive attacks against feeling, thinking and relating and leads to mindlessness and frozen states. In extreme cases we sometimes encounter a hardening of the psychic skin-envelope which becomes impenetrable, rigor-mortis-like. It thus enacts on a somatic level the presence of death within. I think this enacted unconscious phantasy sometimes underlies what Tustin (1981) described as "shell-type" Autistic children.

The paralysis is often accompanied by a difficulty in acknowledging the passage of time or the concept of change. I have noticed that many patients who complain about emptiness, who suffer from a lack of vitality and from blank depression have difficulties in remembering the time of their sessions, in moving between past, present and future tense (usually for them there is no past and no future and an unmoving, stuck present) and they are rigidly unable to face changes. In autistic children the acknowledgement of time is the acknowledgement of separateness. It is therefore attacked and destroyed. The children usually live in a no-time, no-space manner or within a circular or oscillating time. Some of them are fascinated by watches but try to stop them, take them apart or

---

[11] A 5 year old psychotic boy in analysis was extremely afraid of my silences. He would play hide and seek and if I would not find him immediately he would start crying and say that he was stuck "in the lost". When his uncle died he told me that he was not sorry since his uncle was now sleeping peacefully in "the lost".

move them backwards. Others are obsessed with elevators: they try to control their up and down movements and thus combat the anxiety of falling forever in space. Since there is no internal development they are only minimally alive. Their death object is somatic and concrete.

The inner relationship with the death objects is present whenever we encounter psychic states in which the phantasy regarding some form of deadness appears, be it of the self, or of the object. Thus psychic deadness, a dead internal object, the emptying of thoughts, of sensations and withdrawal are often accompanied by a parallel secret relationship with a death object which is very much alive. These relationships and pacts are often well hidden and remote while what is presented to us is an immersion in a sense of futility, emptiness and deadness. In addition, there is sometimes a perverse joy in keeping these relationships a secret-what Joseph described as "a secret world of violence" (1982). In many cases, I've found that the therapeutic temptation to hold and contain these feelings of deadness and emptiness eventually results in an unconscious collaboration of the analyst with the patient's death object, thus unwittingly fulfilling its goal. We must therefore offer our aliveness as an ally to those hidden, threatened parts of the analysand so that we can, thorugh constant interpretation, face together the death object directly.

The more we acquire death-equivalents which are not worked-through, the stronger and more dangerous the death-object becomes, sheltered and protected by denial and fear. This is often the case where traumatized societies without the possibility of or the ability for a proper working-through via mourning, develop monstrous death-objects which are eventually acted-out as murderous attacks and as a death-culture. The social death-equivalents are often dislocation, emigration, poverty, war, social violence and abuse and brutal control of children with the phantasy of eliminating weakness and need through harsh education. Haneke's film "The white ribbon" is a prime example of that as well as Herman Beland's discussion of the inability to mourn in his paper "Collective mourning-who or what frees a collective to mourn?" (2009).

I will attempt to show some different forms of the death-object and the shifts between them in the following clinical vignettes, all taken from a 5 sessions per-week analyses.

Facing death and the death object – Joseph

Joseph was 6 years old when he contracted a rare and quite lethal blood disease. In the course of his analysis he invented a game in which there was a competition between white and red darts. He would throw the darts aiming at a cork board and then he would anxiously count how many red and white darts had reached each side. Each session he would come up with new rules ensuring that the red darts would conquer the white ones. It was apparent that on the conscious level Joseph was enacting the combat between his red and white blood cells, as he was well aware of the details of his medical situation told to him by his parents and by his doctors. I, however, tried to interpret an additional unconscious struggle- between his knowledge regarding the danger of death residing within and his attempt to create new rules and contracts with it so that it would leave him alone. This death-thing inside also forced him to change the rules and ignore reality. Joseph had always been a rather obsessive and compliant boy. I also suggested that now that he had this death-thing in him he can at last try to be bad and break the old rules, and thus achieve a sense of freedom he'd never had before. After a while, Joseph began to add to the game black darts. He insisted that I play too, since my participation was his only chance of winning the game. He claimed that the black darts "rule" and that they do not allow the other darts to play. He would anxiously make me collect all the black darts and put them in my bag so that I can take them home with me and play with my children. This soon developed into an obsessive-phobic relationship with the black darts and with the black color. I drew his attention to the fact that I usually wore black. I said that his disease and the death-thing first attached themselves to the black darts, paralyzing all the other darts, and then- to me. He desperately wanted me to contain and take with me his black death-thing so that it would leave him alone and dominate me and my children instead. By this he also exhibited the envy of the dying towards the living. At the same time he also wanted me to win the game and thus to abolish the threatening death-thing and conquer his disease. However, since I've also become contaminated by the black color he no longer knew whether I was on the death side or on the side of survival which is signified by the good balance

102

between the red and white darts. Soon after, Joseph refused to come to our sessions. When he re-appeared he told me in a whisper about an imaginary friend he had, who looked like the black villain in the film "Star Wars". He said that this friend would soon finish me off for making Joseph so miserable. In addition he confided in me that this imaginary friend was also a good friend of his father's and that he asked him to find a white cat, kill it and burry it in my yard. I suggested that Joseph confided in me and introduced me to the death-thing who was a mixture of daddy and Darth Vader from Star Wars- a death-daddy. A brief explanation is probably needed here: Darth Vader is the chief antagonist in the original film trilogy of Star Wars. He is first depicted as *Darth Vader*, a Dark Lord. He is then revealed to be originally a Knight called *Anakin Skywalker* who falls to the dark side. He also turns out to be the father of both Luke Skywalker and Princess Leia Organa, the two main protagonists of the original trilogy. Luke ultimately redeems his father and Anakin sacrifices himself to save his son. I referred to this and said "now that I know what the death-thing looks like, what his history was and what are his intentions-killing all your white, soft, innocent parts and turning me into a cemetery, there is hope for a rescue. I would have to be a fearless knight and to sacrifice myself for you Joseph. In addition, your father would have to allow you to have a beautiful Princess so that you can live and have brave children of your own". Joseph was quite pleased with this interpretation and in the following sessions there were more open combats – first between me and DD (the new name he found for this death-daddy-object) and then Joseph would join me in an increasingly fearless way. After some time, Joseph's mental and medical conditions improved. On one occasion he remarked that I should have nothing to worry about since he had told his doctor, whom he admired for saving his life, that his analyst, whom he called "the death fighter" was also quite good at frightening the death-things.

The internal death-object, in unconscious phantasy, spreads a double-net: it threatens physical and psychic existence, causing paralysis, loss of the ability to feel, live, think and relate to the other and an obliteration of meaning and meaningfulness. At the same time it offers the allure of a relief from pain, a freedom from the restraints of time, space, from boundaries between self and other, release from the burdens of relatedness or connectedness and a deep, profound stillness. This 'death double-phantasy' is based not only on our primordial ambivalence towards transience and death, but mainly on the compromise we've found in the form of a certain split which pervades human religion, art, conduct and philosophy: the separation of mind from body, the creation of ghosts and spirits and the omnipotent ideas of salvation, re- incarnation, immortality, heaven and hell and of self-realization through death. Merging with death, as is partly the case with the "holy death" of the Shahids (suicide bombers) or any other fundamentalist extremists, could serve as an example for the complicated relationship with the death object and with "death equivalents" which had not been sufficiently mentalized. Many of the interviews which have been carried out with terrorists, who somehow remained alive after the bomb they had carried did not explode, show that many of them experienced the loss of a parent or of a close family member at a tender age. Furthermore, many reported a variety of developmental problems- psychological and physiological. Many times the phobic attitude towards the death object undergoes idealization and erotization and together with a problematic relationship with the father and the deep hatred towards the real enemy becomes an all-powerful death object which offers a final solution to life's misery. Stein (2003, 2006) has linked between a perverted relationship with the father and fundamentalism. In her important contribution she describes two kinds of fear which lead to fundamentalist formations: the fear of death or of personal annihilation and the fear and rage in the face of the very existence of the other human being. Fundamentalism is the attempt to get rid of these fears or to violently transcend them through destructiveness and self-destruction. This is accomplished through processes of idealization and purification in which service destructiveness is being battled, enacted and worshipped. Thus fundamentalism entails a libidinal, homoerotic and perverted father- son relationship in which the persecutory object is transformed into a loving-one and hatred or self-hatred are transformed into idealized love.

Fusion, separateness and the death object

Erlich (1990, 1993, 2008) describes how the major task during adolescence, that of establishing a sense of identity, relies mainly on the adolescent's success in integrating two modes of experience; *doing* (with its developmental achievement of a sense of separateness form the other) and *being* (which implies a capacity for fusion). He writes:" In severe cases, the inability to be in a role, to connect to it and merge with it, is so damaging that it might cause withdrawal and defensive encapsulation. The adolescent refuses 'to do' what is required , even as a response to an external demand, because this might exposed the fact of his 'not-being', his internal emptiness and his feelings of deadness, and this is a risk he can't afford to take" (2008, p.31). I believe that in many such cases the adolescent chooses to withdraw into a phantasised internal fusion with the death-object, often equated with the mother's womb. The patient I'm about to describe used to describe death as "a birth in reverse" This fusion provides a deceptive sense of unity, cohesion and identity leading to disastrous consequences.

Seeking fusion with the death-object
in a suicidal adolescent: Eva

I will present 4 dreams taken from the analysis of Eva, a 15 year old girl. Eva began her analysis suffering from a severe depression. Her life has been full of separations, emigrations and periods of financial well-being followed by near-poverty. Most of her life she just "sailed-through" she said. She was beautiful, talented, a top student. Inside, however, she was hollow, detached, non-feeling, persecuted and lonely. Her mother had a long history of depression. When her mother was Eva's age she tried to commit suicide by cutting her throat and was subsequently hospitalized for long periods. The mother was "in love with death" as Eva commented drily. "She's always had two obsessions- my father and her lover: death". Unconsciously, however, Eva was dangerously identified with this death-couple. About a year into the analysis, during which she was mainly silent and impenetrable she began to talk to me. This opening-up was quickly followed by anorexia and a stubborn determination to starve to death. She lost weight quickly, looking more and more like a skeleton and talking quite frankly about her sadistic joy in having control over her body, over her parents and over me. She told me she enjoyed looking at herself in the mirror and seeing herself resembling a corpse. She was dominated by a murderous, tyrannical death-object.

It became clear after a while that she was doing all in her power to get herself hospitalized and thus to achieve several goals: to repeat her mother's history so that she could both become her and meet her "lover-death". At the same time she wanted to get away from her malignantly symbiotic relationship with her mother by being "taken" from her forcefully and not openly wanting to do so. In this way she tried to reduce her unconscious guilt for deserting her mother. A third goal was to have an affair of her own with this "lover-death" so that she would eventually be able to break away from it, too. Her anorexia, her death-equivalent, which masked and enlivened her depression, was an attempt to conquer not only life but also death. After a suicide attempt she was hospitalized and after a surprisingly short while was released with her weight balanced. She kept contact with me throughout the hospitalization as she claimed contemptuously that "the hospital staff knew nothing about death".

Upon her release from the hospital she resumed her analysis and it became clear that this death-object had resided in her for a very long time, in fact, ever since she could remember. She told me that at last she was able to show it to the world (her skeleton-like appearance) and she associated it mainly with intra-uterine equivalents such as water, boxes, tightly-wrapped blankets[12] and so on. One day she walked by the seashore with her mother and rushed into the water and began swimming with all her clothes on. The terrified mother ran after her trying to pull her back. As the tide was coming in, the waves were quite strong and high. The two of them almost drowned. At last the mother managed to pull her back to shore. I told Eva that it seems as if they were both

---

[12] Eva's grandmother, who was her main caretaker during infancy, used to tightly wrap her in a blanket so that she would feel secure. Eva, who was quite hyperactive, would scream in rage and terror for hours.

longing to drown together, merged together in the warm waves of death. Being saved by her mother was perhaps Eva's wish to be born again and perhaps to even give birth to her mother, not from a death-womb but from the sea or from a man (Jesus), like a born-again Christian. Eva toyed with the idea of converting from Judaism into Christianity for a short while prior to this incident, saying that there was something hypnotizing about the symbol of Christ dying slowly and painfully on the cross.

After a few more months she recounted the following dreams, which were all dreamt during the same night. In the first dream she was visiting her dietician and told her that she wished to remain anorexic since she was not sure she wanted to become healthy. "I want to commit suicide but not to die- I only want *to touch* death". In the second dream she was walking in a shopping mall with two friends from the hospital ward- Boris and Anat. Boris suffered from acute depression and was hospitalized after a suicide attempt. He's had a terrible life, a terrible mother and his existence was one of endless suffering. Eva liked him very much. Anat was a borderline anorexic girl, who used to cut herself till she bled so that she could feel something. Usually she felt nothing. Eva was attracted to her but did not really like her. The mall looked like the psychiatric ward and in the middle there was a nurse station where popcorn could be bought. Eva asked Anat to get her popcorn, which she did. However, before eating it in the dream Eva woke up. She felt terribly hungry and ate a Pizza. Going back to sleep, in her third dream she discovered that her head was full of lice and maggots. She picked one between her fingers, crushed it and ate it. In her last dream she was walking in the street with friends and suddenly she found herself in a small taxi through which she had to crawl on her stomach in order to escape through one of the windows, so that she could return to the street and to her friends. She got stuck in the window, then fell out of it but her dress was caught in the door. The taxi started driving fast and she fell on the road, hanging on to her torn dress while the taxi drove quickly on, ignoring her cries. Finally she managed to disentangle herself. She lay curled up on the road thinking: "when something like this happens, the best thing is to throw-up", which she did. She felt relieved and then met a nice boy, whose name in Hebrew means "Justice". He took her in his car and she thought "Now I'm safe".

I suggested to Eva that the fact that all her dreams presented themselves to her in a succession during one night, probably hinted that they were trying to tell us one story but in encrypted parts. Perhaps this was another trick of the death inside of her: to disintegrate the whole into its fragmented parts so that no complexity and depth would exist and the truth would remain hidden. I suggested that the first "dietician" dream was one where death ran the show, forbidding her to eat, wanting to keep her sadistically alive but starved, alive but nearly dead, like Jesus. It was not just her wish to touch death, her own and that inside her mother, but also death's wish to touch her and abuse her. She was telling me, the dietician who stood for the wish to get well and for the ability to give and to receive food that she was not sure she wanted to live. In this way she was repeating with me the same attitude that death had towards her- keeping me tormented, paralyzed, useless and abused. I became a helpless dietician who failed to feed her.

The second dream, however, expressed her wish to live, though in a heavy conflict with death. Boris stood for the death-equivalent of the suffering part in her, almost identical to her whereas Anat stood for the death-equivalent of her detached, sadistic and violent non-feeling part. Boris wanted *to die so as not to feel so much pain*. Anat wanted *to die so as to try and feel something*. They both represented different roles she gave death- a savior and a tormentor. In the dream she felt hunger which, like pain, is a sign of life, and even managed to convince the Anat-part of her to let her eat. The source of food was the analysis (the nurse station), but the food was pop-corn, a junk-food which was associated in her mind with anorexia. She once described it as "eating cardboard". Although this food was not really good, (her way of attacking the analysis by turning everything I've said into cardboard), it still provoked the death inside which forbade her to eat even this "junk food", and woke her up. But her hunger and her wish to live were stronger. They connected her to life and she ate the Pizza.

When she fell asleep again she discovered herself as a dead corpse, eaten by lice and maggots, which became her death-food. Death punished her for wanting to live and get nutrition from life and from the analysis. As a substitute it provided her with death-food.

In the last dream she expressed her unconscious wish to be reborn out of death together with the acute anxieties this evoked in her. The non-caring, dangerous taxi stood in her phantasy for her mother's womb. She relived her birth experience as being either stuck inside the womb or being carelessly thrown or torn out of it, a lonely and deserted fetus left to die on the road. The tearing of her clothes stood for the experience of being torn apart from her mother's insides, which she experienced as death (a death equivalent). Her idea that she must throw-up and get this death-experience out of her expressed her wish to live. The boy "justice" probably stood for both me and her father, as male figures who were assigned the role of saving her from her deadly internal mother. It is only then that she was able, at last, to feel safe.

Eva seemed to respond well to these interpretations and in the following months produced more valuable material regarding the nature of her death-object and her death-equivalents. She started eating, her anorexia and depression showed marked improvement and eventually she managed to have an age-appropriate romantic relationship with a boy.

Conclusions

Every analyst who undertakes upon himself to confront primitive mental states has to deal, sooner or later, with the presence of death in the internal world. From the beginning of life every infant tries to create a personal, coherent narrative, through unconscious phantasies, in order to deal with the riddles of his birth and of his death. The ability to create such internal, unconscious narratives, always linked to the primary objects, often determines the infant's relation to reality and therefore his mental health. At the outset, the unconscious phantasies concerning death are fragmented, primitive and based on proto-psychological and somatic events which constitute "death equations". These are gradually linked to the object and to the self and eventually become "death equivalents". These are the realization of the infant's pre-conception of death. In the course of development the "death equivalents" are gradually identified with differentiated and animated objects, death objects. Various relationships and pacts are established with these death objects so as to ward off death. The inability to create a death object might lead to nameless dread and nameless grief.

The role of analysis, as a supplier of meaning and connectedness (within the internal world as well as within the total transference situation) has an important life-giving role for the patient in the throes of the death-object.[13] In all ages I find it useful to detect what is the death-object specific to the patient, what death-equivalents build it, describe them in detail, face them without fear (of course this relies heavily on our own relationship with death) and try to contain it within the aliveness, relatedness and meaning of the transference.

Zen picture of skull: "I'm on my way"

References

Abramovitch, A. (2000). "Good Death" and "Bad Death": Therapeutic Implications of Cultural Conceptions of Death and Bereavement. In: Malkinson, R., Rubin, S. & Witztum, E. (Eds.) *Traumatic and Nontraumatic Loss and Bereavement clinical theory and practice*. Madison Conneticut: Psychosocial press p.255-273

Beland, H. (2009). Kollektive Trauer – Wer oder was befreit ein Kollektiv zu seiner Trauer? Annäherung an die Trauer des Selbstverlustes über den Vergleich mit Freuds Empirie und Theoriegeschichte des Trauerns. In: Franz Wellendorf und Thomas Wesle (Hrsg.): *Über die (Un)Möglichkeit zu trauern*. Stuttgart, Klett-Cotta, S. 243-262.

---

[13] Sometimes, especially for patients who are about to confront their death, be it through illness or old age, analysis, as the container of history, emotions and relationships, carries in unconscious phantasy an immortalizing function- much like a life's work, having children or belonging to a group. In such cases, interpreting these phantasies of Symbolic Immortality vis-à-vis the death objects within is of crucial importance.

Bell, D. (2007). *The Death drive: Phenomenological perspectives in contemporary Kleinian theory.* Paper given in the conference "Hanna Segal Today", University College London, December 2nd, 2007.

Bion, W.R. (1970). *Attention and Interpretation.* London: Tavistock

Blattner, W. (2206). *Heidegger's Being and Time.* London: Continuum.

Bott Spillius, E., Milton, J., Carvey, P., Couve, C. & Steiner, D. (2011). *The New Dictionary of Kleinian Thought.* London and New York: Routledge.

Brearley, M. (2005). Making death thinkable Franco De Masi London: Free Association Books. 2004. 157 pp. *Int. J. Psycho-Anal.*, 86:1493-1497.

Chau, T. M. B. (1991).*The Chinese Madhyama Agama and the Pali Majjhima Nikaya.* Delhi: Motilal Banarsidass Publishers.

De Masi, F. (2004). *Making death thinkable.* London: Free Association Books.

Durban, J. (2005). Angst und Sinnhaftigkeit im Schatten des Todes – die Analyse eines 84- jährigen Mannes. *Freie Assoziation,* 8 Jahrgang, Heft 1,2005. Psychosozial Verlag

Durban, J (2011). Shadows, Ghosts and Chimaeras – On some early modes of handling Psycho-Genetic heritage *Int. J. Psychoanal,* **92** (4), 903-24

———. (2014). Despair and hope: on some varieties of countertransference and enactment in the psychoanalysis of ASD (autistic spectrum disorder) children. *J of Child Psychotherapy, Vol. 40, Issue 2*, p. 187-200.

——— (2016). From *The Scream* to *The Pieta*: murderous mourning and evil. In: Lazar, R. (ed) *Talking about Evil psychoanalytic, social and cultural perspectives.* Routledge.

Erlich, H.S. (1990) Boundaries, limitations, and the wish for fusion in the treatment of adolescents. *Psychoanal. Study Child*, 45:195-213

Erlich, H.S. (1993) Reality, fantasy and adolescence. *Psychoanal. Study Child*, 48:200-223

Erlich, H.S. (2008) Trauma, terror and identity. In: *Terror and Aggression in the treatment of adolescents-* collected papers form the Summit Institute conference, Jerusalem 2008, 25-37.

Freud, S. (1915). Thoughts for the Times on War and Death. S.E., 14:273-300. London: Hogarth

Freud, S. (1916). On Transience. S.E., 1: 303-307. London: Hogarth

Freud, S. (1917). Mourning and Melancholia. S.E., 17: 237-258. London: Hogarth

Freud, S. (1919). The Uncanny. S.E., 17: 217-256. London: Hogarth

Freud, S.(1920). Beyond the Pleasure Principle. S.E., 19: 151-204. London: Hogarth

Freud, S. (1922). The Theme of the Three Caskets. S.E.,12:289-302. London: Hogarth

Freud, S. (1923). The Ego and the Id. S.E., 19: 1-66. London: Hogarth

Gottlieb, R.M. (2007). The Reassembly of the Body from Parts: Psychoanalytic Reflections on death, resurrection and cannibalism. *J. Amer. Psychoanal. Assn.*, 55:1217-1251

Green, A. (1986). The dead mother. In: Green, A. *On private madness*. London: Hogarth Press.

Heidegger, M. (1962). *Being and Time.* Translated by John Macquarrie and Edward Robinson. New-York: Harper and Row.

Isaacs, S. (1952) The nature and function of phantasy, In:Klein, M., Heimann, P., Isaacs, S. and Riviere, J. (Eds) *New Developments in Psychoanalysis.* Hogarth Press & The Institute of Psycho- Analysis.

Jaques, E. (1965). Death and the mid-life crisis. In: Bott-Spilius, E. (Ed.). (1988).*Melanie Klein today. Vol. 2: Mainly Practice.* London: The New Library of Psychoanalysis.

Joseph, B. (1982). Addiction to Near-Death. *Int. J. Psycho-Anal.,*63:449-456

Junkers, G (2006). *Is it too late? Key Papers on Psychoanalysis and Ageing.* London: Karnac.

Klein, M. (1930). The importance of symbol-formation in the development of the ego. In: *Love , Guilt and Reparation and Other Works 1921-1945.* London: The Hogarth Press, 1984.

——— (1946). Notes on some schizoid mechanisms. In: *Envy and Gratitude and Other works 1946-1963.* London: the Hogarth Press, 1984.

——— (1948). On the theory of anxiety and guilt. In: *Envy and Gratitude and Other works 1946-1963.* London: the Hogarth Press, 1984

——— (1957). Envy and Gratitude. In: *Envy and Gratitude and Other works 1946-1963.* London: the Hogarth Press, 1984.

Lazar, R. & Erlich, H.S. (1996). Repetition compulsion – A reexamination of the concept and the phenomenon. *Psychoanal. and Contemp. Thought.*, 19: 29-56.

Lazar, R. (1997). Repetition, repetition compulsion, motivation, interpretation. *Israel Journal of Psychiatry*, 35: 9-19.

Lifton, R. J. (1983), *The Broken Connection.* Basic Books.

Meltzer, D. (1976). The child-in-the-family-in-the-community. (with Martha Harris). In:Hahn, A. (Ed.). *Sincerity and other works. The collected papers of Donald Meltzer.*London: Karnac Books.

Money-Kyrle, R. (1955). An inconclusive contribution to the theory of the death instinct. In: Meltzer, D. and O'Shaughnessy, E. (Eds.) *The collected papers of Roger Money-Kyrle.* Perthshire:Clunoe Press.

Ogden, T. H. (1995). Aliveness and deadness in the transference-countertrasference. *Int. J. of Psychoanal.* **76**:695-710.

Proust, M, (1981). *In Search of Lost Time.* Translated by Andreas Mayor & Terence Kilmartin, Revised by D. J. Enright. Vol VI: Time Regained. New-York: The Modern Library.

Razinski, L. (2010). Driving death away. *Psychoanalytic review*, 97:393-424.

Riviere, J. (1936).On the genesis of psychic conflict in earliest infancy. In: Hughes, A (ed) (1991) *The Inner World and Joan Riviere* London, New- York: Karnac Books, p. 279-280.

Rosenfeld, H. (1987) *Impasse and Interpretation.* The New Liblrary of Psychoanalysis ,London: Routledge.

Roth, M. (2017) *Reading the Reader-a psychoanalytic perspective on reading literature,* Jerusalem, Carmel.

Segal, H. (1957), Notes on symbol formation, *Int. J. Psycho-Anal.* 38:391-7

——— (1997). On the clinical usefulness of the concept of the death instinct. In: *Psychoanalysis, Literature and War.* London: The new library of Psychoanalysis.

Sekoff, J. (1999). The undead necromancy and the inner world. In: Kohon, G. (Ed.) *The dead mother: The work of Andre' Green.* London: Routledge.

Stein, R. (2003). Vertical Mystical Homoerosis: An Altered Form of Desire in Fundamentalism. *Studies in Gender and Sexuality.4:38-58*

——— (2007). Fundamentalism, Father and Son, and Vertical desire. *Psychoanal. Rev.,93:210-229*

Steiner, J. (1993). *Psychic Retreats.* London: The New Library of Psychoanalysis.

Steiner, R. (2003). *Unconscious Phantasy.* London & New York: Karnac.

Tustin, F. (1972). Autism and Childhood Psychosis. London: Hogarth Press.

——— (1981). *Autistic States in Children.* London and Boston, MA: Routledge.

——— (1987). *Autistic Barriers in Neurotic Patients.* London: Karnac Books.

——— (1990). *The Protective Shell in Children and Adults.* London: Karnac

——— (1994). The perpetuation of an Error. *Journal of Child Psychotherapy,* 20:1. 3-23.

Willock, B. (2007). Thoughts for our times on transience and transformation. In: Willock, B., Bohm, L.C. and Curtis, R. (Eds.) *On death and Endings.* London: Routledge.

Winnicott D. W. (1952). Ego integration in child development. In: *The maturational processes and the facilitating environment.* London, The Hogarth Press, 1982.

Depleting Language and the Pervertization of Discourse – A Psychoanalytic Observation

Robby Schonberger

El Hombre

It's a strange courage
You give ancient star:

Shine alone in the sunrise
Toward which you lend no part!
(William Carlos Williams)

This article is dedicated to my teacher, mentor, wise opinion giver, and friend, Prof, Shmuel Erlich.

I would like to begin this paper by quoting the words of George Carlin, taken from his standup act, "Euphemisms":

> I don't like words that hide the truth. I don't like words that conceal reality. I don't like euphemisms or euphemistic language. And American English is loaded with euphemisms. Because Americans have a lot of trouble dealing with reality. Americans have trouble facing the truth, so they invent a kind of a soft language to protect themselves from it. And it gets worse with every generation. For some reason, it just keeps getting worse. I'll give you an example of that. There's a condition in combat. Most people know about it. It's when a fighting person's nervous system

has been stressed to its absolute peak and maximum, can't take any more input. The nervous system has either snapped or is about to snap. In the first world war that condition was called shell shock. Simple, honest, direct language. Two syllables. Shell shock. Almost sounds like the guns themselves. That was 70 years ago. Then a whole generation went by. And the second world war came along and the very same combat condition was called battle fatigue. Four syllables now. Takes a little longer to say. Doesn't seem to be as hard to say. Fatigue is a nicer word than shock. Shellshock... battle fatigue. Then we had the war in Korea in 1950. Madison Avenue was riding high by that time. And the very same combat condition was called Operational Exhaustion. Hey we're up to 8 syllables now! And the humanity has been squeezed completely out of the phrase now. It's totally sterile now. Operational Exhaustion: sounds like something that might happen to your car. Then of course came the war in Vietnam, which has only been over for about 16 or 17 years. And thanks to the lies and deceit surrounding that war, I guess it's no surprise that the very same condition was called Post-Traumatic Stress Disorder. Still 8 syllables, but we've added a hyphen. And the pain is completely buried under jargon. Post-Traumatic Stress Disorder. I bet you, if we'd still been calling it shell shock, some of those Vietnam veterans might have gotten the attention they needed at the time. I bet you that. But it didn't happen. And one of the reasons is because we were using that soft language, that language that takes the life out of life.

It might be a shame that one cannot simply go on quoting Carlin's words. He offers a truthful expression of what I wish to describe, but my words are somewhat less articulate. Carlin is not an ordinary standup comedian. His tone is intense and he sometimes sounds downright angry. He often points out some of the well-known mannerisms that surround us and that we seldom pay attention to, for various reasons, perhaps because we use them ourselves. I find the above quotation very useful as it discusses a term borrowed from the realm of psycho-diagnostics. The words he uses to conclude this segment – "that language that takes the life out of life" – mark the subject I wish to tackle here. With great acumen, Carlin is pointing out a process by which language becomes the executor of political-correctness, genteelism, concealment, deception and false pretense, which gradually turn it into an ossified and atrophied jargon and maybe even worse, into a language that is twisted and perverse. I wish, therefore, to take upon myself two tasks which address this state of affairs: to discuss the depletion of words and of language in general and to touch upon the kind of Language that Bionian psychanalysis strives to attain. In addition, I will put forward certain thoughts about what I wish to term "the pervertization of discourse".

In his book, *Transformations*, Bion discusses the analyst's aspiration for what he calls, following John Keats, "the Language of Achievement". This language is supposed to entail various qualities which are not necessarily compatible with each other. First, 'the language of achievement' must enable good communication between colleagues but it must also be endowed with more than that. As the psychoanalyst must experience, in the broadest and deepest way, the emotional experience of the patient's personality by means of his own personality, in order to try and help the patient achieve personal knowledge of himself, the analyst's 'language of achievement' must be communicationally precise, universal, individual and resilient. Thus, according to Bion, a psychoanalytic paper must evoke in the reader the same emotional experience the author has in mind, the paper's evocative power must be resilient and the emotional experience it depicts must be a precise and genuine representation of the psychoanalytic experience the author initially encountered (p. 32). How can anything measure up to such absolutist standards? By borrowing the four synonyms Carlin mentioned in demonstrating the use of euphemisms, one can see that "shell-shock" may be simple, sincere and direct as a term, but it lacks precision, as it only indicates that experience of shock which follows the shelling or the battle, but not the harrowing psychic state which persists in its wake. The two terms "battle fatigue" and "operational exhaustion" are not clinically accurate as they assume that the disorder results from excessive weariness in the organism or the psyche. In and of itself, this is a rather optimistic notion as it suggests that adequate rest is the ultimate cure for such disorders. The final term, "post-traumatic stress disorder" offers a more accurate portrayal of how this psychic disorder endures beyond the particular combat situation, but it essentially omits the immediate shock of sensory overload which overwhelms the combatant. The first three terms have failed the test of time and it is certainly possible that the fourth is but waiting its turn. Therefore, it appears that the standards for 'the language of achievement" are elusive and very difficult to meet. It is thus hardly a surprise that Bion, like Freud and many analysts who followed him, turned to the inspiration offered by poets and artists in order to make his language more sophisticated, precise and charged with meaning. In addition, he uses abstract signifiers, which may assist in universalizing the phenomena they seek to represent, but it seems that there is no escape from failing and faltering in regards to one of his criteria.

In one of his other papers, "Evidence", Bion argues that in order to avoid empty psychologistic chatter, which only has the semblance of interest or meaning, each analyst must shape their own language and terminology, which would creatively and eloquently portray their ways of thinking. It is likely that such a language or such terminology will draw on the analyst's inner world, their own unique realm of associations, experience and imagery. While Bion does not make this particular point, the iterations of one of his concepts can be used to illustrate my claim. The concept of the "container" and its derivative adverb, "containment" are two of Bion's most well known concepts, whose use has spread far beyond the psychoanalytic sphere. Bion drew this concept from certain aspects of his experience as a young officer in the British armored corps during the First World War. In its military sense, "containment" means absorbing the enemy's aggressive actions – either bombardment or infantry forays – without any spontaneous or impulsive response. Such passive absorption prepares the ground for a more opportune time in which response, meaning the counter-attack, would be optimally effective. In other words, containment does not mean paralyzed and terrified entrenchment on the one hand nor an impulsive foray on the other, but passive absorption while awaiting a more auspicious time.

Yet another meaning, that may have inhabited Bion's inner realm of images when he coined this concept, involves the physical structure and the verbal sense of the word 'Tank'. A tank is essentially a container which protects its occupants, but may also turn into a trap for them.

Containment, in a sense that is closer to its tactical meaning, was part of a years-long psychic maneuver that Bion endured in his attempts to mentally process his experiences and memories from that war, in order to overcome them. He talked and wrote at length about the great significance and importance of being able to think under fire. This is tantamount to the ability to psychically absorb bombardment, a life-threatening attack, without reacting either desperately or bravely. He likened such brave responses, which involve a spontaneous and impulsive reaction instead of thinking, to stupidity. I imagine that in listening to his patients, especially to those who were psychotic or to the psychotic core of others, he experienced that familiar difficulty – 'thinking under fire': thinking under the stressful circumstances of the massive projective-identification shot from their turbulent and fragmented psychic worlds. In the consultation room, he **once again** encountered his wish or his familiar impulse to act unthinkingly and in a panic, to say something in a desperate attempt to restore some 'common sense' to the dialogue, to find some momentary solace in what may scarcely be likened to 'cause and effect'. That is, to act stupidly. The words 'container' and 'containment' were also linked to Klein's important intuition concerning the infantile fantasy about what goes on in the internal spaces inside the mother's body and the process of 'projective identification' into these inner spaces. These words became even more valid and significant in the context of clinical theory and analytic practice. The image gradually turned into a metaphor; the mind of the mother (for the infant) and the mind of the analyst (for the analysand) absorbed new qualities and meanings that involved the qualities of their 'contained', becoming something that not only signifies the signified, but is also saturated with some of its qualities and characteristics.

This Bionian concept holds great value for psychoanalytic discourse, in both its explanatory and descriptive functions. However, as is the fate of certain concepts, its use became extensive and widespread, popular and ever more varied, it entered the professional parlance of more and more fields and has been soaking up contexts and meanings from constantly growing circles. I see this soaking up of meaning as an integral and expected process for live concepts, whose explanatory and elucidatory validity has not yet been exhausted; still, this process nevertheless unraveled some of its precise, articulate and distinct qualities. I could thus hear my son's kindergarten teacher tell one of the mothers, whose girl had a crying and raging fit, that she had helped her and 'contained' her. Afterwards, when I asked her what she meant by the word 'contained', she said that she embraced the child until she calmed down. I believe that this is a lovely and refreshing use of the concept, but it already unravels certain aspects of its original meanings. Another form of such unraveling can be seen in the term "post-traumatic stress disorder", mentioned by George Carlin. "Shell shock" was once the lot of certain combatants, among all those who took part in the fighting. Today, "post-traumatic stress disorder" is so common as to include virtually anyone who has had an unpleasant experience.

Even within the psychoanalytic community, one can note such unraveled uses of the concept of containment, which occur when it is confused and mixed up with another highly important and useful concept – "holding". While there is a certain proximity, even an affinity, between the two concepts, there are also essential differences between them. These could be applied to what the kindergarten teacher implied. 'Containment' is an intra-psychic phenomenon, while holding is external, or occurs in the transitional spaces between inside and outside. That is, for the girl to be able to use the hug she received to calm down, she must be able to contain the teacher's attempts at **holding**. Therefore, in line with the present example, the concept of 'containment' has become quite broad and flexible, soaking up various additional meanings. This process by which the concept grows broader and more flexible is necessary in order to keep it fresh and vital. However, as I wish to emphasize, what may be so crucial for its vitality accelerates the process by which the concept withers, grows old and dies; eventually, such changes may cause it to lose its explanatory uniqueness and its heuristic distinction.

By growing broader and more useful, this conceptual clump, much like the dough we knead, is flattened, extended and leveled, often to the point of crumbling altogether. In other words, psychoanalytic concepts are constantly subjected to tests which measure their elasticity in terms of perception and thought. This process is probably inevitable, as a new generation of psychoanalytic concepts, notions and viewpoints wishes to be born, often by presenting the older generation of concepts and views as anachronistic, atrophied and having failed the test of time; the gods must vanquish the titans in order to dominate the new world they are creating. But we are also familiar with the opposite momentum, by which some part of our psyche seeks the wisdom of what came before, the clever and profound life-experience of our founding fathers. Through this momentum, some of us seek to retrieve old concepts, to restore perspectives which, as it were, fell from grace or lost their explanatory capacity. Psychoanalysis has a powerful attraction to things ancient, primitive and primary. It is drawn to etymologies, to the psychological foundation of the development of words, to the way words function in line with the rules of dreamwork, through verbal and pictogram associations, through layering and condensation. Returning once again to the image of dough, one can say that psychoanalysis loves to roll out and extend its conceptual dough and then to fold it and stretch it, to pile it in layers, to see how the new forms yet another layer beside the old, is assimilated into it, how the new introduces novelty, while relishing the depth and multi-layered structure of accumulated tradition and thought. This abundance of layers makes a significant contribution to the creativity and intellectual flexibility of psychoanalysis.

The factors determining whether our professional language will be 'resilient' or 'precarious' entail more than its potential for being sufficiently elastic and stable, its explanatory and descriptive efficacy and the extent to which it measures up to Bion's requirements. Our psychoanalytic language also depends on **our ability** to make lively use of it and to maintain an approach which is inquisitive and exploratory, skeptical and critical, dynamic and evolving. As an illustration, I return to the question I posed to the kindergarten teacher – "what did you mean by…?" This is a very common psychoanalytic question, which is grounded in a comprehensive ethos of exploring and thinking about the patient's inner world. The implicit assumption is that this inner world is not a 'sitting duck' that one may simply shoot down or trap by using common sense or the observant eye of a skillful scholar. The patient's internal world is not something that we can simply grasp with our senses or our standard measuring instruments. Our psyche seeks to be dynamic, constantly changing, becoming, dissolving, growing, restful and restless, excited, passionate, satisfied, abreacting, repulsed, etc. It tends to avoid consistency in terms of what it draws from its environment, from the sources from which it imbibes its motivation, its notions of itself and the world in which it exists, its relation to people and things and its understanding thereof. Therefore, one cannot establish general rules that are too concise about it. Psychoanalysis has been grappling with this since its inception, struggling with the deceptive duality of the desire to characterize and generalize, to conceptualize and encapsulate without losing sight of the subject, the particular and elusive Cogito.

Routine psychoanalytic questions – "what does it mean to you…", "what comes to mind when you're telling me about…", "what does this remind you of…" – are essentially similar to asking "what did you mean by…" By means of what can be consciously and intentionally reported, all these questions are trying to dredge up personal and particular unconscious material which could successfully escape to the surface, or so we hope. As our view of the psyche and especially of its unconscious aspect, is inevitably multi-faceted, dynamic, ever-changing and evolving, making assertions that are **too** decisive concerning its essence, development or guiding motivations is an act of allegorizing and stagnation-inducing ossification. George Carlin is not alone, the general public loves using generic quasi-psychoanalytic statements such as "I wonder what Freud would say about that…", "it goes far deeper than that…" or "I was a victim of failed parental adaptation". Sometimes, those sentences sound like generic standup statements to me.

I will now turn to discuss what I call the 'pervertization of discourse'. In using this conceptualization, I am not referring to a discourse-language that had lost, in the course of its expansion, some of its symbolism or its explanatory elasticity, but to one which intentionally misguides, deceives and deludes its addressee. It is a kind of discourse which uses actual facts and information not as instruments of fictive creativity, which create an imaginary world for artistic purposes, but in order to deceive, disguise, distort and hide a certain truth. For the purpose of discussing this complex subject matter, I will now return to Bion. In a chapter titled "Lies and the Thinker" in his book, *Attention and Interpretation*, Bion (1970) introduces some of his most complex and tricky ideas, those designed to elucidate the status of what he calls 'absolute truth', 'ultimate reality', the godhead and the origin – O, as something which exists independently of a thinker. Even more so, he claims that it is the lie which requires the existence of a thinker. O, the absolute truth – not in its positivistic-scientific sense but it its semi-religious mystical sense, precedes the thinker and is naturally independent of the latter's existence. Bion's definition of O is somewhat muddled, as he always offers a series of consecutive definitions. Alongside the ones mentioned above – "absolute truth", "ultimate reality", "the godhead" and "the origin" – he also adds "**the thing in itself**", which is unknowable and immeasurable and the "**absolute fact**", which may occur in the analytic session, in a work of art or in a state of 'enlightenment'. Due to the nature of O, it cannot be known (by means of K links) nor can there be any defined technique for it's attainment. In this sense, **any** kind of mentalization, symbolization and abstraction is to some degree a mental and cognitive process, which thus leads one away from the ultimate truth. However, moving away from the ultimate truth is not identical to a state of lie. Lies are negative K links, which facilitate the destruction of the capacity to think and the capacity to know. Bion believes that the liar must know quite a bit about truth in order to fabricate the lie. When the link between two psyches leads to the destruction of the capacities for thought and for knowledge, it is the kind of link in which the liar, much like the pervert, needs their audience in order to spread their distortions. What may, at first glance or first listen, appear to be an intelligent, rational, useful and constructive discourse, is nothing other than a furtive and perverse infiltration, which is both domineering and omnipotent, a subduing speech and an elaborate ordeal of deception. This type of discourse may disguise itself as a verbal embrace, as concern, kindness, foreknowledge and sheer disillusioned and unassimilable wisdom, while in fact it is a manifestation of invasive and petrifying conquest, whose sole aim is to plant a flag of omnipotent domination on the pile of debris that is left of the mind of the listener, whose capacity for thought is being corrupted. The listener is not always aware of this, as they are often fraudulently lured into a realm of deception and illusion which is, in my view, the space in which 'the pervertization of discourse' takes place. It is a world of obscured categories, where the self is indistinguishable from other people or the outside world, where wishes and desires are inseparable from external events and where one cannot tell between live objects that seem dead and inanimate objects that appear alive and are used as such. This polyvalent lack of distinction is, in many ways, the result of massive projective identification and violent invasive identification which penetrates the object. These violent processes trap many aspects of the self inside the object, making it impossible for the subject to distinguish between itself and the object. This lack of distinction between subject and object also serves as a fantasy of perfect unity, which seems to perfectly fulfil the wishes of the 'pleasure principle', that constant satisfaction that can never be sated or discharged.

One example of this kind of pervertization of discourse and of immediate transference relations can be seen in Yuval, a man in his mid-twenties who entered intensive psychotherapy complaining of a profound sense of emptiness, which he ceaselessly tried to abate by constantly pursuing random sexual escapades and pornography. Yuval often laughed during the sessions, a kind of shameful, awkward and unpleasant laughter. There was something disturbing and invasive about his habit of staring right into my eyes as he laughed or snickered. He blushed profusely and almost every occurrence or sensory distraction evoked these laughing and snickering responses in him – a door slammed next door, a cat meowing in the yard, a book lying on the shelf: everything aroused this blushed, snickering laughter, even me. The way my face grows serious when I listen, the twin wrinkles between my eyebrows, my sitting position on the chair, the way my legs are crossed with my hand in between, my tone of voice, the words I choose to express myself with, my syntactical structures, recurring words, etc. Without even noticing, I found that I was limiting myself, my actions and my thoughts, dismayed by his laughter and snickering. In our sessions, I felt increasingly trapped in a paralysis that affected my **thought and movement**. It occurred to me that my minor catatonia was, among other things, the expression of his subjugation of my mental array, an act both clandestine and undetectable as well as considerably omnipotent, subversive and forceful. In psychoanalytic terms, this amounted to massive projective identification, which he used to pull my strings and manipulate me according to his wishes and needs. After one of the next snickering laughs, I offered him an interpretation of this subtle dynamic between us. Yuval accepted my words with a mild panic, but then went on to talk about his sexual fantasies, in which he was a subdued object, completely dominated by a woman who commanded him to do her bidding, controlling him with the threat of mockery, for she knew how pathetic he was with his raging sexual fantasies. It gradually became apparent that his shameful snickering was an expression of his attempt to engage me in the same perverse, elaborate and domineering constellation of humiliation and debasement. His snickering laughter at everything around him, including myself, was an expression of condescension, but also an attempt of inducing into me his sense of wretchedness, lowliness and ridicule. Yuval was trying to exert absolute control over the choreography of what was happening in our sessions, dictating a dance of arrogance and lowliness, dominator and dominated, humiliator and humiliated. In other words, this was a kind of unconscious, though quite energetic attempt to cast me in a twofold dynamic role: that of the person being humiliated or debased by being helplessly penetrated and that of the arrogant observer, who witnesses his ridicule and wretchedness, even though I was the one who in reality was constantly mocked. This is not a language in the articulate, symbolic and eloquent sense of the word, but as a unique interpersonal dynamic that Yuval introduced through convoluted psychic means. In this interpersonal dynamic, messages are delivered or, more precisely, inflicted in a subtle though powerful way, while the receiving object seems unaware of being affected by the other, who is now pulling his unseen strings.

This twofold interpersonal dynamic is also manifest in more explicit verbal and linguistic elements. For example, in a direct and verbal manner, Yuval expressed his profound wish that I would know what is going on in his mind and his thoughts without him having to speak: "I would like to have my head hooked up to some big screen so that you could see and know what's going on in my mind, what I'm thinking and imagining, without me having to figure out how to phrase it… without having to feel the shame of saying it… I'd like you to live inside my head so that you could know exactly what you need to do for me and I wouldn't have to explain, explaining is so humiliating…"

On the other hand, alongside this omnipotent wish for me to silently know what is going on in his mind, he also set out, in his unique, invasive and domineering way, to paralyze my thinking, to annihilate my separate presence. I often tried expressing what I had been able to think and gather from the material he shared with me or from his behavior in the consultation room, but all too often his response was just to snicker and blush. On one occasion, when I asked him about his snicker, he said something along the lines of: "I don't know, it just seemed kind of weird all of a sudden… I pictured you like a cloud, or like a whoopy cushion, this balloon that fills up your skin and somehow holds up your clothes… even what you said just now, I couldn't hear a word of it… like a whoopy cushion that's slowly being deflated, so that it talks in farts…" (a blushed and triumphant laugh).

This is a small and perhaps typical example of a way of speaking which is not an expression of broken-down, fragmentary, suspicious or chaotic psychotic thinking, but of omnipotently deceiving, distorting and domineering speech. This kind of discourse may make a small, yet significant addition to the 'euphemisms' mentioned above. It is a kind of discourse which does not only "take the life out of life", but also treats life as if it were denuded of its vitality. In such cases, the collapse of language not only expresses a coquettish wish to elegantly verbally bypass the conflictual and anxiety provoking aspects of our daily life – a bypass manifest in euphemisms and sugar-coating. The kind of speech characteristic of "the pervertization of discourse" is one which abolishes or erases our normal categories of thinking and which infiltrates, furtive

126

and perverse, domineering and omnipotent, through speeches of subjugation that are laden with fraud, deception and false pretense.

Refernces

Bion, W.R. (1965) Transformations. Karnac Books, 1984, London.

——— (1970) attention and Interpretation. Karnac Books, , London.

——— (1987) *Evidence*. In: Clinical Seminars and Four Papers. Fleetwood Press, Abingdon.

Carlin, G. Euphemisms. In: www.youtube.com/watch?v=qvISFZ7bQcE

CHAPTER EIGHT

Thoughts about a New Subject of Psychoanalysis: The 'iGroup'.

Joseph Triest

Dedicated to Shmuel Erlich, with love and appreciation

"Normally, there is nothing of which we are more certain than the feeling of our self, of our own ego. This ego appears to us as something autonomous and unitary, marked off distinctly from everything else [...] such an appearance is deceptive [...]"
(Freud, Civilization and its Discontents, p. 65-66).

At an experiential learning conference[1] devoted to the study of conscious and unconscious group processes, the members of one of the small study-groups are coming back from their lunch break. As groups are wont to do, they leisurely 'trickle' back into the room, supposedly oblivious of the fact that they are several minutes late, as well as of the presence of the consultant, who is already in his chair. In addition to the consultant (a man), the group is comprised of four women and three men. The first two members stride in with linked arms: a woman (1) and a man (A). They are followed by a woman (2) who takes her seat next to the man and who is immediately

---

[1] Modelled after the Tavistock Conferences. These intensive conferences have been held since the 1950's. They were developed by Eric Miller and A. K. Rice, inspired by the work of Wilfred Bion and Kurt Lewin. Such conferences are usually one to two weeks long, during which the conference functions as a 'temporary learning organization', a hive made up of groups with different compositions, tasks and goals, for the purpose of studying the conscious and unconscious dynamic processes taking place inside and between the various groups (see the more elaborate discussion in chapter 17).

followed by another man (B). The consultant is wondering whether this group had been transformed into Noah's Arc during the break. While he is still developing possible 'working hypotheses' regarding the nature and significance of this paired configuration, a third woman (3) walks in. Lingering at the door, she closely examines the temperature on the AC control panel and then, as if to confirm the emerging assumption, sits down next to the man (B). Then the last two enter: a woman (4) and soon after, the third man (C) rushes in and closes the door. The woman – now we can give her a name as well – Alin, has had time to stride around the room in measured steps and to sit down next to... woman (1). The man, who is still standing, finally closes the circle by taking his seat on the other side of the consultant. As the consultant is (sadly) beginning to part with the interpretation he was forming, Alin turns to the man seated next to him – 'say, would you mind changing places with me? The sun is in my eyes and you mentioned earlier that you enjoyed that sun'. The man, eager to please, leaps out of his seat and changes places with Alin. It seems that everyone is breathing a sigh of relief, as if order has been restored: woman-man, woman-man, woman-man, woman (Alin)-consultant (man)... ad infinitum.

The notion suggesting that the group's seating pattern is not incidental but an expression of an unconscious collective Phantasy is one of the underlying axioms of the approach known as 'the group as a whole'. What is it, however, that allows us to treat the group 'as a whole'? Where can we 'locate' that group-subject – 'the whole' – which presents the group as an entity endowed with a uniform identity, a capacity for coordinating complex and synchronized activities, self-reflection and even the ability to develop from 'birth' through 'adulthood' to 'death' (Bennis & Shephard, 1956; Mackenzie and Livesley, 1983; Saravay 1978) What mechanism compelled Alin to change seats according to some unconscious heterosexual pairing choreography? Inversely, one might pose a question that is equally philosophically challenging: who, then, is the subject ('individual') called Alin, who heeded to group's call? Where is she 'located'? If she could have seen herself from without, she might have wondered – 'Who on earth is in charge of my will?', 'Will (my) true self please stand up?' (Triest, 2000)

The subject manifest in (Alin's) individual body and – to the same extent – in the group-body ('the group as a whole'; the social network) is the present chapter's field of inquiry.

*　　*　　*

In his book, *Subjects of Analysis*, Thomas Ogden reviews the dialectic formation of the notion of the analytic subject since Freud, through Klein and Winnicott and to its reestablishment in the contemporary intersubjective field. Ogden studies this process at a point in time which he defines, following T. S. Eliot, as "the present moment of the past in psychoanalysis" (Ogden, 1994, p. 61).

This chapter references the works of Ogden and other authors in an attempt to trace the conceptual evolution that led to the emergence of a portrait of a contemporary, 'hybrid', diffused subject, who comes to life in group space, just as the group – or, more precisely, groupness – lives through it as a 'unified' entity. I have called this subject the *'iGroup'* – among other reasons, as a way to indicate that in order to explore its essence, we must heal the traditional split between individual and group in psychoanalysis. This term imitates the graphics of the *iPhone* brand not only as a formal gimmick but also as a way of closely tying cellular technology to the framework of the new 'body' in which this subject manifests itself, the group-body, which is analogous to the central nervous system as the foundation of the 'psychic apparatus'.

While analytic literature traditionally discusses the emergence of the subject in a dyadic context (as a dialectic process occurring between infant and mother or analyst and analysand, i.e., 'subject' and 'object'), this chapter views the subject as *a function of the field of discourse or, more specifically, the matrix* (Foulkes; 1973). Whether in the singular, as a 'multiple' subject (with 'multiple selves', see Bromberg, 1996; or the product of an 'internal group' of introjects, see Ogden, 1992) – or in the plural, as 'the group as a whole' (a 'group-third' which turns the group into a subject-in-itself), the manifestation of this subject is, first and foremost, the result of reflection (from a 'third' position) which uses the mental maneuvers of *unifying* and *specifying*, in search of the particular in the universal and the universal in the particular[2] – by positing both on a kind of Möbius strip.

While it is later discussed as the product of the social network, the *iGroup* is not in fact limited to any particular group affiliation, rather, as mentioned, it is linked to a form of observation which transgresses boundaries and definitions and is perhaps characteristic of postmodern cultural discourse. It is a 'centaur' (half 'individual' and half embassy of its affiliated group), which may be 'everyman' or 'every-patient', so long as we agree to view them in such a 'multi-focal' manner. When it is lost in 'the garden of forking paths' of the internet and visits our clinic as a patient, it presents a symptomatic picture that is typical of its generation – including an experience of 'emptiness', 'psychic death', 'confusion of identity' and a sense of 'having lost one's way' – so different from the neurotics of the early 20th century, who come to the couch bearing the cross of their neurotic guilt over patricide and incestuous wishes.

In order to know it and acknowledge it, psychoanalysis must assimilate the way the materials comprising 'the place where we live' (Winnicott, 1971) permeate the inner worlds of our patients into its outlook – while also daring to drag its couch outside, to the market squares of postmodernism and cultural studies, in order to meet this subject in its natural habitat, cyberspace.

The Virtual Biography of the Analytic Subject – From Physical Incarnation to Online Manifestation

The analytic subject is a fundamentally dialectic being[3] and is thus

---

[2] In reference to Hegel's notions of 'Besondere' or 'Einzeln' ('singular' or 'particular', 'specified') and 'Algemein' ('general', 'universal').

[3] I am relying on Ogden's definition of this term: "dialectic is a process in which opposing elements each create, preserve and negate the other; each stands in a dynamic, ever-changing relationship to the other. Dialectical movement tends towards integrations that are never achieved. Each potential integration creates a new form of opposition characterized by its own distinct form of dialectical tension. That which is generated dialectically is continuously in motion, perpetually in the process of being created and

essentially elusive. It cannot be reduced to the unconscious (let alone to 'consciousness'), nor even to the 'ego' that is identified with the experiencing subject. It is small wonder that, over the years, it has changed its face and switched between different portraits, along with each model that psychoanalysis has offered throughout its development.

It is constituted by two basic conditions: first, the subject always appears displaced from its own center (decentered) and therefore capable of self-reflection (me-not-me; Ogden, 1994, p. 26); Second, its primary definition as one whose *identity is established through its unconscious sexuality,* forces it to rely on the object in order to know who it is – while simultaneously pressing it, by virtue of being a 'subject', to liberate itself from any definition imposed on it from without. This process sends the subject, which is struggling to establishing itself vis-à-vis and through the object, as a relatively distinct and autonomous being, on an endless journey (Triest, 2013; 2014)

The dialectic view hereby depicted is based on the interaction of recognition and negation – seemingly pushing the subject into constant becoming and change in the attempt to find (inherently partial) solutions for both conceptual contradictions and clinical lacunas in its notion. This developmental process can be likened to a pendulum, swinging back and forth between the pole of the object and the pole of the subject, without necessarily retracing its steps. Every move creates a new model which alters the location of the object in relation to the subject and draws a new portrait of the latter – thus allowing the subject to manifest itself in a different medium each time – *the body, object relations, the intersubjective dyad and, finally, the matrix*. Despite inherent contradictions and inevitable regressions, which preclude any simple scheme encompassing all of its various figures, the subject 'grows in volume' and gradually becomes more 'whole' as it is defined through more and more dimensions.

The *iGroup* can be seen from this perspective as a link in a chain that begins with the removal of the object from the field of vision of both the

---

negated, perpetually in the process of being decentered from static self-evidence" (Ogden, 1994, p. 14).

patient (on the clinical level; Freud, 1913, pp. 132-133) and psychoanalytic theory (on the meta-psychological level of Freud's Drive-model[4]). At the starting point (Bruere, J. & Freud, S., 1895), the object is posited as an anonymous, generalized and faceless entity, located at the position Ogden refers to as 'presence in absence and absence in presence" (Ogden, 1994, pp. 20-21). Devoid of any 'otherness' the body is the object the subject seeks as its libido gradually settles in its 'erogenous zones' (Freud, 1905).

This is where the story of 'the return of the object' begins; first as an internal representation, when Melanie Klein's object-relations model situates it '*inside*', as a matrix of self-representations and object representations, which dynamically constitutes the subject; while American Ego psychology situates it, as it were, '*against*' the subject, as a basis for achieving 'separation and individuation'. In its next iteration, the object appears in its actuality. Winnicott situates it '*in between*', in the intermediary space (the Potential Space), located 'not inside and not outside, both inside and outside'; in Kohut's thinking, the object is present as a new entity that effaces intermediary space by creating the *selfobject*, neither object nor subject and both object and subject. The next stage features the object as a '*subject-in-itself*' – and here is the final reversal this chapter will discuss; the object which constitutes *both subject and object* is no longer clearly demarcated, but is presented as an *intersubjective 'field'* – *as a 'reflective third' which inherently contains the representations of the object and those of the subject, while blurring the boundaries between them.* This (novel, problematic, intriguing) solution which, unlike previous ones, is based on the deconstruction of the notion of boundaries, gives rise to the *iGroup*.

The Transformations of the Notion of the Unconscious and the Demarcation of the Subject

This positioning of the 'field' as the platform (object) which establishes the contemporary subject did not occur in an empty space. It stems from the manner in which the study of the 'unconscious' deconstructed

---

[4] See for example: Freud, s. (1915) Instincts and Their Vicissitudes. *SE* XIV, 109-140.

the notion of the subject. The unconscious was initially depicted as content placed in the individual's body-box; then as a system (the topographic model) which engages in internal communication between the various structures comprising the psychic apparatus (Freud, 1915a); only later, with the introduction of 'projective identification' (Bion, 1961, pp.141 – 191; 1962; Klein, 1946; Ogden, 1994, pp. 42-48) is the unconscious redefined as an 'intersubjective communications array'. Once projective identification entered psychoanalytic theory, *the subject could no longer be confined to the boundaries of its own body*. At first, this phenomenon was discussed solely in the context of the dyad (mother-infant; analyst-analysand), but the solid evidence indicating that a group can coordinate and even contemplate its actions non-verbally and even unconsciously, gave rise to the notion of 'the group unconscious'. The main problem with this notion is that one cannot locate the 'apparatus' whose function can serve as the grounds for our conjectures, unless we consider 'connectedness' as a basic quality of the human mind (Aron, 1996). (After all, one can assume that the human mind can do anything that cellular phones and laptops can do – that is, find and home in on local wi-fi networks). In fact, Freud himself paved the way for such notions in 1915 when he noted that "It is a very remarkable thing that the Ucs. of one human being can react upon that of another, without passing through the Cs." (1915a, p. 194).

Indeed, the large-group of the crowd could have been also discovered in 1921 as the 'royal road' to the 'collective unconscious' – just as the dream showed us the way to the 'individual' unconscious. Freud quotes Le Bon (*The Crowd*, 1895): "The most striking peculiarity presented by a psychological group is the following. Whoever be the individuals that compose it, however like or unlike be their mode of life, their occupations, their character, or their intelligence, the fact that they have been transformed into a group puts them in possession of a sort of *collective mind* which makes them feel, think, and act in a manner quite different from that in which each individual of them would feel, think, and act were he in a state of isolation" (Freud, 1921, p. 72-73; emphasis added).

From this point onwards, the subject is manifest not only in the individual and the dyad but also in large and small groups as well (Bion,

1961; Freud, 1921); in inter-group relations (Rice, 1956; Miller, 1990) and finally in the matrix (Foulkes, 1964; 1973; Foulkes and Antony, 1965) – the unconscious communications network that stretches out into infinity.

The matrix, which is especially important to the matter at hand, was defined by its originator, Foulkes as "a web of communication and relationship in a given group. It is the common shared ground which ultimately determines the meaning and significance of all events and upon which all communications and interpretations, verbal and non-verbal, rest" (Foulkes, 1964, p. 292). The matrix's communication channels are encoded by biology, anatomy and physiology alongside language, culture and social structures.

Authors such as Farhad Dalal (2001), Earl Hopper (2003), Vamik Volkan (2001) and others, have each made their own contribution to the evolving definitions of the 'matrix', while emphasizing the fact that the collective unconscious – which they distinguish from both the 'social' and the 'cultural' unconscious – is not a mere 'container' for norms and customs, for a particular society's chosen traumas or glories (contents), but also actively structures the power-relations between different types of discourse and unconsciously dictates their negotiation.

Defining the 'unconscious' as a hypothetic network which, in fact, describes the quality of inter-mind *connectedness* and thus reaches out into infinity, as if completing the spiral motion of the subject's development, by returning to the individual 'unconscious' at a higher and more complex degree. Matte-Blanco (1988) brought the two together when, following Freud (1900, 1915a), he defined Freud's 'a-logical' laws of unconscious thinking in terms of the axioms of infinitesimal mathematics – just like the matrix. Thus, one scouting the endless spaces of the network finds himself gazing deep into the abyss of his own unconscious. Thereby, the notion of a 'network' effaced the distinction between 'personal' (internal) and 'collective' (external) unconscious, seemingly corroborating Norbert Elias' claim that "Individual and society cannot be separated, they just represent different levels of observation" (Elias, 1990, p. 82-83).

'E Pluribus Unum' – The Perspective of Unity and Multiplicity

According to Winnicott, "when one speaks of a man one speaks of him along with the summation of his cultural experiences. The whole forms a unit" (Winnicott, 1971, p. 99). In light of the above, how are we to fathom the riddle of the subject's many faces, as these are manifest in the portrait of the *iGroup*? What is it that makes it 'multiple' and 'diffuse', while the group in which it is manifest is 'crystallized' into unity?

The perspective which enables both these notions apparently lies in 'the eye of the beholder'. As it traces multiplicity in the presentation of the individual, it creates the diffuse subject; as it traces the common denominator shared by the various phenomena (and meanings) sampled at any given moment in a group's life – it discovers the group as a whole. One should recall that, as far as the subject is concerned, self-reflection is a key factor in its establishment – either conceptually or psychologically-experientially.

First-Person Plural

The notion that the (individual) subject is constituted by a *multiplicity* of factors or an 'internal group' of objects (introjects) can be recognized as a 'trend' in recent psychoanalysis' meta-psychological reflection. Among other sources, it stems from the feeling that Freud's *fixation theory* and *characterology* (which also serve as the foundation of psychoanalytic psycho-diagnostics) fail to contain the vast range of inherent difference evident in the richness of human existence. Daniel Stern (1984, pp. 256-277) proposed a reexamination of this subject by offering the notion of distinct and relatively independent 'self-domains'. Ogden's (1992) commentary on Melanie Klein depicts the subject as the outcome of complex internalized ego-object relations **matrix** (networks), which form internal group affiliations in relation to self and object representations (while different representations of the same object may inhabit different relationships). To this, one may add Bromberg (1996), who studies the subject's 'multiple selves' and finds the focus on 'self-states' to be clinically useful.

137

This preference for multiplicity, for 'having both ways' seems to be the ethical and aesthetic choice of postmodernism – and these psychoanalytic views reflect this influence, even if at the price of creating new clinical as also theoretical problems.

The Group as a Whole

The claim that it is the beholder who in fact *creates* the group-as-a-whole has been taken up by Bion. He explained that viewing a collection of individuals as a single unit is actually the result of a common illusion shared by those group members, who lose awareness of their "individual distinctiveness", due to their considerable regression (Bion, 1961, p. 142). However, the fact that *all* members share the same notion of the group paradoxically turns it into a psychological entity which is 'greater than the sum of its parts' (Bion, 1961, p. 132-133).

Projective identification plays a crucial role in this process. According to Ogden: "Projective identification is understood as a psychological-interpersonal process in which there is a partial collapse of the dialectic of subjectivity and intersubjectivity. The form of intersubjective third that is generated in projective identification is one in which the individual subjectivities [...] to a degree and for a time are subsumed in (subjugated by) the newly created analytic third (Ogden, 1994, p. 9). Although Ogden is here referring to the dyad, his words are just as apt for the group. Similarly, the analytic third could also be converted into a 'group-third', that which engenders the group as a 'whole': "The analytic [group] third is not only a form of experience [...] it is at the same time a form of experiencing I-ness in which (through which) analyst and analysand [or, the group-members] become other than who they had been to that point" (ibid, p. 5).

The Group and the Individual

The relationship between individual and group and the nature of their interaction is crucial to the present discussion and three key narratives have attempted to explain them: regression to the figure of the primordial father

(Freud and his followers); regression to the figure of the primordial mother (Bion and his followers); and construing cultural experience as a 'play' that exists in the potential space between subject and object. All three share the difficulty in representing factors which 'specify' alongside those that 'unify' (despite their essential dialectic polarity), without marginalizing one or the other.

Freud's (1921) narrative 'crushes' the individual; Bion's (1961) narrative tries to offer it some representation through the notion of 'valency' (Bion, 1961, pp. 116-117) vis-à-vis the tremendous power of the mother-group; in my view, the *iGroup* was born through the attempt to save the representations of both individual and group – and, naturally, it risks losing them both.

Freud (1921) depicts the process by which individuals are congregated into a crowd as an archaic Oedipal drama that revolves around the regression to a tyrannical and idolized father figure. His great power causes the tribe members to surrender/submit themselves to him in exchange for his magical protection. Even the aggression inherent in all relationships is marginalized, pushed to the boundaries, and directed against other crowds. Eventually, the crowd grows tired of being thus castrated and its aggression is turned inwards, leading to the father's murder. This murder disrupts not only the fabric of the tribe's cohesion but also the internal organization of the subjects comprising this crowd – giving rise to panic. There follows a process by which the tribe becomes reorganized as families, which are but a pale version of the original structure, while granting members more freedom and autonomy.

Le Bon describes the transformation of the individual forming part of a crowd as some kind of hypnotic process causing "the disappearance of the conscious personality, the predominance of the unconscious personality, the turning by means of suggestion and contagion of feelings and ideas in an identical direction, the tendency to immediately transform the suggested ideas into acts […] He is no longer himself, but has become an automaton who has ceased to be guided by his will" (in Freud, 1921, p. 76).

The dissolution of the boundaries between subject (representations) and object (representations) (horizontal regression) together with identification and internalization processes which focus on the leader as a collective Ego-Ideal substitute, account for this exceptional blurring of identity and loss of individuality. The dissolution of boundaries between the psychical structures (vertical regression), allows the flooding of material from the unconscious to the 'surface'. This is further explained by the Super-Ego's diminished supervision due to the *anonymity* provided by the crowd. In fact, anonymity is reason enough to account for the instinctual outburst, which obeys the pleasure principle. The result is the assimilation of the individual into the crowd.[5] (Freud, 1921, p. 78).

Bion describes the group as an archaic mother (Bion, 1961, p.162) and its members as exhibiting a profound regression to pre-oedipal domains. This allows him to account for the characteristic lack of distinction, the tendency for projective identification, the use of the group-body as a 'toilet breast', i.e., a container for split-off parts that individuals refuse to own and must void and eject into the 'mother-group' as if it was some external and separate object (Group Mentality; Bion, 1961, pp. 50-61). It also explains the group's withdrawal from reality (represented by the 'work group') in favor of a world of Phantasies (the 'basic assumptions' group: 'fight and flight', 'dependency', 'pairing', and later also 'oneness' (Torquet, 1974) and 'me-ness' (Lawrence, Bain & Gould, 1996).

Individuality is represented through the notion of 'Valency' (Bion, 1961, p.175), the individual's a-priori tendency to take part in these various fantasy-based scenarios. In retrospect, this tendency may also represent unconscious attachment strategies in relation to the mother (the 'good' and 'bad' breast). Some overarching structure is required in order to bridge between the needs

---

[5] "A group is impulsive, changeable and irritable. It is led almost exclusively by the unconscious. The impulses which a group obeys may according to circumstances be generous or cruel, heroic or cowardly, but they are always so imperious that no personal interest, not even that of self-preservation, can make itself felt [...] It cannot tolerate any delay between its desire and the fulfilment of what it desires. It has a sense of omnipotence; the notion of impossibility disappears for the individual in a group [... the group] is in no doubt as to what constitutes truth or error [...] it respects force and can only be slightly influenced by kindness, which it regards merely as a form of weakness [...] It wants to be ruled and oppressed" (Freud, 1921, p. 77-78).

of the individual and those of (unconscious) group mentality – this structure is 'culture'. (Bion, 1961, pp. 55-73)

The large-group is perceived as a Faceless Mother – an extremely Uncanny image (Torquet, 1975). It is not castration anxiety but the dread of annihilation and the faceless mother's magical ability to swallow up the identities of group members which triggers regression – whether this regression leads to manic or schizo-paranoid defenses – namely to a mass-orgy, a rock concert or an act of genocide.

The third view is offered by Winnicott, who ascribes the 'environment' (and metaphorically, the group) with the role of the mother who gives her infant its identity. This is manifest in his description of 'the place where we live' as a 'potential space' that has beneficent and growth-promoting qualities that enable the 'play' of culture (in contrast with Freud's and Bion's portrayals). Winnicott pictures "something that is in the common pool of humanity, into which individuals and groups of people may contribute, and from which we may all draw *if we have somewhere to put what we find*" (Winnicott, 1971, p. 99). Winnicott insists on finding out the nature of the place: "where are we (if anywhere at all)? We have used the concepts of inner and outer, and we want a third concept. [...] Can we gain some advantage from an examination of this matter of the possible existence of a place for living that is not properly described by either of the terms 'inner' and 'outer'?" (ibid, p. 105-106).

Cultural experience is located in "the potential space between the individual and the environment", which originates in the object. It is located "between baby and mother, between child and family, between individual and society or the world, depends on experience which leads to trust" (p. 103), it is a space that stretches "between the subjective object and the object objectively perceived, between me-extensions and the not-me" (ibid, p. 100).

I doubt that Winnicott could have foreseen a more fruitful platform for 'me-extensions' and simulations of 'potential space', a more fecund place for the 'play' of the subject's emergence than cyberspace, the birthplace of the *iGroup*.

The *iGroup*

Le Bon's ever pertinent portrayals and the subject's dread of annihilation when facing the faceless mother of the large-group (and modern life) represent group cultures created through powerful – positive or negative – collective transference to a leader *who is perceived as archaic, as an authority and as an omniscient subject;* in fact, it is a subject which represents the entire crowd, it is its face.

It is no wonder that the individual's experience in the group is described as oscillating between an ecstatic-libidinal-oceanic (Freud, 1921) feeling of belonging, power and potency that are 'bigger than life' (*vox populi vox dei*) – and a persecutory-paranoid-stampede stemming from the large-group's tendency to mark an 'enemy', whether real or imaginary, external or internal, and set out to vanquish it, almost always under the auspices of supposedly 'high' religious/national ideologizing.

The present generation has put forth a seemingly new group-culture. Two Major changes, which may be attributed to the psychological impact of recent technological breakthroughs, can be mentioned: the first – authority is no longer viewed as the subject-supposed-to-know (the death of the Father). The second – the formidable faceless mother was given a face – through *Facebook*.

This new configuration seems to have deprived the large group of its key characteristic, *anonymity*, replacing it with virtual identity and relatedness markers. The subject was 'given a face' without being required to meet the other 'face-to-face'.

The implications are vast. The 'social network' (Facebook and its like) has replaced the figure of the leader as the object that constitutes the current iteration of the subject. The social network organizes itself as an enormous-group of *selfies*, creating a reality/illusion by which it is a multitude where 'everyone has a name' (i.e., an identity) and that this multitude (whose *vox* is a *vox dei*) is at the disposal of the individuals comprising it as a kind of Greek choir (Me-ness). Between regression to the father figure and regression to the mother figure, a third option seems to have opened up – regression to peers, whose reciprocity refutes the inherent asymmetry of authority-relations. Thereby, the group is not perceived as necessarily persecutory, but as a kind of selfobject – a gigantic collective mirror, expected to affirm the selfhood of the individuals comprising it ('like').

Three factors form this new (Winnicottian) playful array in which *iGroup* culture is grounded:

1. A Diffused Notion of Boundaries (mostly space and time):

This phenomenon is at the root of the deceptive mixture of inside and outside, 'high' and 'low', copy and original, truth and fiction and even subject and object. Its main characteristics include:

- **Experiencing the Simultaneity of Existence**: The *iGroup* lives in a split screen. As it is not confined by the boundaries of its body, it experiences the addictive freedom to be 'everywhere' at once. However, in the land of endless possibilities, it is destined to suffer a new kind of angst: FOMO (fear of missing out). As a result, the *iGroup* takes on certain traits that can be seen as either 'abilities' or 'dysfunctions' according to context. For example: split attention (as dictated by the omnipresent split screen); emotional shallowness (as a defense against intense stimulation and exposure to events which trigger an impossible range of contradictory emotions); superficiality – adapted to being spread thin across so many parallel options; impatience with long in-depth processes, dictated by the demand and ostensible capacity for instant gratification.
- **A Blurred Distinction between Reality and Imagination**[6], even accompanied by a diminished ability to distinguish the animate from the inanimate. In this context, it is also interesting to note that the natural sciences have begun discussing possibilities that had hitherto seemed science fiction (e.g., Schrodinger's cat, parallel universes, eternal life, creating human beings in laboratories, etc.).

---

[6] This phenomenon is taking place even on a sensory level, as the next generation of virtual reality technology will further enhance the *iGroup's* transcendent experience.

- **The Externalization and Evacuation of Psychic Systems that ostensibly belong to the Inner World**: just as computer files are now stored 'in the cloud', social functions have been replacing intra-psychic regulatory functions and the social network is utilized as a kind of auxiliary-self for the *iGroup*. For example: shame (concerning the fulfillment of narcissistic needs) is being replaced by online shaming. The id is outsourced to porn sites and to the reckless 'city squares' of internet commenters and trolls. The super-ego is deemed detached from a-priori moral standards and seems to have been ousted by 'ratings'.

2. The Collapse of Representations of 'Parental' Authority (as the Subject-Supposed-to-Know)

The reversal of power relations between children and parents (who are inarticulate immigrants in the world of technology) and a lack of recognition of any external authority as the subject-supposed-to-know, liberates the subject from infantile dependence while positing 'his highness the self'[7] and the peer group as the 'overriding authority'. To a certain extent, we are witnessing a new Cartesian revolution, which crowns the 'experiencing self' rather than the 'thinking self' as the bedrock of subjective existence. This process might have been a sign of development if it had not also entailed a denial of the needs of the other. Trump's "America First" (an inverted reaction to 'ask not what your country can do for you, but what you can do for your country') is nothing but a variation on the familiar 'me first'. This legitimized narcissistic self is no longer adapted for delayed gratification; it no longer recognizes the validity of fact and it no longer complies with an external reality that lies outside its control; '*I want, therefore I am*'.

What's more, in the absence of any sanctioned authority, one has no need or ability to decide between different possibilities. Since 'everything goes', one must find a way to live with inherent contradictions. In its pathologically regressed version, this does not mean acknowledging the dialectic nature of thinking but simply ignoring contradictions and

---

[7] Paraphrasing Freud's famous dictum about 'his highness the baby'

avoiding any binding decisions.

3. Gratifying Dependence Needs: given an infinite field of possibilities and the severe existential angst that goes with it, new 'real' ways for gratifying infantile dependence needs have developed, mostly through cellular technology. The western subject is now equipped with a kind of transitional-object, the cell-phone (slyly designed to always be carried in its owner's hand). The 'connectedness' of this devise allows it to be monitored at all times by unseen entities.[8] It seems that, for the *iGroup*, this fact significantly decreases separation anxiety and existential loneliness – rather than gives rise to Orwellian paranoia.

In Conclusion: Some Practical Thoughts about Current Events

This portrait of the *iGroup* confronts psychoanalysis with a serious dilemma. On the one hand, this new structure may attest to the subject's developmental maturation, with its new capabilities and possibilities for self-fulfillment; on the other hand, many of its characteristics are reminiscent of severe personality disorders, according to conventional diagnostic standards. Does exhibitionism and voyeurism – now a commonplace social practice and norm – mark it as 'perverse', or must we reexamine the nature of this pathology? Does its characteristic 'split-attention' constitute an attention deficit disorder, or is it a kind of skill, indicative of its adaptability? Does the subject's relation to its body (which does not contain it anymore), as depicted above, situate it on the 'autistic spectrum'? Does its loose grasp of reality and the collapse of the distance between signifier and signified (symbolic equation) render it 'psychotic'? Does its self-centeredness indicate a narcissistic personality disorder – or, in short, should we consider the *iGroup* a pathogenic mutation?

It seems that psychoanalysis, as a liminal discipline, ought to avoid such rash 'psycho-pathologizing'. These cultural changes are a given and

---

[8] The GPS watches over it with the same patience as Woody Allen's mother, floating above him in the sky in *New York Stories* (1989).

they may also attest to a certain evolution in our notions of ourselves in relation to our (social, object-laden) environment. Nevertheless, psychoanalysis must not recoil from pointing out the perils facing the psyche in this new 'place where we live'. The 'body' as a safe container for the self, the 'psychic skin' that maintains its boundaries; upholding truth and the relation between words and reality; the need for significant relationships and authentic emotional interactions – all these are still the 'main ingredients' of mental wellbeing and replacing them with junk-food, which offers addictively empty calories, is dangerous.

From a clinical perspective, a multi-dimensional view of the subject as both an individual and a group-entity may deepen our understanding of the human psyche. The opening vignette illustrates the importance of elucidating the relationship between individual and collective 'unconscious'.

Later in the session, Alin realizes how switching seats enacted an entire family history. One of her haunting family myths, which hung over her mother's head her entire life, told of how an insignificant and random act of 'trading places' with her sister had saved Alin's mother from the gas chamber. By realizing that this was a 'lifesaving' act, one can similarly construe the group's 'pairing configuration' as an attempt to defend itself against 'scapegoating', which was manifest in the previous session and which some members apparently perceived as threatening to 'kill off' one of the members.

It is naturally hard to estimate the effects of cultural change as it is taking place. My working assumption is that this light, hedonistic culture of the 'selfie' group, creates a dark, unconscious undertone (or 'mentality'), where the price of this 'intolerable lightness of being' in cyberspace keeps accumulating. Lo and behold: in a world which makes light of boundaries – we see the erection of barriers (and walls of iron and stone) that are taller than ever before (one of them crosses Israel from one end to the other, another is about to be built between the US and Mexico); ISIS – at least from a Western perspective – seems to have emerged from the 'caves' of the most archaic, prehistoric unconscious, with their utterly anachronistic practices of 'beheading' people on 'live'

CNN coverage. In a world that celebrates globalization and glorifies the personal freedom to shed off the burden of any collective identity (nationality, religion, gender), terrorism is rampant and gains new footholds every day.

Does psychoanalysis have anything to say about this? One possible answer lies in understanding the world of the *iGroup* – especially the impact of blurring boundaries between subject and object on the 'relatedness-identity' dialectic – causing what I have termed the 'Romeo and Juliet' syndrome.[9] Identity needs the substrate of relationships in order to crystallize, but 'relationships', by their very nature, limit one's ability to select and express a given identity. While globalization extols relationships, connections and 'sharing' by turning the world into 'one small village', all of whose inhabitants gladly cast off the attributes of collective identity – nationality, religion, culture – in favor of crowding under the McDonalds logo and following the Coca-Cola code of 'the good life' – religions gain new momentum and terrorism is on the rise. The latter bring in our commitment to identity at the expense of relationships through the back door. Terrorism, for example, compels the (western) subject to resume its identification with all those identity markers that it would have loved to leave behind – whether it wants it or not. Ignoring the personal, terrorism targets civilians simply for being 'carriers' of collective identity markers (attacks aimed at buses full of 'western tourists', synagogues, rock-concert venues, etc.) – the very markers that globalization wishes to efface to create unity (or the semblance thereof, see under Brexit).

I therefore find that the presence of psychoanalytic thinking outside the consultation room may be more important than ever before. I hope that adding the portrait of the *iGroup* to the 'face-book' of 'subject-portraits' offered by psychoanalysis may help maintain its relevance and influence even at a time when postmodernism is 'doubting the great

---

[9] Taken as a metaphor, Romeo and Juliet cannot fulfil their love (relationship) because of their family identity, which creates an insoluble conflict between the two rival houses. Paradoxically, their death is the one solution that can maintain both their relatedness and their identity- but not their lives.

theories' and lamenting (with crocodile tears?) the death of the subject (Gurevitz, 1997, p.18) – as least the one who have landed on our couch so far.

References

Aron, L. (1996). *A Meeting of Minds – Mutuality in Psychoanalysis.* London: The Analytic Press.

Bennis, W. G. & Shephard, H. A. (1956). A Theory of Group Development. *Human Relations*, 9, 415-437.

Bion, W. R. (1961). *Experiences in Groups And Other Papers.* London: Tavistock Publications Limited.

Bion, W.R. (1962). *Learning from Experience.* New York: Basic Books.

Bromberg, P.M. (1996). Standing in the Spaces: The Multiplicity of Self and the Psychoanalytic Relationship. *Contemp. Psychoanal.*, 32:509-535.

Breuer, J. & Freud, S. (1895). *Studies on Hysteria.* S.E. II, 1-323.

Dalal, F. (2001). The Social Unconscious: A Post-Foulksian Perspective. *Group Analysis* 34: 539-555.

Elias, N. (1990). Reflection on a Life. Cambridge: Polity Press, 1994.

Foulkes, S.H. (1964). *Therapeutic Group Analysis.* London: George Allen & Unwin.

Foulkes, S.H. and Anthony, E. J. (1965): Group Psychotherapy. Second edition. London: Karnac Books.

Foulks, S.H. (1973).The Group as Matrix of the Individual's Mental Life. In: *S.H. Foulkes, Selected Papers, Psychoanalysis and Group-analysis.* Ed. E.T.Foulks. London: Karnac Books, 1990.

Freud, S. (1900). The Interpretation of Dreams. *S.E.* IV, 1-338.

Freud, s., (1905). Three Essays on the Theory of Sexuality. *S.E.* VII, 125-245.

Freud, S. (1913). On Beginning the Treatment (Further Recommendations on the Technique of Psycho-Analysis I). *SE,* Vol. XII (1911-1913) p. 121-144.

Freud, S. (1915). Instincts and Their Vicissitudes. *S.E.* XIV, 109-140.

Freud, S. (1915a). The Unconscious. *SE*, Vol. XIV, p. 159-215.

Freud, S. (1921). Group Psychology and the Analysis of the Ego. *SE*, Vol. XVIII, p. 65-144.

Freud, S. (1930). Civilization and its Discontents. *SE*, Vol. XXI, p. 57-146.

Gurevitz, D. (1997). *Postmodernism – Culture and Literature at the End of the 20th Century.* Tel Aviv: Dvir Publishing House.

Hopper, E. (2003). *The Social Unconscious.* London: Jessica Kingsley.

Klein, M. (1946) Notes on Some Schizoid Mechanisms. In: *Envy and Gratitude and Other Works, 1946-1963, pp.* 1-24. New York: Delacorte, 1975.

Lawrence, W.G., Bain, A. & Gould, L. (1996). The Fifth Basic Assumption. Free Associations 6/1 37: 28-55.

Mackenzie, K. R. and Livesley, W. J. (1983). A Developmental Model for Brief Group Therapy. In R. R. Dies and K. R. Mackenzie (eds.) *Advances in Group Psychotherapy.* New York: International universities Press, p. 101-116.

Matte-Blanco, I. (1988). *Thinking, Feeling, and Being.* David Tuckett (Ed.), London & New York: Routledge.

Miller. E.J. (1990) Experiential Learning in Groups I: the Development of the Leicester Model. In: E.L. Trist & Murray (Eds.). *The Social Engagement of Social Science. A Tavistock Anthology.* Vol. I: The Socio Psychological Perspective (pp. 165-185). London: Free Associations.

Ogden, T. H. (1992). *The Matrix of the Mind.* New York. Karnac Books.

Ogden, T. H. (1994). *Subjects of Analysis.* New York: Jason Aaronson.

Rice, A.K. (1965). *Learning for Leadership.* London: Tavistock Publications.

Saravay, M. S. (1978). *A psychoanalytic Theory of Group Development. International Journal of Group Psychotherapy.* Vol.28 (4): 481-507.

Stern, N, D. (1984). *The Interpersonal World of the Infant – A view From Psychoanalysis and Developmental Psychology.* United States: Basic Books, Inc.

Torquet, P.M. (1974). Leadership: The Individual and the Group. In: Gibbard G.S. et al, Eds. *The Large Group: Therapy and Dynamics.* San Franciscoand London: Jossey Bass.

Torquet, P.M. (1975). Threats to Identity in the Large Group. In: *The Large Group: Dynamics and Therapy.* (ed. L. Kreeger). London: Constable.

Triest, J. (2000). Will the Real Self Please Stand-up – Self Revelation in Psychodynamic Psychotherapy. *Sihot* – Vol. 14 (2): 84-92.

Triest, J. (2013). Sexuality and its Unique Role in Constituting the Psychoanalytic Subject in Terms of Body-Ego and Object Ego. *Maarag – The Israel Annual of Psychoanalysis.* Vol 4: 137-175.

Triest, J. (2014). The Witch and the Child – Reflections about the Changing Notions and Theoretical Development of Subject and Object in Psychoanalysis. *Sihot* – Vol. 29 (1): 27-42.

Volkan. V. (2001). Transgenerational Transmissions and Chosen Traumas: An Aspect of Large group Identity. *Group Analysis* 34 (1): 79-97.

Winnicott, D. W. (1971). *Playing and Reality.* London: Tavistock Publications.

CHAPTER NINE

Literature's Keys "Before the Law" of Trauma[1]

Merav Roth[2]

In her article "Modes of Memory, Modes of Recovery – When Language Meets the Traumatic Lacuna,"[3] the psychoanalyst Dana Amir proposes four modes of witnessing trauma: The Excessive mode, the Metonymical mode, the Muselmannic mode, and the Metaphorical mode. In this article I will show how different modes of witnessing take place within the mind, and how transformations occur in the mode of witnessing as a result of psychological development. I will demonstrate this using Otto Dov Kulka's book (his testimony) **"Landscapes of the Metropolis of Death".**[4] In addition, I will point to the centrality of the movement between the axis of 'emergent being' and that of 'continuous doing' in the mind – as a crucial factor in the consolidation of the different forms of witnessing. Finally, I will seek to show how reading literature promotes the transformational movement between internal modes of witnessing, and the formation of the metaphoric internal witness function in the mind.

---

[1] The English title is "Before the Law". In Hebrew it is "Before the Gate of the Law," which is also the name used in the English translation of Kulka's text.

[2] To my teacher and mentor Shmuel Erlich, with love and gratitude. This article is based on a chapter from my book: Roth, M. (2017). Reading the Reader – a psychoanalytic perspective on reading literature. Edited by Avi Sagi and Aner Govrin, Jerusalem: Carmel."

[3] The article "Modes of Memory, Modes of Recovery – When Language Meets the Traumatic Lacuna" by Dr. Dana Amir is currently in press.

[4] Kulka, O. D. (2013). *Landscapes of the Metropolis of Death.* First Harvard University Press edition. Cambridge, Massachusetts: The Belknap Press of Harvard University Press.

I hope that these thoughts would free up space for clinical reflections on the stories of our patients, which are always told from one register of testimony or another, and from a particular equilibrium and balance between the axis of 'continuous doing' and that of 'emergent being' in their internalised object relations, in their transference relations, and in their daily life.

I shall start with a dream taken from Kulka's book:

That night dream always brings me back to the same immutable law by which I end up back inside the crematorium and, by some roundabout way, through canals of dark water, through trenches and hidden openings, I dig beneath the barbed wire and reach freedom and board a train, and at one desolate station at night a loudspeaker calls my name, and I am returned to the place I am bound to reach: the crematorium. And however much I know that I must be caught, I always know, too, that I must be spared. It's a kind of circle, a cycle of Tantalus or Sisyphus, or of whatever myth we choose to invoke that is germane here, which returns in an endless vicious circle to the same place.[5]

Kulka was born in Czechoslovakia in 1933, and had been in Auschwitz at the age of ten and eleven. Eventually he became a Professor Emeritus of History at the Hebrew University of Jerusalem, and studies modern anti-Semitism from the early modern period, and up to the "Final Solution". In the last decade of the 20th century he recorded and then arranged into a book what he says is not a historical but a personal witness account, or in his own words, a viewing of **"those fragments of memory and imagination that have remained from the world of the wondering child of ten to eleven that I had once been."**[6]

When Kulka the child arrived in Theresienstadt, he was put, together with his mother, in the "families camp" which is the "exemplary camp" used in attempts to refute charges of Nazi war crimes. They were unaware that within six months all will be exterminated, upon arrival of the next

[5] Kulka, O. D., (2013), pp. 34-35.
[6] Kulka, O. D., (2013), pp. 14-15.

human transport. All, except those who were by chance sick, as was the young Kulka who that day lay in hospital and so did not walk down the stairs leading to the crematoria, along with everyone else. Surprisingly and at the same time understandably, throughout his life Kulka has repeatedly dreamt of entering that place into which he had never entered in reality.

I shall return to the dream.

Following the modal classification proposed by Amir, this dreamt and narrated witnessing by Kulka belongs to the Metonymical witnessing mode. In her definition, the Metonymical mode collapses into repetition, never leaving any space within it for the reflective subject. It produces an experiential continuity in between itself and the traumatic events, whilst remaining effectively trapped within this sustenance, without the freedom of movement to stand in an observer's position towards itself, or in a position that would enable the reconstruction of events in retrospect.

Following on from Amir's analysis, it is possible to think that Kulka's dream on the one hand expresses the guilt of the survivor, but beyond that also the intolerability of his arbitrary, coincidental survival, and an attempt to claim belonging and ownership of it, and of his own life's particular fate.

In his words it is as follows:

[W]here I seemingly lived and remained always, from that day to this, and I am held captive there as a life prisoner, bound and fettered with chains that cannot be undone. Were it not so grating, I would say, 'like Prometheus bound'. But I am after all a child, who was bound with those chains as a child and remained bound by them throughout every stage of growing up. I say that I was bound and remained bound, or fettered by chains, but that is because I was never there, because my foot never stepped into those courtyards, inside those buildings. I circled them as a moth circles a flame, knowing that falling into it was inevitable, yet I kept on circling outside, willingly or unwillingly – it was not up to me – all my friends, the butterflies, not all of them, but almost all of them, were there and did not come out of there.[7]

With exceptional skill, Kulka describes here how the Metonymical witnessing mode is experienced from inside; How he is caught in the centrifuge of his private post-traumatic Claustrum,[8] which repeatedly sounds its voice in the dream, imposing a recurrent act of dreamt witnessing of an "observed without an observer."[9]

The Metonymical form of witnessing is not the only witnessing mode in Kulka's book. For many years Kulka has lived in a split between two central modes of witnessing: Alongside the Metonymical witnessing expressed in his recurrent dream, Kulka the historian adopted an Excessive mode of witnessing: Amir describes the Excessive mode as illusive, in that it is typically formalized with eloquent language and employs a highly developed rhetoric, while in effect it is a disguise of a complete witness account, and does not enable transformation to take place. The historian's work is not necessarily identified with the Excessive mode, which in its extreme is regarded as a psychotic witnessing mode. But the manner in which Kulka reveals his witnessing, positions it on the excessive continuum, as it is indicative of his use of historiographical witnessing for the purpose of distancing and blocking linkage and movement: **"[R]eaders of my historical publications will have identified me unequivocally with an attitude of strict and impersonally remote research, always conducted within well-defined historical categories, as a kind of self-contained method unto itself."**[10]

The split between these two witnessing forms (the Metonymical and the Excessive) is derived from another split in Kulka's mind, which is crucially related to these. The split between the two axes of psychological dialectics: the 'emergent being' on the one hand, and the 'continuous doing' on the other.

---

[7] Kulka, O. D., (2013), pp. 30-31.

[8] Meltzer, D. (1992). *The Claustrum*. Perthshire: Clunie Press.

[9] As opposed to Amir's designation of the "observer within the observed" as the precondition and expression of the individual's witnessing function (Amir, D. (2012). Thom Safa (Language Abyss), Magnes Press, Jerusalem, p.105. Free trans. By C. Wagner & T. Tlalim)

[10] Kulka, O. D., (2013), p. 14.

The dialectic of 'Continuous doing' versus 'emergent being' in the mind.

Kulka's witness account sheds light on the centrality of the dialectical-psychic axis of 'emergent being' contrasted with that of 'continuous doing' for the formation of particular forms of witnessing in each individual.[11] This axis is not an addition to these modes, but is interwoven with them, so that the structure and proportion between the 'emergent being' and 'continuous doing,' is one of the crucial factors determining the mode of witnessing.

The axes of doing and of being are described by Winnicott, and in continuation to him, albeit differently, the psychoanalyst Shmuel Erlich who asserts that the nature of all experience is dualistic – and is formed in the midst, between the mode of doing and that of being. Existence's mode of doing enables us to construct our lives – to respond to bodily needs, to encounter the actual world, to survive, to learn, and to form both practical and mental links and relations. Alongside it, **"Being' mode is inherently involved in and silently underpins our sense of aliveness as well as connectedness with everything — relationships, nature, life, ideals and values — without which our psychological life is seriously impoverished and hampered"**[12]

The axis of being is related to primary unintegration and, from there on, the strings lead toward the individual's ability to create and enjoy creativity. The psychoanalyst Eigen writes that **"acting out of unintegration [entails] forming oneself anew out of the drift, coming together freshly, seeing things with new intensity, throwing oneself into the fullness of experiencing, … [it] means letting built-up versions of self go so that one can drift."**[13] Yet at the same time this psychic mode comes bound with the dread of disintegration, and therefore evokes both attraction and anxiety at once. The pronouncing power

---

[11] I would like to thank Shmuel Erlich for directing my attention, quite some years ago, to the relevance of the axis terms of doing and of being in the mind, for literature reading.

[12] Erlich, H.S. (2003). Experience—What is it?. *Int. J. Psycho-Anal., 84*:p 1144.

[13] Eigen, Michael. *Psychic Deadness*. London: Karnac Books, 2004. p. 77.

of the word enables written works to expose the reader to that unique space, which has the power to liberate from the habitual and open the reader towards what Heidegger defines as the "the opening-up of the open and the clearing of being"[14] which may be similar to what Bion terms the "O".[15]

On the other hand, the axis of doing – to which I will refer henceforth as "continuous doing" – anchors the individual in his world, yet without the axis of being, this anchor risks becoming chained to the secondary law and order, and left without any spirit, creation or dreaming.

Dana Amir writes about the lyrical dimension of the mind as the capacity to integrate between these two axes: **"The lyrical dimension is that very dimension which transforms the psyche from a plane whose two axes form the continuous axis of experience – toward a space which contains these two axes in integration. The experience of the inside, which is formed by means of this integration, is in fact the experience of self: our experience of ourselves as having a boundary, depth and meaning."**[16]

I shall now return to the problem of the witnessing of trauma. The researcher and psychoanalyst Dori Laub asks:

> **"How to bear witness to historic truth *from inside the radical deception* (amplified by self-deception) by which one was separated from historic truth at the very moment one was most involved in it? [...] As the locus of a silence and as the vanishing point of the voice, the inside is *untransmitable* [...] Who would be in a position, then, to tell? [...] If it is indeed impossible to bear witness to the holocaust from inside, it is even more impossible to testify to it from the outside."**[17]

---

[14] Heidegger, M. (1968). *The Question Concerning Technique*, Trans Roger Berkowitz and Philippe Nonet. 2006. (unpublished) p. 54. Available on www.academia.edu/2083177/The_Origin_of_the_Work_of_Art_by_Martin_Heidegger

[15] Bion, W.R. (1965). *Transformations*. London: Heinemann.

[16] Amir, D. On the Lyricism of the Mind. Magness.

[17] Felman, Shoshana, and Dori Laub. Testimony: Crises of Witnessing in Literature, Psychoanalysis and History. New York: Routledge, 1992.

And Jorge Semprún, the writer survivor of the Buchenwald concentration camp, determines: **"I imagine there'll be flood of accounts... everything in these books will be true. . . except that they won't contain the essential truth, which no historical reconstruction will ever be able to grasp, no matter how thorough and all-inclusive it may be..."[18]**

Like others, Semprún finds answers within the transitional space of literary fiction:

"Literary narratives... that will go beyond simple eyewitness accounts, that will let you imagine, even if they can't let you see... What's problematic is not the description of this horror. Not just that, anyway – not even mostly that. What's at stake here is the exploration of the human soul in the horror of evil. . . . We'll need a Dostoyevsky!"[19]

Literature is called to the witness stand. The metaphorical mode to which literature is accustomed is not only characterized by secondary, symbolic thinking, but rather in its ability to bear witness to the wider domain of dialectic motion of the mind in between the modes described above and additional axes of psychological existence – the paranoid-schizoid and the depressive, the familiar and the uncanny, the present and the absent, the symbolic order and madness, and others; the metaphorical mode takes place within a wider array of contours that surround both the deficient and the developed areas of the mind, the bruised and the healed, the traumatic and the healthy, and integrates them. The metaphorical mode indicates a mental contact with, and an expressive capacity of, and in between the various areas of experience. That is why many consider the power of the fictional literary witnessing a most reliable witness, paradoxically, of traumatic experience. Bearing witness to muted experiences is precisely the strength of fiction, experiences that in the traumatic psychic reality are characterized by a hole, a tear or a

---

[18] Semprún J. (1994). **Literature or Life.** New-York: Penguin books, 1997, pp. 124-125.
[19] Semprún J. (1994), p. 127.

distortion. Fiction is able to exceed the traumatic time and space, which are accompanied by collapse and characterized by either a perforated or an overly dense witnessing, which either way does not represent the completeness of human experience.

The mind's relation to time, space and death are some of the characteristics that differentiate between continuous doing and emergent being. The researcher Yoel Pearl makes a distinction between Freud and Martin Heidegger, as representatives of this difference, where Freud consistently refers primarily to linear time,[20] which develops phase by phase, and to which one's relation as such, shapes his development over time.[21] Vis-à-vis him, the mode of existence of the emergent being is related to nonlinear time, which faces the horizon of the present and not the concrete present. "In the blink of an eye" is a term that captures and distills the standing within time of emergent being. In the words of Avi Sagi "The blink of an eye connotes the look of the eye, which captures reality itself in its entirety."[22] The words of the philosopher Søren Kierkegaard focus on the co-occurrence of the momentary and the eternal, the passing and the whole, that all manifest in that moment of the blink: **"And now the moment. […] It is brief and temporal indeed, like every moment; it is transient as all moments are; […] And yet it is decisive, and filled with the Eternal […] let us call it *the Fullness of Time*."[23]**

When Kulka brings together these two forms of temporal relations within him – the historian who assesses events along a linear temporal axis, with the child who is captive within the Claustrum of time, which

---

[20] The claim that Freud primarily refers to linear time is not simplistic and acknowledges the fact that Freud, for example, refers to the appearance of the past in the present in relations of transference, to the possibility of regression and fixation – yet Pearl shows that these all align and move along the continuum of the linear axis of internal time (M.R.).

[21] Pearl, Y. A. (2011). *A Question of Time: Freud in Light of Heidegger's Temporality*. Bar Ilan University Press, Ramat Gan

[22] Sagi, A. (2009). *The Human Quest for Meaning: A hermeneutic philosophical study of works of literature*. Bar Ilan University Press, Ramat Gan, p. 105 (free translation by C. Wagner & T. Tlalim)

[23] Kierkegaard, S., 1985. Philosophical Fragments. Trs & Ed: Howard V. Hong and Edna Hong, Princeton University Press, p 18.

spins to infinity around that single point – they observe one another as witnesses and help germinate the witness function within his mind.

Literature's Keys "Before the Law" of Otto Dov Kulka's Trauma

Unlike a history book, Kulka's book is not written linearly but as a "chronotope,"[24] which moves forward and backwards, in between the present time and space and that of the past, and in between the objective and subjective. He exposes the dilemma between 'reliving death,' which means being in touch with his internal truth but dying with it time and time again; and between the attempt to go through life detached from death, 'leaving it behind', which paradoxically sentences him to a psychic death, since the most fundamental parts in his psyche are projected out of it in this path, leaving it void of affinity and significance.

Years after his physical liberation from Auschwitz, Kulka, who still remains trapped within its gates, tells of a number of reading experiences which I will soon describe. These experiences exemplify the power of literature to support the renewal of the mental movement between the time of the eye's blink, and that of continuous time; In between openness to the unknown and the grasping of the familiar and comprehensible. These reading experiences, and above all the reading of Kafka's parable – "Before the Law,"[25] led to what Kulka refers to as "an epiphany,"[26] which had altered the pattern of psychic witnessing in which he had previously been captive. They paved the way (up until the 'opening of the gates') for the constitution of the internal witness function, which is the constitution of the metaphorical mode in his psyche. Only at the point where he was finally able to deliver his metaphorical witnessing in "Landscapes of the Metropolis of Death" could the Holocaust child finally

---

[24] Bakhtin, M. (1975). *Forms of Time and of the Chronotope in the Novel. Kinneret, Zmora-Bitan, Dvir, Or Yehuda, 2007.*

[25] Kafka, F. (1925). *The Trial.* Hebrew translation by Avraham Carmel, Schocken books, Jerusalem and Tel Aviv, 1992, pp 205-206.

[26] Kulka, O. D., (2013).

meet face to face with the researcher in him, and the past could meet the present. Kulka seems almost apologetic: **"The hidden meaning of the metaphoric language of the central, recurrent motifs in the book, such as 'immutable law of death', the 'Great Death', the 'Metropolis of Death', reaches beyond the experience of the world of Auschwitz."**[27] He is well aware that this time around, his mind remembers, devises, struggles, observes; since this time he does not only recall but also reimagines, and also remembers his imaginings, and imagines his memories.

In the process of becoming able to give a metaphorical witnessing account, which lays out his experiences as a boy in Auschwitz from a personal perspective, Kulka describes three experiences of reading literature that have led to a transformation in the shapes of his experience and witnessing facing the trauma he had gone through:

First transformation – following the reading of stories by von Kleist[28]

The first movement, which I will only mention briefly due to the scope of this paper, takes form through Kulka's reading of Von Kleist's stories "Michael Kohlhaas" and "An Earthquake in Chile." In both of these stories, the law (the church, the judicial system, the nobility) acts in a cruel and arbitrary manner towards the simple individual. In both cases the protagonists try, and fail, to fight against the power of the law. Kulka finds his witness-double in Von Kleist's stories, and in the encounter with these tragic heroes who futilely try to rebel against the deformations of the law –serves for him as a meaning-endowing reflection of his many boundless internal visits into the eternal laws of death:

Many years later, here in Jerusalem, when I read the stories of Kleist, it seemed to me that I understood cognitively what I

---

[27] Kulka, O. D., (2013), p. 16.

[28] Von Kleist, H. (2002). Kohlhaas and Others – all of the novels. From German: Ran Hacohen. Tel Aviv: The New Library.

had then intuited. I understood the great and terrible impulse toward such returning and resignation, […] to order and to the terrifying law […] against which every revolt always remains no more than a small, desperate, hopeless deferment.[29]

Second Transformation – following the reading of "In the Penal Colony" by Kafka

The second movement where the realization which started with reading Von Kleist deepens, takes place when Kulka reads Kafka's story "In the Penal Colony."[30] In Kafka's story, a travelling researcher arrives at the Penal Colony and discovers that the legal system there, which was determined by the "former commander", is that any criminal finds out what his verdict is through a machine that engraves the verdict on his body, and following six hours of torture the written words are revealed to him and he realizes his fate. There, there is no room for trials since the guilt is known in advance. It is a jurisprudence that accepts no appeal, and from which there is no escape. As Kulka reads "In the Penal Colony," the story of punishment by flogging to death, which was carried out in the concentration camp, resurfaces in his mind after years of amnesia. He writes:

I probably would not have recalled this incident, would not have engraved the scene and its import in my memory, had it not loomed before me again much later when I read Kafka's story 'In der Strafkolonie' – 'In the Penal Colony'.[31]

Kulka describes in meticulous details the situation, which years later he had recalled, where a prisoner was flogged to death in front of all of the other prisoners, in complete silence. He was beaten on his head, with each blow leaving a new red mark on his skull, just like the engraving of

---

[29] Kulka, O. D., (2013), p. 87.
[30] Kafka, F. (2011). *In the Penal Colony*. Penguin UK.
[31] Kulka, O. D., (2013), p. 98.

the punishment on the body of the condemned in Kafka's "Penal Colony." Only that it was not the recollection which had become transformative of the reading of the story, but the realization that there and then, and against his will, Kulka the child had himself become a "researcher-traveler" observing from outside at this jurisprudence which is so utterly absolute, that

> **[it] can exist without any connection to the strange landscape the traveler chances upon, and can be transposed to the landscape of the camp on that foggy morning, in Auschwitz itself. And from Auschwitz itself, might infiltrate into every possible situation, as though it is an autonomous system, utterly divorced from any feeling [...] even the distinction between victim and perpetrator seems to disappear here completely.[32]**

The story "In the Penal Colony" penetrates through Kulka's selective amnesia. The previous order is weakened, and he starts to become aware of the alienation in his psyche:

> **Actually, certain episodes of this kind do inhabit my consciousness. Earlier, I described, in passing, the piles of skeletons, the bodies – bones covered with skin – which were heaped up behind the barracks before dawn and which we children sidestepped, skirted, on the way to the youth barracks in the special camp.[33]**

Skirting the skeletons had in fact become an act of denial or a 'skipping' over the upsetting sights, as part of the greater efforts by the boy's mind to outlast the daily trauma without collapsing – physically or emotionally. But the price of the skip is that it had made the world arbitrary and reality such, that no negotiation remained possible between it and the consciousness of a human being. A divide between the continuous doing and emergent being, between the Excessive witness-

---

[32] Kulka, O. D., (2013), p. 99.
[33] Kulka, O. D., (2013), p. 93.

ing, and the Metonymical witnessing. The language that had served him became a concrete language, or a pseudo-language, in the sense that it either did not evoke any emotion due to the level of trauma involved, or that it forbade emotion from surfacing, so as to guard itself from its devastating power. There is no place for reproof, rebellion, doubt, alarm, pain; In the words of Kulka, "an autonomous system, utterly divorced from any feeling."[34] According to the literary view of this arbitrary situation, where everyone responds to the greater logic of death without disputing it, His reading of Kafka exposes an internal death sentence with which Kulka has so far identified – a death sentence to the mind's capacity to be a present, responsive, reflexive counterpart to the happening and recollection within him. Following the experience of reading and the insight which followed it, Kulka begins to search for events that exceeded the arbitrary monotonicity of the grand death – human moments of involvement in the process of an emergent being which had dared to lift its head in the midst of the inferno, and to express a different voice, from a derelict terrain of human values and of protest. He describes a whole list of such events that begin to overwhelm his consciousness and to instigate motion within it. Due to the limited space I will not specify them here.

Final movement – following the reading of "Before the Law" by Kafka

One of the properties of the stringent defenses of the continuous doing is a split between the singular, the particular, and the general or universal, and the inability to integrate them. Throughout the years Kulka had entirely refrained from any kind of subjective or artistic Holocaust witnessing. He had felt complete alienation from other Holocaust stories, and had believed that his own story would be perceived similarly. In 1989 he was invited to attend a university colleague's lecture on the subject "The Holocaust in Literature." In preparation for this invitation he picked up a book on the Holocaust, and once again felt that terrible

---

[34] Kulka, O. D., (2013), p. 99.

alienation, whereby he could not find any affinity between "his own" Auschwitz, and the one described in the book, and in his frustration – he had turned to Kafka. He describes the procedure as follows:

> The only response I feel able to express is alienation; all that is authentic is the authenticity of the alienation. Therefore I ask: *in what am I different? Something is wrong with me!* And then, as so often, as almost always during periods of distress, I escape to Kafka, […] I always open randomly – I opened at the ending of the wonderful story of the man standing before the Gate of the Law. This man who stands before the Gate of the Law actually asks the same question […] He asks: 'Tell me, after all this is the Gate of the Law, and the Gate of the Law is open to everyone.' To which the gatekeeper says: 'Yes, that is so.' Then the man says […] 'Yet in all the years I have been sitting here no one has entered the gate.' And the gatekeeper nods his head and says: 'Indeed.' The man asks him to explain this puzzling fact, and the gatekeeper does him this one last mercy "and says: 'This gate is open only for you, it exists only for you, and now I am going to close it.

And Kulka continues as follows:

> Accordingly, everything I have recorded here – all these landscapes, this whole private mythology, this Metropolis, Auschwitz – this Auschwitz that was recorded here, which speaks here from my words, is the only entrance and exit – an exit, perhaps, or a closing – the only one that exists for me alone. I take this to mean that I cannot enter by any other way, by any other gate to that place. Will others be able to enter through the gate that I opened here, that remains open for me? It is possible that they will, because this gate that Kafka opened, which was intended for only one person, for K., Josef K., is actually open to almost everyone. But for him there was only one gate into his private mythology.[…] I don't know whether this analogy is valid here, but this is the only meaning

I can find for the puzzle of the occupation of my present with that past, which I experience constantly [...] and, at least to this mystifying matter, seems to have found an answer at last. It's not much, a marginal thing, really, but it is impossible not to convey these things, not to puzzle over them, not to believe in them, for without that belief the whole memory of my childhood landscapes, the landscapes in which I always find freedom – my last but one freedom – would be lost.[35]

The experience of reading Kafka had led to a paradox, which is the core of the miracle of reading: the story of the other tells the innermost and most private story of the reader. All of a sudden he feels familiar, touched, and treated by the text and its writer. He begins to search, in the words of Amir, **"for the 'language of the individual,' one of the most particular details that have been assimilated, and faded into the generalisations, and into the shared 'language of the plural.'"**[36]

Aharon Appelfeld writes that this is in fact the very guardianship of literature:

literature [...] and her greatest guardianship: the individual [...] That very individual, whose expression had been erased in the public eye and who had become one amongst many, this individual is the gist and the essence of any literary vision.[37]

And he adds that:

Forever, its greatest concern is the individual, his first name, his weakness or loftiness. When the doubters appear and question what the concern of art might be in a sphere where either deeds or silence are called for, I answer to myself; who would

---

[35] Kulka, O. D., (2013), pp. 166-169

[36] Amir, D., (2012), p. 24

[37] Appelfeld, A. (1979). *Essays in the First Person*. World Zionist Organisation, Jerusalem, pp. 90-91. (Free trans. By C. Wagner and Tom Tlalim)

redeem the anxieties, the pains, and the torments from the shadows, the obscured beliefs, the feelings of insignificance and those of eternity. Who would let them out of the darkness and bestow a bit of warmth and dignity on them, if not this art, which toils so much on the choosing of words, which is ever so mindful of any emotion and of any shadow of a feeling.[38]

Due to this nature, literature makes a fertile ground for what I refer to as **"The reader's art of mourning."**[39] As possible to learn from Kulka's witness account, this is an active and creative form of mourning. When the reader dares to outlast the daring entry into the realms of phantasy, the deep identifications with catastrophically threatening life situations and the direct confrontation with the limits of existence expressed in the contents and in the forms of consciousness enfolded in them, then he would have the opportunity to mourn in the arms of literature. Reading can become a process of slow but active mourning for the reader, through his efforts to 'create the story' within him facing the impossible and ultimate suffering, the contradictory and the chaotic nature of existence and consciousness. This while being part of the creation of the aesthetical, the good and the beautiful, whilst recalling the good internal objects and the possibility of encountering life from a position of meaning, peace and acceptance, and also of creativity and fulfillment. The reflection, introspection and creativity exercised by the reader when encountering the "life" he experiences in the reading, constitute the reader's "art of mourning." The reader is enlivened, is coping, and is invited to face the dialectical challenges of his existence, and to exceed them using the transcendental potential provided by the practice of reading, and once again the reader struggles with their framework until he can find a new balance, which better acknowledges the

---

[38] Appelfeld, A., (1979), p. 98. (Free trans. By C. Wagner and Tom Tlalim)

[39] Roth. M. (2017). Reading the Reader – a psychoanalytic perspective on reading literature, edited by Avi Sagi and Aner Govrin, Jerusalem: Carmel, pp.310-311. This terminology is inspired by Ogden's article "Borges and the Art of Mourning represents the strive of the individual to encounter, to come to terms with, and to do justice to the fullness and complexity of his relation with what he had lost and the experience of loss itself: Ogden, T.H. (2000). <u>Borges and the Art of Mourning</u>. *Psychoanal. Dial., 10*: pp 65-88.

limitations of his existence and his possibilities. As he is no longer required to protect himself from the abundant artillery of his mind, additional mental energy becomes available with which to be more creative, more relaxed and more alive, whilst becoming more at peace with the permanent presence of the eternal existential tenants – death, pain, border and a portion of exile in the uncanny space of the living and of the psyche. That is the reader's art of mourning – and his creation is a new integration of the dialectical poles with which he is grappling – of the absent and the present in life; of the familiar and the uncanny; of the symbolic order and madness and of the emergent being and continuous doing. Reading's art of mourning leads to the creation of a new equilibrium within the multi-dialectical space of the reader's psyche.

Kulka's reading experiences, which culminate in "Before the Law," have exposed him to the transcendence of existence which, the more private it is, so it becomes universal, belonging to no one and to everyone at once. Out of this break out of a present experience, which transgressed his internal barbed wire fences, hope had sprang in him and a movement towards the capacity to tell his story before the gate of his own life and death, which is no longer experienced as singular but as personal, and as such it touches the general as well. The integration of doing and being, of the continuous and the blink of an eye, had led him, after almost 60 years of preoccupation with the Holocaust, to bear a metaphorical witnessing which unfolds his personal story. In doing so he could finally begin the process of mourning which characterizes the depressive position, which involves a movement and integration of the dialectical aspects of the mind: the I and the other, phantasy and reality, the particular and the general individual and the public, the familiar and the uncanny, present and absent, madness and symbolic, linear and timeless, permanent and fleeting and more.

From within the process of mourning, the yet unsuccessful dimension of reparation in the psyche changes as well. Kulka writes:

> **I have dwelt on the duality, the methodological distancing, and all the rest. Yet the truth, as it seems to me now, is that I only tried to bypass here the barrier of that gate, to enter it with the**

whole force of my being, in the guise of, or in the metamorphosis of, perhaps, a Trojan horse, intended, finally, to smash the gate and shatter the invisible wall of the city forbidden to me, outside whose domain I had decreed that I would remain.[40]

Kulka in fact understands that the repetition of the metonymical witness did not merely represent an act of repetition compulsion belonging to the death instinct. With profound illumination, he realizes retrospectively that both the post-traumatic metonymical repetition, and the excessive witnessing along the axis of continuous doing, are concealing a secret striving of the mind to break through the gates of the law of trauma, towards the voice which asks to diverge, his internal voice which asks to continue to live and to create and to observe, and who there and then would be capable of beginning a new process of mourning and integration. Similarly to any defense mechanism, that was the best possible ad hoc solution that the mental system had found, and where the **wish for reparation** had resided as well; a wish to escape from the internal dungeon. The scientist was a Trojan horse built by the child who had wished to break through, paving a way towards the other areas of his psyche.

Kulka borrows on Kafka's gate in order to pass through the gate of his own story, which shines new light into him. The end of Kafka's story had transformed within Kulka the reader, who had also changed as a consequence of his reading:

Was that my gate to the law? To the law of the world? One of the two massive iron doors of that gate, a gate that is open day and night? And now, as the gatekeeper said to the man, 'I am going to close it.' Yet it seems to me that story also tells, that in those moments it appeared to the man that beyond that gate there shone, or glowed dimly, a new light, such as he had never before seen in his life.[41]

---

[40] Kulka, O. D., (2013), pp. 170-171
[41] Kulka, O. D., (2013), p. 173

In her last article "On the Sense of Loneliness"[42] Melanie Klein writes that one's loneliness is a fundamental aspect, which never entirely vanishes, yet it's path differs from the isolation of one part from other parts of the self. Such isolation stems from an internal splitting of one part that the self expels for various reasons. In Kulka's case, the return of the young boy from his internal exile into the arms of the other parts of the self, also brings back the representations of the self into a living relation with the internal object representations, and in doing so also restores the internal witnessing function in the mind. That is not the conclusion of the processing of mourning, but its beginning/renewal, whose tasks would only be completed in the end of life itself.

References

Amir, D. (2008). *On the Lyricism of the Mind*. The Hebrew University Press, Magness.

Amir, D. (2014[2013]). *Cleft Tongue*, London: Karnac.

Appelfeld, A. (1979). *Essays in the First Person*. World Zionist Organisation, Jerusalem.

Bakhtin, M. (1975). *Forms of Time and of the Chronotope in the Novel. Kinneret, Zmora-Bitan, Dvir, Or Yehuda, 2007.*

Bion, W.R. (1965). *Transformations.* London: Heinemann.

Eigen, M. (2004). *Psychic Deadness.* London: Karnac Books.

Erlich, H.S. (2003). Experience—What is it?. *Int. J. Psycho-Anal., 84.*

Felman, Shoshana, and Dori Laub. Testimony: Crises of Witnessing in Literature, Psychoanalysis and History. New York: Routledge, 1992.

Heidegger, M. (1968). *The Question Concerning Technique*, Trans Roger Berkowitz and Philippe Nonet. 2006. (unpublished) Available on https://www.academia.edu/2083177/The_Origin_of_the_Work_of_Art_by_Martin_Heide gger

Kafka, F. (2011). *In the Penal Colony.* Penguin UK.

---

[42] Klein, M. (1963). On the Sense of Loneliness. In: *Envy and Gratitude and Other Works: 1946-1963.* London: Vintage, 1997.

Kafka, F. (1925). *The Trial*. Hebrew translation by Avraham Carmel, Schocken books, Jerusalem and Tel Aviv, 1992.

Kierkegaard, S., 1985. *Philosophical Fragments*. Trs & Ed: Howard V. Hong and Edna Hong, Princeton University Press.

Klein, M. (1963). On the Sense of Loneliness. In: *Envy and Gratitude and Other Works: 1946- 1963*. London: Vintage, 1997.

Von Kleist, H. (2002). *Kohlhaas and Others – all of the novels*. From German: Ran Hacohen. Tel Aviv: The New Library.

Kulka, O. D. (2013). *Landscapes of the Metropolis of Death*. First Harvard University Press edition. Cambridge, Massachusetts: The Belknap Press of Harvard University Press.

Meltzer, D. (1992). *The Claustrum*. Perthshire: Clunie Press.

Ogden, T.H. (2000). Borges and the Art of Mourning. *Psychoanal. Dial., 10*.

Pearl, Y. A. (2011). *A Question of Time: Freud in Light of Heidegger's Temporality*. Bar Ilan University Press, Ramat Gan.

Roth, M. (2017). *Reading the Reader – a Psychoanalytic Perspective on Reading Literature*. Edited by Avi Sagi and Aner Govrin. Jerusalem: Carmel.

Sagi, A. (2009). *The Human Quest for Meaning: A hermeneutic philosophical study of works of literature*. Bar Ilan University Press, Ramat Gan.

Semprún J. (1994). Literature or Life. New-York: Penguin books, 1997.

III. From Theory to Practice

CHAPTER TEN

Hiding in the Dyad:
What is a Manageable Frame?

Edward R. Shapiro

Introduction: Shmuel Erlich is first and foremost a master clinician. Beginning with his training with very disturbed patients at the Austen Riggs Center, Shmuel has become an internationally known and widely published psychoanalyst, applying his broad learning to the problems of institutional standards and the pressures of our larger society. In his career and in his writings, Shmuel has consistently focused attention on "the third": that aspect of any dyadic engagement that connects us to reality. We lose this connection at our peril. This paper discusses a problemmatic and infamous treatment that underlined the dangers of losing touch with a tradition. I offer it in tribute to Shmuel's teaching about the dangers of hiding in the dyad.

In 1991, as I was entering Austen Riggs as the Medical Director/CEO, a psychoanalyst in Boston lost her way in a heroic treatment with a young man. The publicity around this case destroyed this young clinician's career and led to speeches in professional societies and two books (Maltzberger, 1993; Chavetz, 1995; McNamara, 2009). Dr. Margaret Bean-Bayog took a risk with this very disturbed young man, offering him a murky framework. The patient punished her efforts by killing himself. She was then crucified by the family, the media, and the profession. Her extensive data, the prominence of the case, and the importance of the issues raised suggest their increasing relevance to our profession today.

Why did this case become so notorious? I will review some of the boundary dilemmas in this case and suggest that this treatment is symbolic of a profession in transition, where all boundaries are up for negotiation. The way Dr. Bean-Bayog got lost with this patient reflects some of the difficulties in our field. These difficulties in turn reflect problems in the larger society. I will suggest that the transition in psychoanalysis from the relatively isolated study of the patient to the study of the dyad has unexpected dangers for the treatment of disturbed patients. Irwin Hoffman (1994) has commented on the commonalities in case reports that attend to the therapist's necessary involvement with the patient. These reports often include, implicitly or explicitly, a feeling of deviation from a commonly accepted way of working, a feeling of "throwing away the Book." He states, " . . . those of us who [are] part of this movement [are] in trouble. After all, how often could we throw away, retrieve, and throw away the same Book?" (P.188).

The intensity of the work with disturbed patients and the dangers of irrationality in an isolated dyad require a third perspective (Brickman. 1993). This can be provided by an institution, supervision, or consultation. In some cases, the traditional framework itself, with its historical connections to an interpretive task, can provide the third. This sense of perspective is marked, in Hoffman's words, ". . . by a sense of struggle with uncertainty . . . and an openness to consideration of the unconscious meanings, for the analyst and patient, of whatever course has been taken." (P. 200-201). Without this perspective, we run the risk of developing two grandiose fantasies. The first is that an isolated dyad can fully grasp its own irrationality. The second is that patients' difficult past experiences can be corrected through a consistent use of the empathic mode. I see some evidence that these fantasies were enacted in this case. In this case, the relative absence of a third precluded perspective on the changing role of the therapist, allowed the pair to be seduced into a myth of corrective experience, and obscured the need for a holding context for the treatment.

The Framework of Personality Disorder

In my studies of families whose members have personality disorders, I have found that family members often form rigid defenses against recognizing limitations in themselves, in others, and in the availability of resources (Shapiro, 1982a). These defenses, manifest by inflexible or aberrant personal and family boundaries, protect them from feelings of helplessness, anxiety, rage, and grief (Shapiro, et al, 1975; Shapiro, 1982b, 1991). When defenses fail, these affects emerge. The world does not ordinarily conform to the individual's needs. In response, the identified patient in the family escalates his demands, demonstrating the lack of anxiety tolerance, difficulty with delay, and poor impulse control that characterize the illness. Limitations in the world cause these patients to become symptomatic. For example, obsessive patients faced with time limitations can become anxious, narcissistic patients confronting the unavailability of significant people can withdraw or become angry.

Clearly defined task and role boundaries in therapy – mutually agreed upon markers of the frame – help patients experience these feelings and interactions so that they can fully articulate and acknowledge them. These boundaries slow the interactions. The obsessive can notice how his efforts to control contribute to his anxiety. The narcissist can recognize his need for the other's attention. For patients, experiencing and studying transactions across these therapeutic boundaries offers an opportunity for learning (Bion, 1962). Patients begin to recognize their desperate efforts to change the outside world to fit their needs. With this recognition, they have a chance to get perspective on their childhood and current maladaptive style and notice that the world requires negotiation.

The Therapeutic Framework

Over the years, psychoanalysts have increasingly learned to define and manage a therapeutic framework within which a deepening treatment can take place (Milner, 1957; Baranger, 1966; Langs, 1973, 1976). Milner (1957) noted that the frame has a crucial boundary function, in that it ". . . marks off an area within which what is perceived has to be taken symbolically, while what is outside the frame is taken literally (p. 158)." Managing this framework is our responsibility. It includes confidentiality and role boundaries, time, place, setting, financial arrangements, and vacations. We structure these arrangements in the outer world of our contractual negotiation with another adult, who agrees to take up the patient role. We do all of this both to take care of ourselves and to support an interpretive treatment task.

The framework thus has footholds in external reality and in the analytic dyad. For example, we set our fees according to our needs, pressures in our outer world, and assessment of where we stand in relation to others. In other words, we set fees in response to the market and our patients' resources. Fees, vacations, the management of missed sessions – all of the framework issues – are the context within which our patients make sense of us. The way in which the analyst manages these issues is a reflection of how he or she manages the boundary between the inner and outer worlds. It, therefore, provides information to the patient about the analyst's character (Langs, 1976). The patient's interpretation of the analyst's management is a reflection of the patient's inner world. We meet our patients at this intimate management boundary to engage in the task of interpretive treatment.

When patient and analyst mutually negotiate a structured framework, they respectfully address this complexity and provide a safe, predictable, transitional space for therapeutic work. With this security, an individual can take up the patient role and risk a symbolic regression in which an interpretable transference to the analyst can evolve. Though the management structures of the framework quickly enter the patient's inner world of private meaning and what Ogden calls "the third of the analyst-patient intersubjectivity (Ogden, 1994)," the analyst is responsible for establishing and maintaining them.

For neurotic patients, the framework is largely a silent aspect of the work. These patients have internalized a stable psychic structure. Patients with severe personality disorders are different. They crash against boundaries. Many live from crisis to crisis because of their inability to manage a stable and secure framework for their lives outside. Quite often, then, it is within and around the framework of treatment that these patients enact their psychopathology. These interactions impinge on us at our management boundary, evoking our countertransference reactions and framework errors. The study of these mutual enactments has deepened our learning about the fine distinctions between transference and countertransference. In such treatments, our authority for the framework, our ability to manage it and to notice when we don't, and our commitment to holding the interpretive treatment task as primary become crucial.

All of these issues are relevant to this case. Because of what I believe were unmanageable pressures, Dr. Bean altered her framework – particularly her role boundaries, fees, beginnings and ends of sessions, and management of vacations – with consequences for what could be safely interpreted. She unwittingly revealed – as we all do – elements of her conflicts and character to her patient. The patient's irrational use of her character provided the drama of this case, but it was enacted in an unexamined framework where the drama could not be interpreted by her, the patient, or the rest of us.

Terry Maltzberger (1993), in his Presidential address to the American Association of Suicidology, reviewed the case, describing the altered framework. He said, "Dr. Bean, with misgivings, gave her patient children's books and wrote, 'Love, Mom' and similar now notorious inscriptions. [In the treatment notes] she repeatedly reminded the patient that she was not his mother and could not be his mother. He seemed to understand this, but claimed he found it comforting when away from her to pretend [a] mother had really given him the books, loved him, and wanted him to be comforted. The much deplored cards described by the press had the same origin. These were written at the patient's dictation, and when they were being written, he was reminded that they represented fantasies, not facts." He adds, "The toys, the blanket, the books, and the cards were fixtures in profoundly regressed periods and . . . the patient was psychotic in the transference." Dr. Maltzberger stated, "I would not have written those inscriptions nor those cards. Read out of context they do indeed sound too tender, too intimate, like a mother speaking to a frightened child. Yet I am a man, and Dr. Bean-Bayog a woman. She was there and I was not."

He states that Dr. Bean-Bayog repeatedly consulted other psychiatrists about the use of transitional objects, but there are indications that she did not mention the specifics of her approach. Everything suggests that these were interventions she kept solely within the dyad and did not present to a third party for reality testing. Dr. Maltzberger thinks that the transitional objects were useful in that the patient's symptoms improved and he no longer needed the hospital during the period they were used. But the deeper meaning of these interventions remains unclear. We will never really know what they meant to either party, but the issues raised demand our professional speculation.

The transference became erotic, and the patient brought in aggressively dominated explicit sexual fantasies. Dr. Bean developed countertransference fantasies in similar detail, working out the affective implications of sexual submission. Perhaps she was trying to understand her patient, but the links to the therapy are unclear. She wrote her fantasies down. The patient broke into her office and stole his records, including these explicit countertransference fantasies. He began to threaten Dr. Bean-Bayog with suicide. He said he would leave written documents that implicated her for his family to find. His regression escalated, including drugs, alcohol, and psychosis. Dr. Bean-Bayog ultimately transferred his care while he was hospitalized.

As the work unfolded, it became clear that the treatment of this patient was a severe risk. But the patient had unusual strengths: high intelligence, high motivation, and a wish for help. It was probably worth a try. Medications – and, as it proved, ECT, were of limited value. The patient needed a way to make sense of his life, to take charge of his experience. He needed a reliable framework to make sense of his experience. He was being driven crazy by his own idiosyncratic interpretations of his world.

Dr. Bean-Bayog's framework choices, and the personal dilemmas of patient and therapist – made public – triggered every specter around dynamic treatment: low or no fee, endless availability, the feelings of mother and child evoked between two adults, different cultures, painful personal experiences of failed motherhood in the therapist's life, the possibility of parental molestation of the patient as child, perverse sexual fantasies in both doctor and patient, and endless, detailed, publicly available notes, cards, and books. In a world where our once-reliable frameworks for managing dependency – the family, religion, education, and health care – have failed, dependency itself has become a threatened dynamic. When the framework is not secure, dependency becomes more frightening. We have seen neighbors turn on neighbors, leadership mocked, resources for the poor cut off, and medicine deciding that it has for too long provided "excessive care." Dr. Bean-Bayog became the symbol of the dangers of trusting another person. She paid a high price as an icon of failed dependency.

She did not kill her patient. He killed himself. Her surrender of her license was a severe punishment for her problematic technique. We who continue to treat these patients know that our technical and personal failures often provide critical learning for us and our patients. "How was the patient right and how did we get it wrong this time?" is a recurrent theme for all of us. When the treatment is effective, it is because our frameworks hold, and we manage to sustain the presence of the third perspective.

In considering this case, we are now "the third" to this case. Dr. Bean's extraordinarily detailed treatment notes, the two books that have been written about the case and the issues played out in the media provide an opportunity for the case to be used within the profession for its symbolic, communicative value to the profession and the public. In what follows, I will briefly take up some of the altered boundaries in this case and offer my own perspectives and speculations. I will address two aspects. The first is the negative transference, including responsibility for the patient's life and the use of transitional space. The second is the outside world: the family, consultants, and the public.

The Negative Transference

A mutually agreed upon framework that protects both the therapist's and the patient's reality provides a relatively safe space to examine the negative transference. Severely characterologically disturbed patients – borderline and narcissistic – struggle to integrate their aggressive experiences. These patients often feel they are victims of others' mistreatment. And many of them have been. Their family experience has often been abusive, unempathic, unresponsive. They have found no way to get beyond these early experiences, they cannot justify or face their rage, and they recreate this trauma in their relationships.

We have learned to take seriously patients' stories of abuse as one central context for their tortured lives and conflicted enacted rage. Their stories evoke sympathy and a wish to repair the damage. Such feelings can cause us to shift our framework toward illusory repair instead of acknowledgment and perspective. The trauma in many of these patients' lives has come as a consequence of corrupt family frameworks. Unclear boundaries and the narcissistic use of children to represent aspects of parental conflict (Shapiro, et al 1975) may have been the daily experience for these patients. Parents lose sight of a shared developmental task in the service of regressive self-protection. When, as therapists, we "throw away the Book," we run the risk of losing the therapeutic task, colluding in recreating a familiar, pathological developmental setting.

Too often, we do not attend to the ways in which the denied and enacted rage of these patients contributes to their becoming abusers, in identification with those who abused them. This identification protects them from their conflicted rage at their beloved and needed abusers. When they recognize their own aggression, our patients can gain access to their past and develop an ability to take charge of their lives. If the therapist's boundaries are clear enough for the patient to recognize his or her attacks on the framework of treatment, there is a possibility for this perspective.

With these patients, therapists' empathic identification with the victim can lead to compensatory efforts to provide a "good enough Mother." This countertransference – where the therapist avoids the negative transference and attempts to compensate contributes to so-called "helpful" techniques, beyond the standard framework. As Slavin and Kriegman (1992) note, ". . . patients know, or come to know, that another human being whose only substantial utterances take the form of validating affirmations of the patient's own subjective world and developmental strivings are likely, themselves, to be engaged in one or another form of self-deception and deception (p. 250). [An] immersion in the patient's subjective world must be complemented, at times, by what is, in effect, the open expression of the analyst's reality . . . (p. 253)"

Attention to the therapist's reality was hard to find in this case. The patient did not pay, he called her in the middle of the night, demanded to see her on weekends, imposed on her vacations, bought a gun, threatened to sue her, robbed her office, and barraged her home and her family. For a long time, none of these assaults led her to confront his aggression or indicate that he was threatening her ability to continue the therapy. There appeared to be nothing he could do that would evoke her limits and allow him to see his impact on her. She remained available, supportive, and giving. She interpreted his behavior as evidence of his despair, not of his rage. This difficulty in confronting aggression has consequences for the treatment of those patients who require clear boundaries in order to grasp their effect on others and the degree of their aggressive feelings. Running into the therapist's clear limits can clarify for the patient the distinction between fantasized and experienced aggression and real damage.

Instead of confronting and interpreting the negative transference, Dr. Bean-Bayog expanded the frame by taking up a "cognitive" approach, where she created a corrective persona according to the patient's dictation. She became what he created, rather than examining his efforts to remake her. She gave the patient a blanket from her office, then expanded to books, flash cards, phone calls, and an enacted drama about "Mom" and "The Child." On one occasion, at the patient's request, she even became a representation of his girlfriend, writing to him about "terrific sex." She reified the transitional space, rather than keeping it illusory. She played "the good Mom," attempting to provide a sense of support and availability to compensate for the patient's bleak despair. She created this persona in the context of her extended vacation "to keep the patient alive."

It is worth noting that Winnicott, who articulated the notion of transitional space, had a complex view of the therapist's contribution. He noted (1954) that "[The therapist's love is shown] in the positive interest taken, and [his] hate in the strict start and finish and in the matter of fees." (P. 285). As best we can tell, Dr. Bean-Bayog felt that her interventions were examples of "playing" in a transitional space, and that the patient knew it was just a game. But at the same time, she believed that these "unusual" interventions were necessary to keep the patient alive throughout her vacation. It is here that she lost her way. By herself, she could not hold the negative transference in which he would hate her for abandoning him and punish her with his fantasized and attempted suicide. I'm not sure that any of us could. Her desperate effort to calm her patient instead of confronting his hated contributed, I believe, to the difficulty the patient had in testing reality. In the end, there appeared to be little he had responsibility for, including his own life and his relentless impingement on the therapist's life.

Dr. Bean appeared quite confident that her "countertransference mom" was not herself, it was a "psychiatric conceptualization." But who else could it be? In the transference, the patient projects the most difficult aspects of his experience into the therapist. In order to make an empathic connection with the projection, the therapist must find aspects of herself that link to it. After all, the transference/countertransference is a joint creation of patient and therapist, and therapists have an unconscious. Dr. Bean-Bayog's open confidence about her interventions indicate to me that she had lost the uncertainty necessary for maintaining a relatively safe transitional space.

The second loss of this space came when Dr. Bean detailed in writing her sexual fantasies. I believe her that she was attempting to gain perspective on the process. But the extent of the perverse details, the absence of any corresponding written interpretation, and the preservation of these documents in her files, indicate her inability to hold an external perspective. She did not think of others seeing these documents. She had lost "the third" necessary for preserving reality testing and the illusory nature of the transference and countertransference.

The therapist's responsibility is for the framework, not for the patient's life. This is an aspect of the negotiation, where two adults agree to take up different roles so that a process can develop between them for the purposes of the patient's learning (Shapiro, 1996). An interpretive treatment cannot proceed if the therapist holds the anxiety for the patient's life; his life belongs to him. In this case from time to time, an unworkable framework evolved in which the patient's role was to threaten death, the therapist's to keep him alive.

When this patient indicated that he could no longer keep himself safe and planned to kill himself, the treatment had to stop or the setting be changed. It is strenuous enough for the therapist to hold responsibility for the framework, his or her own process, and an interpretive stance toward the processes between them. A patient's concrete suicidal plan becomes a medical emergency, requiring the therapist to make a management intervention. If, on the other hand, the therapy is engaged and the alliance solid, acute suicidal preoccupation can be understood as an interactive communication and an attack on the treatment. If the patient is dead, the therapist's work of interpretation is destroyed. In many cases, if the patient is safe, and held accountable for this attack in the transference, this can be explored and worked through as a manifestation of the patient's hatred (Plakun, 1994).

I think that Dr. Bean-Bayog took too much responsibility – for the fees, the patient's life, and the burden on her own life. In Winnicott's terms, she did not "survive" the patient's aggression – in her therapeutic role, in a grounded technique. Winnicott (1947) notes, "It seems to me doubtful whether a human child as he develops is capable of tolerating the full extent of his own hate in a sentimental environment. He needs hate to hate (p.202)." The managed framework of the treatment symbolizes this structured aggression. In this case, I believe, the pressures on the frame were more than Dr. Bean-Bayog could stand. She shifted her role to become the patient's creation, a framework which left him unclear about her limits, raised questions about the task, and failed to hold his aggression.

The Outside World

When working with an adult patient who can manage the treatment framework, it is within the patient's prerogative to insist on a boundary between the therapy and the outside world. Adult patients can decide to preclude the family. The therapist must respect this. If the family calls, the therapist must inform them that the patient will not allow him to discuss the treatment. This does not preclude the therapist's listening to the family's concerns and the messages from the patient that induced them to call. This boundary is important from several perspectives. The patient needs a space to explore a full range of feelings about the family without being overwhelmed by their presence and involvement. The therapist must have a space to engage fully with the patient's experience without the immediate correction and influence of the family.

If the patient can manage his side of the framework – fee, safety, life management, and management of the family's interventions – this boundary can be preserved. If, however, the patient cannot manage the fee, requires additional structure and support, endangers his life, and cannot preserve the therapist from the family's involvement, the therapist cannot accept the patient's conscious wish to exclude the family. In such cases, the patient is challenging the framework of treatment, implicitly asking the therapist to take over family functions: structure, finances, life protection. The therapist must interpret this, suggesting that if the patient cannot manage it, outside involvement will be necessary. The patient is free at this point to fire the therapist, but this is the therapist's reality limitation. In effect, the therapist says to the patient, "The severity of your struggle is inviting your family into our work or asking me to take over their role. If I do that, it will interfere with my being your therapist. How would you like to proceed?"

Bion (1961, 1962) notes that an "an isolated pair runs the risk of being delusional." The third to the therapeutic dyad can be the task, the framework, the outside world. The therapist's role differentiates the therapist from the patient. The role is a function of the therapeutic task of reflecting on chaotic experience in the service of understanding the patient. When the role is lost, the therapy is in trouble. This crisis requires an external third: the family for resources, and the consultant or institution for perspective.

In this case, Dr. Bean's use of a consultant appeared not as an effort on her part to get perspective on her treatment. She was looking for support for her efforts to withstand the pressures of the hospital that was asking her to examine her intensive involvement, a "third" both therapist and consultant ignored. She apparently had no such question for herself. Following one consultation, she even constructed the consultant's note for him to sign. This is strikingly similar to her patient's dictating the flash cards for her to sign as "Mom." These collusions appear to me to obliterate a genuinely external third that represents reality.

Summary

Dynamic treatment opens the irrational, the unconscious, the frightening aspects of an internal world not in our control. It is resisted by all of us. In the past, psychoanalysts spoke of these issues to themselves in jargon. We had the internal world to ourselves. Popularizers held up only the most palatable or sensational syntheses for others. Now, the barricades have fallen, anyone can be a therapist, there is no agreed upon framework or theory for treatment, and the psychiatric world has turned to mechanical approaches. Dynamic treatment is exposed to the outside world. If we are to survive, we must publicly discuss our failures and incorporate into our theory the role of the third, the external, the larger context. The Bean-Bayog case illuminates the price we will pay for hiding in the dyad.

References

Baranger, M. and Baranger, W. 1966. Insight in the analytic situation. In: *Psychoanalysis in the Americas*. Ed. R. Litman. New York: International Universities Press, pp/ 56-72.

Bion, W. R. 1961. *Experiences in Groups*. London: Tavistock.

Bion, W. R. 1962. Learning from experience. In *Seven Servants*. New York: Aronson, 1977.

Brickman, H.R. 1993. 'Between the devil and the deep blue sea': the dyad and the triad in psychoanalytic thought. *Int. J. Psycho-Anal.* 74:905-915.

Chavetz, G. 1994. *Obsession: The Bizarre Relationship Between a Prominent Harvard Psychiatrist and Her Suicidal Patient.*, NY: Crown.

Hoffman, I. Z. 1994. Dialectical thinking and therapeutic action in the psychoanalytic process. *Psychoanal. Quarterly* 63: 187-218.

Langs, Robert, 1973. *The Technique of Psychoanalytic Psychotherapy*. New York: Aronson.

Langs, R. 1976. *The Bipersonal Field.* New York: Aronson.

Maltzberger, J.T. 1993. Presidential Address to the American Society for Suicidology. Unpublished.

McNamara, E. 2009. *Breakdown: Sex, Suicide and the Harvard Psychiatrist.* NY: Gallery Books.

Milner, M. 1957. *On Not Being Able to Paint.* N.Y. International Universities Press.

Ogden, T. H. 1994. The analytical third: working with intersubjective clinical facts. *Int J Psychoanal* 75:3-20.

Plakun, E. 1994. Principles in the psychotherapy of self-destructive borderline patients. *J. Psychotherapy Practice and Research* 3:138-148.

Shapiro, E.R. 1982a. The holding environment and family therapy with acting out adolescents. *Int J Psychoanal Psychother* 9:209-226.

Shapiro, E.R. 1982b. On curiosity: intrapsychic and interpersonal boundary formation in family life. *Int J Family Psychiatry.* 3: 69-89.

Shapiro, E.R. and Carr, A.W. 1991. *Lost in Familiar Places: Creating New Connections between the Individual and Society.* New Haven and London: Yale University Press.

Shapiro, E.R., Zinner, J. Shapiro, R.L. and Berkowitz, D.A. 1975. The influence of family experience on borderline personality development. *Int Rev Psychoanal* 2:399-411.

Shapiro, E.R. 1996 (in press). The boundaries are changing: renegotiating the therapeutic frame. In Shapiro, E.R. ed. *The Inner World in the Outer World: Psychoanalytic Perspectives.* New Haven and London: Yale University Press.

Slavin, M.O. and Kriegman, D. 1992. *The Adaptive Design of the Human Psyche.* New York: Guilford Press.

Winnicott, D.W. (1954) Metapsychological and clinical aspects of regression within the psychoanalytical set-up. In: *Through Pediatrics to Psychoanalysis.* New York: Basic, 1958

Winnicott, D.W. (1947) Hate in the countertransference. In: *Through Pediatrics to Psychoanalysis.* New York: Basic, 1958

CHAPTER ELEVEN

From Consciousness to Awareness: the Lia's Case[1]

Stefano Bolognini

To my friend Shmuel, with sincere esteem and authentic admiration for his intelligence, creativity and personal simpathy, as a memory of many years we shared working together inside and for our beloved psychoanalytic institutions.

In this clinical presentation I would like to explore the relations between the Ego and the Self in revisiting the traumatic area during analysis.

In this specific clinical experience, such revisitation is undergone through auditory experience.

I am going to describe a condition of relative split between the cognitive Ego and the experiential Self. This also corresponds to a partial psyche-soma split, where only the body, through the senses, seems able to remember and then re-start the "talking": the mind appears to need the senses and the body, the split experiential container, to recover its wholeness.

Analysis is the treatment of choice (albeit lengthy and problematic) for reintegrating these very deep, dramatic splits.

I will also highlight a certain difficulty in Italian, usually such a rich language, in finding specific terms to define the different levels of activity and mental integration that I am trying to represent.

---

[1] This is a part of a longer chapter published in German: "Inauditum/Unerhoert!!!". Gewissen, Bewusstsein, Integration. Die Analyse als posttraumatische Erfahrung". In "Unherhoert – Vom Hoeren un Verstehen", edited by I. Bozetti, I. Focke, I. Hahn. Fachbuch Klett-Cotta, Stuttgart, 2014.

In Italian the terms "*coscienza*" ("consciousness") and "*consapevolezza*" ("awareness"), when used as adjectives, do not seem sufficiently differentiated to define very different levels of complex functioning.

Clinical material

Lia is able to describe in great detail the car crash she was involved in eight years ago when she was 19. She fractured her pelvis, spine and both legs, but it cost her fiancé, Gabriele, his life.

She remembers almost everything about the accident up to the moment she went into a coma which lasted several days.

But she cannot exactly recall what happened inside their car, after the terrible impact with the other vehicle, during the twenty interminable minutes when she and Gabriele were trapped upside-down in a ditch, waiting for someone to spot them and summon help. Nor does she remember when exactly she lost consciousness and went into a coma, but she knows that it happened before she was pulled from the wreckage.

A few days later in hospital, once she had regained consciousness, Lia gave a very lucid account to the police, which they regarded as realistic and convincing.

Gabriele had had a bit to drink at dinner with friends and was excited, as he usually was on Saturday nights. They were to go to a discotheque and she knew that if she told him to slow down, he would only get angry and it would make matters worse.

He was overtaking at almost 90 mph on a minor road when a Land Rover came towards them round a bend. It was a head-on collision.

After the terrible impact, their car span round and round before crashing into a ditch, where it was later spotted with difficulty by rescuers.

She told me about the crash with similar lucidity in our first encounter, when she asked me for analysis "*for professional reasons*": after the accident she had abandoned law school and become a psychologist. She wanted to become a psychotherapist.

From that moment on, we never spoke of the accident and its tragic consequences, except very rarely and then only in practical and rational terms.

As often happens in analysis, very important items which are reported in the first encounter disappear or remain in the background for a long time. It almost seems as if the analytic couple have 'forgotten' about them.

For three years Lia produced a torrent of stories concerning her turbulent love-life, which came across as somewhat superficial and less than genuine. She appeared to be committed to building a "permanent" relationship with two successive boy-friends, but there was always something shallow about these affairs.

I have a very clear impression of the first years of analysis: they were rather repetitive.

She would tell me of her busy love-life and in all honesty I would not feel totally involved. All the attention was focused on these affairs in a hyper-real atmosphere which was completely cut off from the past. It was in a certain sense two-dimensional.

I paid attention to the possible transference implications (shifting of transference etc.), but did so almost out of a sense of duty, as if I deliberately sought out what was lacking, because I was unable to do much with the material, as far as our relationship was concerned.

If anything, I felt called upon to act as a pre-personal witness/container; my presence seemed to be my only contribution.

What is more, I have to admit that I too was enmeshed in this shallow network of anecdotes, and often wondered before the session began what new events had happened in the meantime, as if I were about to watch with relatively little interest the umpteenth episode of a soap opera.

However, I was there and I realized one thing: the patient attached great importance to coming to sessions and to my presence. The importance she attached was greater than I felt I deserved for what I was able to do for her.

Curiously, I found myself thinking that, because of the way she used me in analysis and was happy with our work, Lia seemed less intelligent than I had first considered her.

In a series of sessions at the start of the fourth year, she appeared to be in a state of real anxiety about the last days of her dog, who was dying of cancer.

She took care of him at home, and asked herself about his possible elimination by the veterinary or not; in principle she wouldn't have been against, but something impeded her from doing that.

So she was close to him till his last breath.

And after the animal's death, in the course of a dramatic session which took us both by surprise, a door opened within her and she made contact again with the rest of herself.

Lia was deeply disturbed by a sombre sensorial element. Intense and oppressive, it took over her thoughts and seemed to fill the consulting room.

This sensorial element was the laboured breathing of her dog as death approached. She spent a long time talking to me about it.

She spoke with difficulty and a clear sense of alarm, but she seemed to be unable to get it off her mind.

She could not help but speak of it, even against her will. She insisted and it was not long before I understood why.

It triggered off the association she had been trying for years to avoid: *"It was Gabriele's breathing."*

Suddenly, she broke down and cried desperately, talking, weeping and shouting all at once: *"I remember it. His face was close to mine, he made a terrible sound, it was the blood going up and down into his lungs. I screamed and shouted:* **GABRIELE! GABRIELE!!!**, *but he didn't look at me. His eyes were turned inwards and there was a terrible sound. That same sound…the blood formed bubbles…it was unbearable!* **UNBEARABLE!!!…***"*.

Lia's screams were terrifying and I was more than a little disturbed by them.

I protected myself through a "technical" thought : I told myself it might be a hysterical way of overawing the other person, perhaps a cover for something else.

But I realized this was not the case; I was just trying to defend myself.

At the end of the session she was pale and trembling, still shaken.

I believe I can imagine what they must have experienced, the first people on the scene after the accident, as well as the paramedics and the police.

*   *   *

The Italian language, so rich in vocabulary and nuance, seems to encounter some difficulty when it comes to differentiating between specific levels of integration of conscious mental functioning.

We have two terms: "conscio" and "consapevole", which appear poorly differentiated.

In this case, the English language seems to be somewhat better equipped.

The COLLINS COBUILD "ESSENTIAL ENGLISH DICTIONARY", with suitably "essential" Anglo-Saxon pragmatism and conciseness, defines these two terms in a way that is by no means trivial for an analyst:

AWARE: "If you are aware of something, you realize that it is present or happening because *you hear it, see it, smell it, or feel it*". (my italics).
CONSCIOUS: "Someone who is conscious is awake rather than asleep or unconscious".

The two English terms seem to be slightly more specific than the Italian ones in distinguishing between the different types and degrees of the subject's participation in cognition, and between the prevalence of the cognitive and representational functions of the Ego or the experiential conditions of the Self, and their integration.

When distinguishing the different types and degrees of the subject's participation in cognition, the problem lies in the prevalence of the noetic and representational functions of the Ego, or the experiential conditions of the Self, and the integration of the two aspects.

In rare, optimal conditions, the subject's Central Ego (Fairbairn, 1952) harmoniously integrates the various levels and functions, forming an overall experience which respects and fulfils the cognitive potentialities of the human being.

More often, particularly where the situation is traumatic or post-traumatic, people defend themselves from the experience they have undergone by repressing it, splitting the Self or the object, and thus losing their natural integration of Ego and Self, and/or dissociating themselves as regards their Ego functions.

"How much reality can you bear?" is the very apt title of a paper on this theme by Loredana Micati (1993).

In the course of our analytic work, we ask ourselves not only which specific defence mechanisms are activated at any one moment, but also what are the general conditions of the conscious and unconscious Defensive Ego that enable the patient to accede to possible and adequate levels of profundity (Busch, 2003; 2004) at that particular moment, in the analysis in question.

When the analyst's personal integration is good and there is intra- and interpsychic contact with the correct degree of separateness, then he or she is in a position to perceive and represent empathically the relations which hold at that moment between the patient's Defensive Ego, Central Ego and experiential Self (Bolognini, 2002; 2004).

The approach route to the traumatic area or the second encounter with the trauma may then be monitored as complex dynamic processes, of which the analyst may have either theoretical and clinical knowledge (*consciousness*) or full and integrated experiential cognisance (*awareness*).

In many situations, we can perceive and represent to ourselves the way the patient experiences the object/analyst, in the fluctuating nature of relations, given the complexity of the various functional levels of both parties.

When there is a greater degree of integration, we are able to experience, by sharing, what the other person is going through at that moment, in that given situation.

This may be connected to events which took place some time in the past, but which subjectively are fully present and perhaps still overwhelming even.

Unfortunately, from the point of view of countertransference, we are also involved in the sharing of our patient's specific unconscious defences (A. Freud, 1936). It is part of our analytic work to tolerate this temporary inability to function, while awaiting better times.

Perhaps we should not underestimate an extract from the DSM IV – a text we analysts usually look down on, justifiably – which says that "…*post traumatic stress disorder affects those who experience the trauma, those who witness it and those who are confronted with it*" (my underlining)…

Coming to the specific topic of this paper, the issue I intend to investigate, using the case of Lia as a springboard, is the following: why after three years of analysis did the trauma re-emerge experientially? Why had we apparently 'forgotten' about it for all that time? Why was the missing part, i.e. the emotional experience, added to the noetic, informative and conceptual knowledge of the trauma only years later?

My hypothesis is that in order to stay constitutionally and functionally whole, or become so again, the patient requires, first and foremost, the support of an object capable of sharing the sensorial and emotional contents of the raw traumatic experience which the patient carries within him but has not integrated.

Clearly, in analysis this sharing is often 'recorded' rather than 'live', but the sharing is fundamental, and it is not the same as comprehension. Rather, it is a necessary precursor to it.

I cannot possibly know whether Lia went into a coma for reasons which were exclusively neuropathological (cerebral oedema, etc.) or because she could no longer stand all that unbearable reality.

In my mind it was a necessary defensive coma, of protective benefit to her Ego.

The body, the Self, remain repositories of the split experience.

I only know that she found herself for some time alone with her dying fiancé who could no longer respond in any way to her.

I also know that later, in hospital, she recovered her lucidity and gave an account of the matter which satisfied the investigators, whose job it was to establish what had objectively occurred, and who were not interested in her emotional integration (indeed, as far as they were concerned any emotional interference would have detracted from her testimony).

I have reason to believe that Lia had regained her mental lucidity at that point, but that the relationship between her Ego and her Self was no longer integrated (Bolognini, 2002; 2008): her Self was left "upside-down" and her Ego, overwhelmed with anguish, took leave of her.

I also believe that Lia had unconsciously chosen to train as a psychotherapist in order to recover the subjective sense of what had happened to her: and I consider her career choice to be a "sensible" one, in the sense that it made sense.

In my view, Lia needed those first three years of analysis to return to the (mental) scene of the accident in such a state as to be able to stand the impact with an almost unutterable sense of death. It was not the fact of seeing a dead person, but the act of watching a dear one dying before one's very eyes.

With hindsight, I think that in those first three years the analytic couple shared the experience of a defensive 'coma' which excluded any degree of depth, while waiting for developments in the analytic relation necessary for a possible re-awakening.

I can only imagine that for Lia those three years were needed to assure herself about the person who was taking her back to the trauma area, someone who would not say: "Just don't think about it!", or who would not run away when faced with that terrible scenario; someone who would not bureaucratically require all the details in order to write up an accurate report.

That someone also had to prove himself to be a sturdy, but prudent, travel companion, one who would not race ahead "at 90 miles an hour" during analysis, nor rush to reopen the trauma.

Her interlocutor should agree, perhaps reluctantly, to hear that death rattle and put himself in her shoes, to some extent at least.

He should be an *object/co-subject* who is able to share to some degree the experience she found it hardest to bear, as in a system of communicating vessels, without a complete decantation from one to another, without total evacuation.

I am struck by another aspect of the clinical picture: the re-integrative movements aimed at regaining contact with what has been split and projected afar are always amazing, and they follow unexpected paths precisely because they are truly unconscious.

Lia's dog was kept at home until the end.

Knowing Lia, who is practical by nature, I believe that her not wanting to put the dog to sleep with the vet's help was not insignificant, especially since she loved him very much and watching him suffer made her suffer greatly.

I think if her analysis had been at an earlier stage, Lia's dog would have been put down.

She held him a lot, in the final stages: she did what she had been unable to do with Gabriele; this was not just about "righting herself" from upside-down to right-side-up, she also needed to rediscover her arms so that she could touch someone else, her "emotional arms" that had been lost.

I also had to be in a position to "touch" my patient, as nurses do in intensive care units when a patient is comatose or semi-comatose, with the relational equivalents that are typical of the analytical session.

Three years in analysis is not long, but neither is it a brief period. One wonders what passed between us from the interpsychic viewpoint in that period of time, since very little took place interpersonally.

What discreet reverie, what subtle nutritional processes or even what basic containing functions of a pre-natal nature were silently at work to make it possible, or even inevitable, for us to re-encounter the trauma?

What could have enabled the shift from a defective and incomplete consciousness (a protective feature which partially anaesthetised the Self) to integrated and humanising awareness, achieved at the cost of re-experiencing the pain and suffering?

These questions remain unanswered, at least as far as I am concerned.

What I know for sure is that the sensory part of thought (the "beginning" of thought) is easier for small children, less so for adults.

In analysis, we rediscover and regain contact with it in adults. Before we can attribute a meaning to it, we must be willing to hear it, to listen to it, to feel it.

References

Bolognini, S. (2002). *Die Psychoanalytische Einfühlung.* Psychosozial Verlag: Gießen

Bolognini, S. (2004). Intrapsychic-Interpsychic. *Int. J. Psycho-Anal.,* 85:337-358.

Bolognini, S. (2008). Verborgene Wege. Die Beziehung zwischen Analytiker und Patient

Busch, F. (2003). Telling Stories. *J. Amer. Psychoanal. Assn.,* 51:25-42.

Busch, F. (2004). A missing link in psychoanalytic technique: Psychoanalytic consciousness. *Int. J. Psycho-Anal.,* 85:567-572

Fairbairn, W.D. (1952). *Psychoanalytic Studies of the Personality.* London: Tavistock publications Limited.

Freud, A. (1936). *The ego and the mechanisms of defense,* New York: Int. Univ. Press, 1946

Micati, L. (1993). Quanta realtà può essere tollerata?. *Rivista Psicoanal.,*

39:153-163.

CHAPTER TWELVE

Keeping in Mind:
The Forgotten Patient

Irene Melnick

I was very pleased and honored to contribute to a book of essays to cele-
brate Prof. Shmuel Erlich. He was my supervisor in my psychoanalytic
training, and although I have developed a somewhat different approach to
clinical psychoanalysis, throughout the years, he has been very influential
in my thinking. I will always be grateful to him for giving me the funda-
mentals of psychoanalytic thinking together with the freedom to be myself.

In this paper I want to explore issues that have to do with distraction
and forgetting the patient as an expression of the analyst dissociative states, and the ways they may appear in the clinical situation
through the transference-countertransference configurations that occur
between patient and analyst

The conscious and unconscious encounter between the mind of the analyst and the mind of the patient and the influences upon this encounter
are the motor that propels the psychoanalytic process. Assuming that most
analysts are not chronically absentminded, especially forgetful, and basically more or less organized, it is safe to say that we have the capacity to keep
our patients in our mind for long periods of time and in each session, and
this ability is one of the most difficult tasks of the analyst. It is revealed
through our capacity to listen, to hold in our mind the analytic setting,
verbal and nonverbal communications, conscious and unconscious narratives, from the patient and from within ourselves, and to give meaningful
and hopefully transformative interpretations, based upon the exploration of
the transference countertransference dynamics.

We want to assume that most of the time the analyst mind is in what I want to call a "whole" integrated state, but this assumption has been challenged by contemporary psychoanalysis, like Bromberg who considers the unity of the mind, an illusion. In everyday life, we have words that describe the disruptions of the whole, integrated mind: "My mind was not there", "I was absent minded", "My mind was boggled" "I was mindless" "I was losing my mind", "It slipped my mind", etc.

As clinicians, we have all met the slips of our minds, either by commission or by omission. These failures range from everyday small events to major catastrophic ones such as the ones I will describe. Sometimes we have forgotten the name of a patient, or a changed appointment. Sometimes our minds are "elsewhere" when our patient is talking. Sometimes we have felt that our mind is in a chaotic state when listening to a particular overwhelming account.

The idea of writing this paper germinated not from my clinical experience, but, when listening the news about a number of cases of parents which had left their babies in a closed car in the hot summer and as a consequence the babies died. I was horrified by these news, and since then I have been trying to understand what had happened in the mind of those parents that led to this tragic events. What kind of forgetfulness are we dealing with? Are these examples of extreme dissociation? Are these expressions of repressed hostility towards their own children that "cause" a dissociative split of such great proportions? Are these parents' psychopaths?

These accidents have received the name of the Forgotten Baby Syndrome, (FBS) and there are psychological and neurological researches on this syndrome. David Diamond, professor of psychology, molecular pharmacology and physiology at the University at South Florida, says each day people perform tasks that become routine, involving little conscious thought and are therefore governed by a part of the brain called the motor cortex. A good example is driving home from work each day using the same route. Eventually, we can do it seemingly without thinking. Dr. Diamond explains, that our motor memory frees us up to think about the future while completing the task at hand. Then there is the part of the brain responsible for making a clear decision, for example, to stop at the store on your way home from work. This is called the hippocampus, and it controls the cognitive portion of our brains. Dr. Diamond explains that in FBS, the motor memory part of our brain competes against the cognitive part of the brain, overruling it. In this example, that would mean leaving work with the intent of stopping at the store and then finding yourself in your garage having forgotten that you intended to make a stop elsewhere. This phenomenon happens as a normal part of our brain's function and not because there is something wrong with our brain structure. The competition between the two brains would explain FBS, mainly in parents that changed routines when taking care of their babies.

The main reaction of the media to these news was to bring experts of all kinds who have developed different gadgets, techniques and systems to put in cars, to alert the parents not to forget their babies, the assumption being that this could happen to any of us, because we live in an era of overwhelming stimulation and pressure that leads to distraction, the use of smart phones was also blamed for these events because our brain is structurally wired to induce distraction, especially when we change routines.

I have not met personally any of these parents, so I have no way of knowing their inner struggles, and probably there are different parents, in different circumstances, with different problems and minds. But there is no doubt that for some reason, these parents had obliterated their babies, their complete dependency upon them and their capacity to hold them in their minds, sometimes for many hours. Dr. Diamond's findings seem to go along with the theories that have placed dissociation as a central mechanism of the mind in contemporary psychoanalytic thinking. These terrible stories are extreme examples of the failure to keep in mind important others and they led me to think about failures of these kind, not only in everyday life, as parents, spouses but as analysts towards our patients, in the clinical situation. These failures which may occur in the relationship between adults, may not lead necessarily to death, but they may affect these relationships sometimes in irreparable ways.

Many years ago, when I was doing my internship, there was a case presentation in the hospital I was working. One of the senior psychologists was consulting about a very difficult case with a patient who had called that very same morning with the intention of committing suicide. The consultation went for about one hour, the psychologist was extremely worried, and I remembered thinking why she was here talking to us, instead of being with her patient. Although I could not formulate this idea then, in retrospect, I think that this was an example of a dissociative process in the psychologist mind.

Dissociation as a mental phenomenon is a mechanism that describes the disruptions and splitting of the mind. Since the beginning of psychoanalysis, there was interest in this phenomenon of the mind. Janet was the first theoretician that placed dissociation as central to his theory, and linked between trauma and dissociation, describing phenomena which are known today as PTSD. (1907). Freud wrote of dissociation as a splitting of consciousness (1894), as a kind of repression, as a split between the ego and the super ego, (1917) and as a split of the ego (1927). His conceptualization of dissociation is basically one of defensive function within the self. Ferenczi described how psychic trauma causes a split in the mind (1949), and Fairbairn who assumed that the psyche is originally whole, based his theory around splitting and internalization in order to survive attachments with intolerably frustrating objects. (1943).

Sullivan, an interpersonalist developed his theory based on anxiety, trauma and dissociation. In his model of the self, dissociation was central, but as a defense from traumatic events (1953).

In Contemporary Psychoanalysis, Philip Bromberg has articulated a model of dissociation and multiple self-states. He writes about the "dissociative structure of the human mind" (1998- p.8). According to Bromberg, dissociative processes are central in the human mind and are the underlying condition of all personality disorders (1995). He writes: " *The concept of personality "disorder" might be usefully defined as the characterological outcome of the inordinate use of dissociation, and that independent of type (narcissistic, schizoid, borderline, paranoid, etc.), it constitutes a personality structure organized as a proactive, defensive response to the potential repetition of childhood trauma*" (1995) p200.

According to Bromberg, personality growth in treatment is an "*interpersonal process of broadening a patient's perceptual range of reality within a relational field, so that the transformation from dissociation to analyzable intrapsychic conflict is able to take place"* (1998 p.8)

At the beginning of her comprehensive book about dissociation Elizabeth Howell (2005) contends that "dissociation pervades psychic life, and the capacity for it is built into our DNA" (p.vii) and it helps different parts of the self "know" different things. Stern (1997) contends that the reason for not knowing has to do with a kind of refusal to formulate the "unknown-known" experience, due to anxiety or past traumatic events. This is the reason of the importance of helping the patient to formulate his experiences in the analytical situation.

Both analysts and patients have different self-states, partly dissociated, which they encounter in the analytic situation, mainly through enactments of past relationships. The ability of the analyst to hold the different self-states of the patient, as well as to reflect upon his own dissociated states and to transform them in words promotes growth.

Clinical Vignette 1.

Hanna started treatment after a painful divorce from her husband to whom she had been married for 10 years. Although she still cared for him, she felt that she could not go on living with him. They had 2 small children. During the first month she talked about the divorce, her concern for the children, but in spite of the fact that she seemed to be talking about important matters, I could not have a clear idea of what she wanted to gain from treatment. She talked in a very low and monotonous voice, she sat at the border of the armchair, conveying something between wanting to get closer, fear of not being heard, and getting ready to leave at any moment.

I found myself becoming sleepy, bored and slightly impatient. I did not say much, but once in a while I asked questions about her relationship with her husband, trying to understand why she had decided to end the marriage. I noticed that when looking in my appointment book I felt somewhat surprised that I had a session with her, and for some seconds, I could not remember who she was. I attributed this state of affairs to the fact that she was a new and unobtrusive patient. Then, after months of treatment, nothing much had changed, and one day after the patient before her cancelled, I booked an appointment at the hairdresser and I forgot the appointment (it was the last hour of the day). At the hairdresser I got a phone call from Hanna, asking me whether she "had the wrong hour", because she had come and I was not there" Had we changed the hour? Was something wrong with me?" I was so embarrassed that her existence had slipped my mind, that I felt tempted to tell her about an emergency or something of the sort, but I resisted the temptation, and told her that I had forgot our session, and suggested an alternative, which she immediately accepted.

At this session she came on time, and talked about how worried she was when she had arrived and I did not answer, she thought that "something terrible has happened". She gave no signs of being upset or angry with me. I told her that indeed something terrible had happened, that I had forgotten her session, and I was surprised that she did not seemed to be angry with me. She smiled, and told me "I am used to it". During the next sessions, and for a long time in the treatment (who eventually became an analysis) we talked about her being used to be forgotten. It transpired that her husband was a very busy person, and he always seemed to forget what she asked for, and once he forgot to pick one of the children from nursery school when she asked him to do so, because she had an appointment to the doctor.

I realized that we had become entangled in this enactment, through which I had enacted the role of disinterested and forgetful mother, a mother who erases her daughter's existence and who was not particularly interested in this compliant, "good" little girl, who was so very accommodating. The working through of these unformulated experiences, was helpful for Hanna who began to be more "present" in the sessions and in life.

The part of me which did not want to think about my "erasing her existence" from my mind, due to embarrassment and guilt, was responsible for this enactment, and only when I could think about this, it was possible to talk with her about this experience.

Clinical Vignette 2

Sara came to analysis 5 years ago. She was very depressed and agitated after being abandoned by her former husband, who announced abruptly that he was leaving her after many years of marriage. He told her "he could not stand any longer being married with her". She is a very wounded and difficult patient, and this is a very long and stormy analysis, with many breaks, disruptions caused mainly by Sara's poor state of health, which sometimes prevents her from arriving to the sessions. At these times, we have had some periods of phone conversations. It is not the place of this paper to expand on the whole process and I will focus on events that have taken place the last two years, and that relate mainly on issues of our disrupted minds. These last years, after "accepting me as her analyst" (a process that took a long time, and was characterized by her profound terror of making me angry and "dropping" her like her former husband), she became very dependent, and gave the feeling that she could not do nor decide anything for herself. Most of the sessions were filled with questions about "what to do" and "where to find". For example, if she wanted to find a person to take care of her elderly mother, she would ask me how to do this, where to look for such an information. If she wanted to find information about anything at all (such as how much money should she spend on a present, or a pair of shoes or where to find a hotel in a city abroad, etc.), these questions would fill the sessions. It is important to say that she is a very intelligent and educated woman, who has travelled, and is well acquainted with the Internet. I could not understand what was happening, and after a while, I interpreted her wish to become completely dependent on me, so that I would become "her mind". She was very hurt and frightened by this interpretation, since it felt to her as if as I was attributing her with some kind of conscious agency, in other words, she felt blamed and accused of doing it on purpose. She told me that she felt that there was something wrong in her mind, that she kept forgetting things, and she needed me to remind her. In fact she started forgetting appointments with clients in her job, to pay her fees, because she forgot the amount. She forgot many times my phone number, or that she had promised her daughter to babysit for her. She became convinced that she had Alzheimer, and was terrified to go to the doctor to check this out. She started to write me lengthy messages asking me questions about the previous sessions which she did not remember, and blaming me for my insensitivity and abandonment, when I refused to answer these messages, always inviting her to talk about them in our sessions. I had become very irritated by these regressive behaviors, her dependency was very straining and it affected my capacity to hold her in my mind in a positive way. I felt bombarded by her questions, fears, complaints, and accusations. Sometimes I got angry with her, "forgetting" that I was her analyst, and a part of me wanted to get rid of her or to get rid of her in my mind. I wanted to forget her, and she would not let me. A couple of times I lost my patience, when she demanded from me concrete advice on issues that were trivial and inappropriate from a person from her age and education. On these occasions, she would express terrible fears that I would throw her out from the treatment, and she would insist that her mind was completely erased, and she did not have control on her forgetfulness. I felt differently, because I found that she never forgot the hour of our sessions, she never forgot an injury, and when she fought with me she was very sharp and clear minded. After a long time of encounters of this kind, I started feeling that we were stuck, she was becoming more and more regressive, and I began to understand that we had developed a routine that apparently was comfortable for both of us, but that was not helping. I asked myself what it was that we were reenacting, and in what ways I was forgetting my role as an analyst. In fact I was becoming more and more like an impatient mother, who could not tolerate childish behavior, and who wanted to get rid of her impossibly demanding and whining child. Thinking about the strong feelings that Sara evoked in me, aroused my anxiety and guilt, so for a long time, I was not able to formulate my experience, and offer her my thoughts in a way that was helpful and growth promoting. When I was able to reflect on these feelings I found out that they corresponded to the experience that Sara had through all her life of being an unwanted and forgotten child. She remembered early experiences of her mother letting her cry for hours, and saying to her father "don't pay attention to her, forget about her, she is impossible".

It was only when I could formulate my own dissociative experience of wanting to erase her from my mind, of wanted to get rid of her , the movement in the treatment continued, allowing her to confront her fears about something that had already happened in her early childhood. She began to remember early childhood experiences where she had refused to eat what her mother offered, was very obstinate, and her mother had reacted in ways that corresponded to her fears that she was an unwanted child. She began to see the connections between her "forgetfulness" and issues she was scared to think about and as a result, her complaints about losing her mind and her memory diminished.

Summary and Conclusions

In these two vignettes, I have tried to share the ways in which disruptions in the mind of the analyst are expressed through enactments in the relationship between himself and the patient. These enactments are inevitable, they can be short lived or long term experiences and are one of the reasons for a sense of stalemate in the psychoanalytic process. The ability and willingness of the analyst to overcome his anxiety, guilt and shame about these unwanted emotions, and to think about his own dissociative states are important for the progress in analytic treatment, since it enables him to formulate his experience, and therefore give words to the patient's unformulated experiences which have become dissociated. Once the experiences are being put into words, they can become integrated memories.

References

Diamond, D. 2014 http://psychology.usf.edu/faculty/data/ddiamond /baby-sy.pdf

Janet, P. (1907), *The Major Symptoms of Hysteria*. New York: Macmillan

Freud, S. (1894), The Neuropsychoses of Defense. S.E., 3:45-61. London: Hogarth Press,1962

Freud, S (1917), Mourning and Melancholia. S.E., 14:237-258. London: Hogarth Press,1957

Freud, S. (1927), Fetishism. S.E., 21:149-157. London: Hogarth Press,1961

Ferenczi, S. (1949), Confusion of Tongues between the adult and the child. *Internat. J. Psycho-Anal.*,30:225-231

Fairbairn, W.R.D. (1943), The repression and the return of bad objects. In: *Psychoanalytic Studies of the Personality*. Boston: Routledge & Kegan Paul, 1952

Sullivan, H.S. (1953), *The Interpersonal Theory of Psychiatry*. New York: Norton

Bromberg,P. (1995), Psychoanalysis, dissociation and personality organization. In: *Standing in the Spaces: Essays on Clinical Process, Trauma and Dissociation*. Hillsdale, NJ: The Analytic Press, 1998, pp 189-204.

Bromberg, P. (1998) Staying the same while changing: Reflections on Clinical Judgement. In: *Standing in the Spaces: Essays on Clinical Process, Trauma and Dissociation*. Hillsdale, NJ: The Analytic Press, 1998, pp291-308.

Howell E, F. (2005) *The Dissociative Mind*. Routledge. Taylor & Francis Group, New York, London.

Stern, D.B. (1997) Unformulated Experience: *From Dissociation to Imagination in Psychoanalysis*. Hillsdale, NJ: The Analytic Press. .

CHAPTER THIRTEEN

On the edge: The psychoanalyst's countertransference experience

Noga Badanes

To Shmuel,
> *My mentor and teacher who taught me about the mysteries of psychoanalysis and Freud.*
> *For his stimulating thoughts and his valued being over many years.*

"But now, my unknowing is perceived as valuable, as a guarantee for authenticity and subjective truthfulness. This unknowing protects me from futile repetitiveness that does not ask itself what it is attempting to say in each moment and each word... In my internal dialogue with my own knowing and unknowing, I have touched my most internal, personal boundaries. In fact, I have touched the other inside me". S. Erlich, 2001.

"Actually, the term "mind" is in itself objectifying what should better be studied as an "experience"". S. Erlich, 2003.

It is very rare to find in Freud's writings references to what he called "countertransference". Freud saw in countertransference "a result of the analysand's influence on [the physician's] unconscious feelings" and emphasized that "every psychoanalyst only gets as far as his own complexes and inner resistances allow" (Freud, 1910). This had led to the conclusion that analysts should undergo personal analysis.

Freud's psychoanalysis, according to which analyst's gaze is directed first and foremost at his analysand, formed the epistemic core of the classic psychoanalytic model. The derivatives of this model included aspiration to objectivity, neutrality ("blank screen"), lack of actual emotional involvement on the part of the analyst, anonymity, abstinence and a carefully defined setting.

In his advocacy of objectivity (a periodic paradigm that viewed reality as "objective"), Freud (1912) forbade the analyst from feeling any emotions towards his analysands. In the case that emotions did emerge, he advised the analyst to return to personal analysis. Ferenczi (1933), one of Freud's first disciples, was perhaps the first to criticize the image of the analyst as a neutral "blank screen", whose sole role is to offer correct intellectual interpretations. He urged to renounce "professional hypocrisy", expressed in the denial of the "slips" perceived by the analysand, and in the automatic ascribing of analysand's fears or vulnerabilities to his own sensitivity and past traumas. The analyst's willingness to admit his mistakes, Ferenczi believed, will strengthen the analysand's trust in the analyst and create an atmosphere different from the false atmosphere in which – in many cases – he had grown up.

Margaret Little (in Faimberg, 1989) was, too, one of the first to object to this view and argue that the impersonal analyst is a myth, and that countertransference is not only a matter of the analyst's unresolved neurotic conflicts. Paula Heiman went even further, arguing that countertransference is not an exclusive creation of the analysand (even though he plays a significant part in it), but an element connecting to another element, which belongs to the unconscious of the analyst. She interpreted Freud's words as meaning not that the analyst should be cold and distant, but that he should use his emotional reactions as a key for understanding the unconscious of the analysand. The goal of psychoanalysis is not to turn the analyst's mind into a "mechanic mind" that delivers intellectual interpretations, but to allow him to hold and contain the feelings aroused in him by the psychoanalytic session.

It seems that Freud underestimated the importance of the analyst's internal world and sacrificed it on the altar of idealization of his theory. However, in his metapsychological papers, he emphasized over and over again how remarkable it is that the "unconscious of one human being can react upon that of another, without passing through the conscious", that way establishing the only communication that is truly psychoanalytic (Freud, 1915). And in Bion's words: "In every consulting room there ought to be two rather frightened people: the analysand and the psychoanalyst. If they are not, one wonders why they are bothering to find out what everyone knows" (Bion, 1974).

In his 1923 paper, Freud developed the idea of the unconscious and discussed memories that were never repressed, or prehistorical (phylogenetic) traumas that cannot be known by the conscious mind. Knowing is possible only though their connecting to representations (memory traces) so that they can be integrated in representation networks. In other words, Freud related to certain forces that reside as a foreign body, with no shape, content or representation and surely no memory, which can be expressed through repetition compulsion, acting out, hallucination or intense affective experience. Along the same line, dream can not only constitute the return of the repressed but also the expression of materials that were never represented to begin with, materials that were poured out despite the "dream's navel, the spot where it reaches down into the unknown .any definite endings; bound to branch out in every direction into the intricate network of our world of thought" Freud 1900.

How does one come in contact with such primary materials that have no mental representation, but are yet active and very influential in mental life? How are they transferred? This is not the case of the revival of early relationships displaced onto the analyst, but a singular revival within the mind of the analyst.

Freud did not develop a method for working with such regressive materials, something that perhaps explains why the "countertransference" concept was marginal in early psychoanalysis. The discussion of this complex term started with the progressive understanding of psychoanalytic practice as a two-person relationship (Laplanche and Pontalis, 1967). In recent years, the legitimate boundaries of the presence of the analyst's internal world are rarely questioned, and it seems that everyone agrees that the analyst can no longer remain "suffocated in artificial caricatures of analytic neutrality" (Bollas, 1987; Casement, 1985; Ogden, 1995).

There is no doubt that the starting point for attempting to understand the stories that are told in myriad different forms began with Freud's constitutive discovery of transference.

Later, many terms were proposed in the attempt to capture intersubjective processes pertaining to the psychoanalytic dialogue, that is, the transference-countertransference interaction: "projection", "introjection", "projective identification", "containment", "reverie" (a state of absent-minded daydreaming, a term borrowed by Bion and in its Latin origin meaning also wild conduct, madness), "container-contained relationship" (Bion, 1959), "intuitive perception of evolution", "empathy", "vicarious introspection", "the analytic third" (Ogden, 1994), "role responsiveness" (Sandler, 1976), "intergenerational transmission" and "radioactive transmission" (Gampel, 2010), terms that became our working tools.

In this paper, I engage in the studying of the mental activity of the analyst, that is, his countertransference work. I am particularly interested here in a specific psychological experience in which the analyst feels himself pushed to an emotional edge that is experienced as going mad (temporary psychosis) or an uncontrollable physical turmoil. In such an experience, an abundant, intolerable affective experience is forced onto the analyst and thus he feels that his own mind is at risk. This unrepresented, meaningless experience occurs closer to his body, to the id (Ogden, 2001; Green, 1975). In its silent force, it activates violence and thus instinctively elicits a desire to get rid of it. The main part of this experience is unconscious and cannot be thought of or represented. Drawing on McDougal (1988), Bion (1967), Ogden (1994), Botella & Botella (2013) and others, I will argue that the ability of the analyst to tolerate this experience is perhaps the only way to connect to the unrepresented unconscious of the analysand. This connection is in essence part of the analyst's countertransference work, done in his attempt to transform the languages of body and behavior to symbolic language. The analyst offers meaning and makes new intrapersonal and interpersonal connections in an atmosphere of silent, burdening communication that lacks associations (Aisensetein, 2013). During "classical" psychoanalyses, the action of the analyst is focused on listening to free associations and being immersed in reverie, and this allows him to do the work of interpretation and integration. Associations are composed of images and allow for the making of associative connections that are integrated into figurability, the transformation of unconscious to preconscious material and to representation.

Ogden (1994) described this process as follows: the psychoanalytic process is created by both analyst and analysand, and in it the analysand is not only a subject of analytic exploration but at the same time its initiator, since his self-reflection is vital and essential to the process. Likewise, the analyst cannot simply be a subject who observes the endeavor, since his subjective, countertransference experience is part of the endeavor and is the only possible way of knowing something about the relationship he is attempting to understand. In other words, the analyst and analysand are interdependent, but their relationship is not a symmetrical one! (Since as subjects, they both create and are being created, destroy and are being destroyed... But it is the analyst who is supposed to be receptive, who needs to "digest" the materials, turn them into representations and offer interpretations).

But what is unique about the work with difficult patients, those who had been described by Bion as residing outside the neurotic spectrum? What tools do we, psychoanalysts, have at our disposal for dealing with the psychological phenomena residing outside the spectrum, beyond representation, falling out of time? Contemporary psychoanalysts are preoccupied with these questions.

Often our patients come to us with stories: both explicit, elaborate stories and stories that cannot be told. In fact, people come to therapy with stories that they themselves are not aware of. They tell them through their actions, through symptoms, body and dreams, but mainly, they communicate their story through the experience they arouse in their therapist, including identifications, anxieties, and bizarre affects. The intensity and specificity of these experiences, even when they are not yet known, is felt very distinguishingly despite the absence of verbal symbolization (representation)!

McDougal (1978) described it beautifully: "we were faced with a screen-discourse, impregnated with messages that have never been elaborated verbally, and that can in the first instance, only be captured by the arousal of countertransference affect".

Bion did not emphasize countertransference as a term in itself, but he compared the mother-infant relationship to the analytic relationship in what he called "container-contained interaction" and assigned it a central role in mental development. According to Bion (1962), the personality is composed of two components: container and contained. This is a dynamic state, in which the contained seeks a container and the two engage in relationships of varying nature (commensal, symbiotic, and parasitic). Bion emphasized that affective experiences are dreamt in an intersubjective field, when every occurrence that takes place in one of its members is echoed in the dyadic relationship. In this state, echoing which like dreaming and thinking is an almost autonomous action, creates and continues the relationship between two people. The work required of the analyst is impossible, since only the intuition – which is unconscious, by nature – is what allows perception of the emotional reality of both analysand and analyst. This intuition yields and creates a special memory that Bion called evolution-development, a memory bursting from the darkness and formlessness. It has a dreamlike quality that feels whole and intensely real, yet is elusive. Bion (1967) emphasized the hard work required of the analyst to be capable of working with this unconscious intuition, which is usually hidden behind desire and memory that constitute our everyday practice, but are obstructing and distorting the attentive capacity necessary for doing psychoanalytic work.

The countertransference experience when working with regressive patients elicits an experience so intense that it may reach the point of derealization. Words lose their power and the analyst finds himself in a terrifying, unrepresentable, nightmare-like void. This can be a disintegrating experience for the analyst, who defends against it through denial or offering of ineffective interpretations (saturated with desire and memory). The assumption is that the countertransference work of the analyst allows him to remain for a longer period of time in a state of unknowing, and from inside that state, to attempt to make a certain perception and bring it to the sphere of representation, thinking and words. Thus, our work with severe conditions, in which associations are notably absent because there are is no representation nor regression, is constituted in our ability to feel the anxiety and affects that perhaps communicate an early trauma that was never registered in the analysand's chain of representations.

It was not registered because it was never repressed. These are perhaps prenatal traumatic intrusions of unrepresented parental scenes that were registered with debilitating urgency or aroused such a terrifying sensory fantasy that the individual was not able to defend against it and created a void so distressing that it must be concealed by compulsive actions, which are evidence of something living that wants to emerge and seeks a durable container.[1]

Such extreme circumstances can lead to a regression in the analyst, which is similar to dream work or to a hallucination that for a moment may even seem understandable, connecting affects that were perceived and transferred by the patient in the analytic encounter. Thus, the analyst can integrate the different levels of experience to form a new representation, one that did not exist until then (Botella, 2014), and try to create psychological continuity.

Countertransference work, thus, is driven by the effort to connect to what is beyond language, which had collapsed into a nonverbal phase; it is an attempt to try to formulate verbally the nameless dread that does not converge into meaning. It acts through one's willingness not to know, to experience regressive madness and revive stagnant, blocked, unrepresented areas (Botella & Botella, 2013). Its purpose is to push towards a meeting of minds, to connect to our minds and to those of our patients (Klein said that countertransference is the best of servants but the worst of masters), and through the human-mental connection to allow for representation, transformation and change to occur. The goal is to transform what was before a series of cruel, inhuman psychological and bodily events, that were experienced lonelily and could not be expressed or thought about, into something human (Ogden, 1994).

---

[1] In 1925, Freud wrote on the mystic writing-pad, in which notes of an external origin can be written on its receptive surface and be erased while at the same time storing memory traces in the unconscious, thus clearing space for new stimuli. Drawing on this metaphor, could it be that difficult situations (intergenerational traumas, massive projections) leave their marks on the upper layer of the mind, without the "protective shield" of the erasing mental apparatus, the one that is supposed to lift the "wax paper" and protect one from "tearing" and "crumpling" stimuli? This process, perhaps, leaves the mind with strange, threatening, undigested remainders.

Clinical illustration

Years have passed since those first two sessions with Ziv, two meaningful, strange sessions that took place two weeks apart. Those two sessions had left me wondering what had happened in the first session that had led to the second session and to the beginning of a long analysis.

What had happened in those two sessions, of which I remembered an 'uncanny' experience that persisted throughout the years that followed?

When I tried to think of countertransference experiences, a memory of these sessions emerged in me, like a dream calling for associations, arousing in me curiosity and desire to know more about the process of working in and with countertransference, from the first analytic sessions onward.

Ziv was in her thirties when she had made an appointment with me, to see if I was worthy of being her analyst.

It is not an unusual request in our practice, but in this case it emerged surprisingly, only in the second half of the first session. When we had spoken on the phone, she had told me, or at least I thought that she had told me (as I'm writing, I'm already experiencing some uncertainty as to what had really happened) that she wanted to begin psychotherapy and most likely convert to psychoanalysis in the future.

Ziv was a boyish, slender woman, her beautiful young face hidden behind long, soft, curly hair that was revealed as she gracefully shook her head in obvious awareness of her beauty. In my notebook, I wrote: "a Madonna-like face that combined confusing contradictions: was she a young woman or a girl, a tomboy or seductress? Was she fragile or powerful, hard-natured or soft?"

Ziv sought therapy because of what she had described as anxiety and despair concerning her motherhood and interpersonal relationships. She said that she has to mature and grow, become capable of taking responsibility, if only for the sake of her children – even though she wishes she could stay a little girl. She spoke fluently and decisively and focused on her goal and on the central conflict of her life.

I remember myself listening with much interest, feeling that the way she had been talking was evasive, perhaps even concealing, but at the same time, it was also flowing and free. I thought that this first session anticipated a curious journey into the uncertainty of Ziv's unconscious life, as well as my own.

After talking for about twenty or thirty minutes, she mentioned haphazardly that she had come to "check me out", to see if she likes me, and that in fact she was "shopping for therapists" and when she is done, she would let me know her decision.

My heart skipped a beat! My reaction made me realize that something unusual was going on, something that was beyond the content of looking for a decent therapist.

I felt a mixture of somatic-sensory experiences that made thinking difficult. My feelings shifted between vertigo, helplessness, anger, rejection, feeling deceived, fear – and I felt humiliated. I could not transform any of these feelings into words. Her mentioning of shopping aroused in me a desire to be chosen, immediately followed by a desire not to choose Ziv, to get rid of her. I felt the frustrating aspect of the desire that was aroused in me following Ziv's request, which immediately attacked my inner ability to relate (Bion, 1967).

What was I supposed to do for her to want me and choose me? Is there a death wish present in our first session, even before the analysis is born, even before the baby is born, even before pregnancy? All my efforts to reflect on what I had felt seemed to me rather limited.

For a moment, violence and muteness were intertwined and interlocked. I found myself struggling to think, to find some sort of transition from this overwhelming feeling to a form of thinking that will be able to collect, digest and interpret something particular and minor, appropriate for this experience that had occurred in our first session, that could very well be our last. The attempt to think of the "correct interpretation" was in itself indicative of my persecutory experience.

Was it an exchange between action and remembering? Were they random expressions of unconscious identifications? What should I relate to? What should I interpret? Or, perhaps, I should not interpret at all just yet?

In **"On 'wild analysis'"**, Freud (1910) wrote: "Since, however, psychoanalysis cannot dispense with giving this information, it lays down that this shall not be done before two conditions have been fulfilled. First, the analysand must, through preparation, himself have reached the neighborhood of what he has repressed, and secondly, he must have formed a sufficient attachment (transference) to the physician for his emotional relationship to him to make a fresh flight impossible. Psycho-analytic intervention, therefore, absolutely requires a **fairly long period of contact** with the analysand. Attempts to rush him **at first consultation**… mostly bring their own punishment by inspiring a hearty enmity towards the physician on the analysand's part and cutting him off from having any further influence".

Ziv resumed her fluent speech and seemed unaware of how shaken I had been. Was this how things were transferred to Ziv, was she a passive recipient? I found myself hearing only the music of her words, a far echo of her presence, as I was struggling over a piece of emerging intuition, over some sort of sanity…. struggling to connect. And then I thought that through this shaking experience, Ziv communicated to me something that her fluent speech masked. This way, she managed to communicate silent psychic terror, ultimate psychological pain, a feeling of falling into an erotic, death-ridden psychological darkness.

Ziv continued talking and after a few minutes that felt like forever to me, I chose to interrupt her speech. (In my work, I only rarely interrupt a flow of associations).

I interrupted her and interpreted that she did not need to go on telling me about herself and her life story. I said that she was letting me know how frightened she was that I would not be able to hold her and survive the life and death terror that she feels inside, how terri-fied she is of being rejected, and thus she feels that she must choose well and is so afraid of making a mistake.

And I added – **that until she decides, I advise her to take care of herself… and to protect herself from me, also.**

This was the first silence in our first session.

The session ended rather peacefully, and as she left, she promised that she would let me know her decision soon.

Thoughts

Did I actually choose to interpret? Or perhaps I was pushed (in counter acting out) to interrupt her fluent speech because I felt that I was getting "too comfortable" with her verbalism, that had felt like an anesthetic, like I could spend the time we had left with what seemed to me as empty words filling an empty space. Her speech felt like words that were not said by a person speaking to a person, but as if they were said by no one speaking to no one, perhaps not even to herself, and thus, I wanted to get rid of my intense, bothersome countertransference affects, which threatened my own sanity.

I interrupted her because there was something troubling in the way she expressed herself, in her projections and manic-omnipotent thoughts about decision making. I thought that if I had not interrupted her and interpreted, I would have risked "dropping" her and reenacting something that I have not yet learned about her. I felt the seductive-orgastic quality of her surrender, which stood in contrast with my shaking traumatic experience. Only in retrospect, I could understand this as a terrible trauma, that as Winnicott (1963) had assumed, was never forgotten but could not be remembered. There were tremendous longing and fear of passive-masochistic surrender to me, that is, to her mother figure: a mother who suffered from psychotic depression that made her leave home for long periods of time, even before Ziv was born. Ziv was a baby that had had to separate from her mother prematurely, separation that felt like eternity and that left in her confusion between self and object and a desperate need to project the unbearable, undifferentiated fear. This was a terrible fear of a mother that perhaps wanted her dead (unconscious maternal projection) even before she was born. The occurrences of the first session were the cacophonic noise of her repressed internal objects and voices, traces of a murderous, depressed, manic mother interweaved with traces of a crying, tormented baby (secondary fragmentation; Bion, 1967); an inseparable and yet split dyad, fighting for life and death.

It seems to me that this drama was inserted and condensed into me in the first session (Condensation of generations; Faimberg, 2005). It seemed to me that pain or terror that were buried deep inside her as an ambiguous unexperienced, unrepresented experience and therefore could only be communicated through activating in me contradictory, condensed uncanny sensations and images, helplessness and sadistic omnipotence.

I chose to interpret and formulate the one experience that had been clear to me in that moment.

After my interpretation, the fluent speech stopped and turned into a heavy silence that perhaps contained what she had tried to push away (Abjection? Kristeva, 1980). And so, I waited.

Did my interpretation mark a stopping point, driven by my counter-transference, when I had felt that my anxiety, and perhaps hers as well, was unbearable? When had I felt an experience that was impossible, that had no sense, that was unrepresentable in the human mind?

I wondered whether in my interpretation I acted out the fantasy of the ideal analyst (an analyst who can grasp the actual experience and who possesses the most accurate intuition and interpretative ability, which captures a truth that underlies the symptom or is found below the surface) – a fantasy shared by both Ziv and I. I suppose that I, too, had experienced the emergence of a grandiose, manic-omnipotent fantasy.

Since I had already realized that the theme of our first session had been the question of my appointment to the role of **the** analyst, we were both trapped in a dramatic caesura that involved the potential for either an abrupt termination or, perhaps, continuation.

Thought in retrospect: This momentary experience of insight or discovery elicits in the analyst excitement and even a sense of accomplishment but in fact, sometimes, the moment he comes up with an interpretation, he loses his confidence in it. Doubt, guilt and other feelings (pertaining to Klein's depressive position) emerge and form an inseparable part of the experience. The sense of confidence in one's hypothesis and its undermining both constitute an inseparable part of interpretative psychoanalytic work. The moment one comes up with an interpretation is the very same moment that relinquishes the possibility of absolute knowing. Then, the listening to the patient's reaction to one's interpretation becomes crucial, and in Ziv's case, it was all the more crucial!

Only if these conditions are fulfilled, one can recognize the resistances that had led to repression and unknowing, and then gain control over these processes.

A week later, Ziv informed me that she had chosen me, and we scheduled a second session, after which she started – or to put it more accurately – we continued her psychoanalysis.

My thoughts after Ziv's phone call

The discovery that I was the "chosen analyst" aroused in me contradictory, colliding affects: on the one hand, narcissistic relief, and on the other hand, fear. The narcissistic relief involved manic feelings of excitement, idealization, victory and grandiosity. The fear involved a sense of suffocation, a feeling of being trapped in a world whose laws I do not know but that involves the temptation for mutual idealization, perhaps as defense against psychotic depression (Meltzer, 1992).

I had associations to selection to life or death, the holocaust, heavy annihilating burden and annihilation anxiety (Klein, 1937).

What was it in the session that had led to her decision? In the second session, Ziv told me with a mischievous smile that had a sadistic quality about it, that she had felt my anxiety, that she liked the smell of the flowers in the vase on my table and added that one of the other 'candidates' was much more accurate than I had been… but somewhat "dry"… and that was why she had chosen me.

I felt how the terror that I had experienced in the first session now turned into a lightheaded manic feeling, some sort of seductive flirtation, into something vivacious. I felt that Ziv was enjoying a sensory pleasure that stood in striking contrast to the "to be or not to be" atmosphere of the first session.

Then, I had the thought that Ziv came, made herself known and disappeared – was it a display of the mother/therapist (a narcissistic, withdrawn, depressed mother who projects into her daughter) she was afraid of surrendering to? Or perhaps a dead mother, who speaks a "dead" language (accurate language, with agreed symbols but no connection to what it symbolizes, like "dry" psychologistic clichés)? Did her return express her individualized hysterical and deceiving infantile solution, one that tries to disown the suffering? Did she protect herself from a manic-flirtatious intrusion of split objects? Did she choose me intuitively, hoping that I would take her in and keep inside me her destructiveness, or her goodness? There is no self without an object and there is no object without a self.

What is the origin of such condensed transmissions-caesuras (Bion, 1977)? (Intergenerational transmission of inextricably condensed psychological and historical aspects; Faimberg, 2005).

There is no doubt that her explicit desire to be a better mother had been present ever since the first session, expressed in the (M)otherhood (Palgi-Hecker, 2005) drama she had aroused in me.

I interpreted that she had chosen a live (sexual) analyst, who could feel the terrible anxiety she was bearing inside. And I added that anxiety and odors make life vital and that they are better than a depressed, unsexual mother (and baby) that perhaps only "recycles" accurate knowledge retrieved from memory; "recycles" accurate but dry, detached and empty (dead) words.

The content of this interpretation had stayed with us for years:

The intuitiveness with which she had chosen me as a mother who survived her "selection" and aroused in me feelings that I had turned into a thought and an interpretation – that is, the thought that she feels that she must protect herself from unknown destructiveness (and protect herself from me and my interpretations) – instilled in her hope to find a place where she can connect to parts of herself that have been repressed, denied and forgotten, parts that she never knew of but that were nevertheless reenacted in the disturbing situation I had described.

The experience of abandonment by a psychotically depressed mother, disguised by eroticism – which had been relived in the first session – this time aroused something that sparked liveliness.

Ziv lived with a compulsive defense she had developed in an attempt to get rid of her intrusive psychotically depressed mother; unable to "digest" the projections, she either identified with her or clung to her desperately. She had tried to fix her in manic-erotic-obsessive-omnipotent ways that failed every time. The persisting internal maternal object remained active inside her, and any attempt to control it increased its persecutory nature.

This compulsive-claustrophobic cycle was reenacted almost in full in our first session. I survived her, barely, when I responded to what she could not then experience as part of herself. She was a tormented, confused baby, welded together with her object, not knowing what belongs to whom. Was I the possessor of the milk who was supposed to feed the flirtatiously screaming baby or was she a baby who was supposed to feed me, who was depressed and dry; was she a murderer or victim?

I believe that Ziv had felt (in retrospect) that she could communicate something about her mental catastrophe in various ways that Freud (1900) defined as being on the verge of representability, such as dreams, hyper-verbalism, fast and chatty speech, changing ideas, spaces, and mainly in her ability to elicit in me intense countertransference reactions. These reactions communicated an experience of liveliness that had a chance to exist in the room, in contrast to its substitutive structures, such as manic excitement or perverse jouissance that attempted to mask the lack of liveliness (dryness) with which she had come to the first session.

I believe that my ability to feel something of these remnants that had no traces or memory but emerged through a mysterious, stimulating presence (Botella, 2014; Gampel, 2010) were what had allowed her to continue this analysis.

The art of interpretation usually focuses on the practical activity itself and is not inspired by systematic consciousness and awareness (it lacks reflectiveness). However, in psychoanalysis, interpretation becomes an independent objective. Only then, the focus is shifted from a scene of practical activity to the theoretic arena, which is necessarily reflective.

This transition marks the beginning of the systematic work invested in deciphering, analysis and description of the areas of verbal, emotional and semiotic human activity, in which interpretation is implicitly implicated.

The interpretative cycle has a dialectic nature, that is, the interpretation is interpreted by the analysand, who is in turn being interpreted by the analyst. Something unconscious is awakened in the analysand's mind when he listens to an interpretation and in that sense, the first meaning presented by the analyst is later transformed, allowing the opening of unexpected channels, which will reveal a condensed, unconscious identification (Faimberg, 1981).

Years later, the position I had taken in those two sessions turned out to be accurate.

To paraphrase Freud (Constructions in Analysis, 1937), it seems to me that only during the course of the analysis, I could find out whether my interpretation was useful and correct. At the time, I did not see her choosing of me (only) as a confirmation of the correctness of my interpretation, but as an associative reaction to it and to my willingness to let her affect me. I realized that my attitude and willingness to be with her emotionally aroused in Ziv curiosity regarding the meaning of her experience. As such, it presented psychoanalysis as an interpersonal drama that is a focus of authentic exploration, and as an invitation for bringing dramas still unformulated, but that nevertheless arouse simultaneous anxiety and rejoicing. The interpretation communicated that there will be something that will stop the familiar drama (acting in and acting out, in and outside the analysis), which serves as a substitute for unconscious materials, thus allowing her to take the time to be, reflect and connect. In that sense, in retrospect, my interruption was perhaps the important part of the interpretation.

Three years later, it is a Sunday, a particularly rainy winter day (I describe here only the parts that are relevant for the subject of this paper).

Ziv lies down on the couch and tells me a strange dream, in which she has to catch a bus. She is waiting at the central station but every time a bus comes, something strange happens to the ticket. "Every time, the numbers change and then I can't get on the bus. I realize that someone, some guy that has an issue with me, that maybe I hurt some time ago, is responsible for the bus tickets".

And then, silence. Ziv continues, she says that regardless of the dream, she now remembered that she was told that her cousin had cancer, that she is going through chemotherapy and has a good chance of recovering... and that she does not have the energy to call her.

Besides, she keeps hearing a song playing in her head, a song from "The Jungle Book", in which the panther, Mowgli's friend, is singing a dramatic, passionate song: "If you don't have teeth and you don't have claws, you can't live here". Ziv sings the song to me. (In the past, Ziv and I shared special, intimate moments, in which she sang to me songs that she loved and that had meant something to her. Those were special moments of intimacy, admiration and softness. This time, the lyrics of the song reminded me of mothers' lullabies that disguise hate by singing a sweet song such as this one). While singing, she remembers the film "Brother Bear" that she had watched with her son, which is about a little bear who lost his mother. She is enthused by her son, telling me how sweet he had been, that while watching the film, he started crying without understanding why. Is that so?

My feelings shifted between tension and sleepiness, which was strange considering the contents she had presented…And so, I said something somewhat banal. I said that perhaps she felt anxious about losing me during the weekend, that she had wanted to be here and that it felt a little like a nightmare.

Ziv reacted immediately. She said that the dream was a nightmare and that she remembers reading a book about dreams once, and she thinks that it said that a bus symbolizes dependence needs. The person getting on the bus surrenders completely to the bus driver. And she also thought that this guy reminded her of someone she had been seriously involved with. She said that yesterday she had spoken to her sister, who had asked her where I lived, and she had told her that I live in a good neighborhood that has parking. Then, she remembered that the guy in the dream lived in a neighborhood that had no parking and that every time she had come over, she got parking tickets.

I said that she wanted to surrender to me (the bus), but was afraid of someone hurting and punishing her. (I stayed on the oedipal level that masked her fear of surrendering to me, the seducing/abandoning object).

In return, she told me various stories that I cannot remember and then, to my surprise, she said that on Thursday she felt again that she wanted to die. She did not remember how the thought had come to her mind, perhaps it had emerged after the conversation she had had with her cousin, but all she knew was just that she wanted to die.

As I listened to her, I thought about the first sessions and about her desire to find a mother who would offer her a "parking space" inside her. I remembered the terrible fear aroused by the life-or-death selection. Then, I remembered my father, who during World War II was "selected" to stay in hiding and when he returned, there was nothing left of his family. I remembered her omnipotent-manic defense when she had thought that she could make a good choice, that she could disown the nightmare and emotional pain. Consciously, she had told her sister that I have concrete parking, while in her tormented, fragmented internal world, she was hinting that perhaps she would be better off to escape my parking and maintain the (split-off) omnipotent illusion that the parking (surrender) she is longing for is not yet available. The reason for this was that the surrender to me involved a terrible fear from aggressive, murderous motherhood (this was a time of terror attacks on buses in Jerusalem), as well as depressive motherhood of a mother who was not interested in her unborn baby and perhaps even wished her dead. Ziv had a younger brother, who had been abandoned by their depressed mother, and after the mother had left them both, Ziv became his devoted caregiver. The brother died at young age.

But this time, three years later, she was working through these contents with more psychic space, which allowed her to tolerate pain, as well as her destructiveness, desires, angers and perhaps also the beginning of her surrender. These were no longer beta elements through which she emptied herself or that served as internal noise in our aforementioned first session, in which she had acted out of a position of arrogant "therapist shopping", while I had tried to contain the intolerability and interpreted it. Now she had dream thoughts, an indication of unconscious psychological work.

And therefore, after she had talked with me about the "The Jungle Book" song and had shared her associations, I told her:

"When I disappear on you, for a moment, you are not sure whether I had died because you devoured me with your anger, your claws... you discover that you are left all alone and then you want to die, to join me."

She replied: "you know, I had a dream about parking spots once, and I had told the dream to a friend of mine, the one who reminded me of the person who was in charge of the tickets in the dream... he told me that I was trying to figure out whether he has "parking" for me in his heart... I don't know why I had just thought of this, it doesn't connect."

Me: "Perhaps the feeling that you don't have "parking" here over the weekend awakened an old fear of being abandoned, the nightmare of being left alone in terrible dread, with no mother around... and then, maybe you are tempted to stay with the flirtatious ticket man, who is changing numbers, and perhaps seduces with numbers – anything, just not to feel my disappearance, not to feel that maybe it was I who discounted you (the dry mother had been reintroduced into the transference-countertransference space).

Ziv: "In my head, I know for certain that this analysis will end prematurely."

Me: "Why?"

Ziv became very upset. "I'm not thinking rationally, it is just a kind of real internal certainty. For you to stay with me as much as I need in order to grow – it's not even an option! I know it!"

I thought that Ziv was regressing to the magic-omnipotent thinking that perhaps reemerged in the very moment of the encounter with the good object, the moment she had experienced dependence and neediness, which had immediately led to idealization of the bad object and to an attack on the psychoanalysis (Sodre, 2004). When one faces his need for the breast, the ideal solution is the annihilation of the breast one craves, and from there the road is short to envy, persecution and annihilation anxiety. The bad breast-object is a primitive, splitting attempt to hold on to the good (Klein).

I said: "Perhaps it was the terror that had kept you from surrendering and taking the bus, perhaps you did not want to find out what kind of bus-mother-Noga you would encounter: a dead and deadening one, or a reviving, facilitative one..."

(I also thought that she had been scared that the bus-mother could explode, an experience I was familiar with in her analysis, in which death was repaired through erotization and excitement).

She replied: "but my mother was not there. She had never waited for me... she did not want me...". And then, silence.

The session continued. It was raining outside and she said that she did not have an umbrella.

I remembered a similar situation that had occurred during the second analysis I conducted at the psychoanalytic institute, in which I offered the analysand an umbrella. My supervisor, who had been a mother figure to me, said to me in our supervisory session: "Noga, it is sufficient that you be a good enough mother, and not an omnipotent mother who knows what her patient needs. Let him ask you..." I thought whether I had not paid sufficient attention to the good parking (the first signs of positive transference) that Ziv felt she had received here, and that perhaps was the reason she experienced me as rejecting her?

So, I asked Ziv **if this was her way of asking me for an umbrella that would protect her**. "Do you have a spare one?", she asked with a calm smile.

Thoughts

The analytic space involves several simultaneous dimensions. Countertransference work occurs in all of them, between the words, feelings, speech rhythms, spaces, silence, stories, dreams and associations of the analysand, and the reactions, internal work, associations, physical sensations, recurring thoughts, daydreams, emerging theoretical models of the analyst.

The analysand's unconscious recognition of our internal space as necessary for the analysis of the transference allows him to use us in this form of relating and knowing. I use the term transference to describe a relationship between analyst and analysand that is at the same time a renewed transferal of unconscious contents, the sole purpose of which is to regressively relive and revive the analysand's past, and an attempt to give the analysand an emotional experience that contains the early unmentalized memories and gives meaning to somatic or unrepresented experiences that cause the analysand much suffering.

In such moments, when the analyst knows something about the oc-currences inside him, when he has his internal reflective processes at his disposal, even if only in hindsight, then the integration between the internal life of the analysand that is forced onto the analyst, and analyst's own new experiences undergo subjectivization (Erlich, 2003). Then, interpretative work becomes the **returning** of something that was silenced and/or annihilated and/or was never represented. The capacity of the analyst to tolerate disintegrated thoughts and unrepresented experiences during a physical and emotional turmoil is crucial for the potential to transform the analysand presentations into representations – into interpretations that offer and provide meaning.[2]

This means that the analyst should get lost in the world of the analysand, which is condensed into him, arousing chaos; that is, he needs to be in a condition of not knowing what his affects and internal experiences are in any given moment. But he also needs to know for certain that their remembering and storage for the sake of future under-standing will allow the analysand to experience his different voices in the transference.

When the analysand feels that his analyst is emotionally reserved, even if only in his attempt to listen attentively to what the analysand is saying or to reach a better understanding of his life story – this can

---

[2] In my second session with Ziv, I had felt myself struggling with two acute questions: the first had been what I was supposed to <u>do</u>; the second was what I was supposed to <u>know</u> and that I could not think. It seems to me that these two questions contain two working modes that occur during the psychoanalytic process and that were pointed out by Freud already in 'The Interpretation of Dreams'. The first question concerns the process of <u>presentation</u> of the unconscious, while the second refers to representation, the issue of how unconscious ideas are represented and transferred. Both modes occur simultaneously during the analytic session and depend on the analyst's ability to engage in countertransference work. The first mode involves concealed pressure and elicits intense affects, nameless dread and claustrophobic sensation. Reactions of this sort usually arouse in the analyst a need to act, and so I had asked – what do I do. My second question resulted from a difficult feeling of losing my mind, an attack on my ability to think the emotions that had arisen in me. It was as if I had felt qualities that were on the verge of my ability to represent them, qualities that I perceived as all that was left of Ziv's unconscious experience: <u>unrepresented</u> experience.

interrupt the transference experience and keep a significant, and perhaps one-time occurrence from happening.

Concluding thoughts

The questions that had preoccupied me and that are at the heart of our work as psychoanalysts are: how do we listen to, hear and follow the living materials that are nevertheless unrepresented, and perhaps disowned by the forcing of external or internal worlds? How do we listen to our own internal mental processes?

One cannot predefine what might constitute a good interpretation. The interpretation does not express a priori knowledge meant to force itself or get something from the analysand (exaggerated, saturated narrative).

A partial answer is found in the ability to sustain an internal dialogue with our knowing and unknowing, to try to accept the other's influence, to host the stranger residing inside and outside ourselves, to let ourselves be led by him while at the same time leading him, to issue an invitation for a joint exploration even at moments of meaningless, unrepresentable experience, to stimulate an infinite process of finding and inventing, of infinite mental experience (Erlich, 2003).

References

Aisenstein, M. (2013). Drive, representation, and the demands of representation. (175-189) in: *Unpresented States and the Construction of Meaning* by ed: H.B Levine, G. S. Reed & D Scarfone Karnac London

Bion, W.R. (1967). On hallucination. in: *Second Thoughts*, Jason Aronson

Bion, W R. (1974). *Brazillan lectures*. Rio de Janerio, Imago

Botella. C. (2014). On remembering: The notion of memory without recollection. *Int. J. Psycho- Anal.* 95: 911-936

Botella C&Botella S (2013). Psychic figurability and unpresented states. In: *Unrepresented states and the construction of meaning* by ed: H.B Levine, G.S Reed & S. Scarfone. Karnac Books London

Casement, P. (1985). *On learning from the patient.* London, Tavistock

Erlich, S. H. (2001). Otherness, Boundaries and Dialogue – Reflections. In: Deutch, H. & Ben- Sasson, M. (ed.*) The Other, Between Man and Himself , Between Man and his Fellow Man.* Yedioth Ahronoth Books, Israel.

Erlich, S.H. (2003). Experience. *Int. J. Psycho-Anal.* 84, 1125-1147

Freud, S. (1900). The Interpretations of Dreams. S.E., 4,5: London: Hogarth

Freud, S. (1910). The Future Prospects of Psycho –Analytic Therapy. S.E., 11: 139-152: London: Hogarth

Freud, S. (1910). Wild Analysis. S.E., 11: 219-228: London: Hogarth

Freud, S. (1915). The Unconscious. S.E., 14: 159-215: London: Hogarth

Faimberg, H. (2005). The Telescoping of Generations: A Genealogy of Alienated Identifications (1981-5) in: *The Telescoping of Generations,* Routledge London

Faimberg, H. (2005). The Countertransference Position and the Countertransference, (1989) in *The Telescoping of Generations.* Routledge London

Green, A. (1975). The analyst, symbolization and absence in the analytic setting. in: *On Private Madness.* Karnac

Heiman, P. (1950) On counter- transference. *International J. of psychoanalysis* 31: 81-84

Meltzer, D. (1992) Life in the Claustrum. in: *The Claustrum.* The Clunie Press, Perthshire

McDougall, J. (1978) Countertransference and Primitive Communication. 247-299 in: *Plea for a Measure of Abnormality.* Free Association London

Ogden, T. (1994) The analytic third: Working with intersubjective clinical facts. in: *On not being able to Dream. Essays,* 1994- 2005 Jason Aronson

Palgi-Haker, A. (2005) *From Motherhood to (M)otherhood.* Am Oved Israel

Sodre, I. (2004). Who's who? Notes on pathological identifications, in: Spillius, E. and O'Shaughnessy, E. (ed) *Projective Identification the Fate of a Concept,* London: Routledge

Segal, H. (1993). Countertransference. In Alexandris, A., Vaslamatzis, G. (ed). *Countertransference: Theory, technique, teaching.* London Karnac

Racher, H. (1953). A Contribution to the Problem of Counter- Transference. *In .of Psychoanalysis* 34: 313- 24

Racher, H (1968). *Transference and Countertransference.* New York, International Universities Press

Winnicott D.W. (1963) The fear of breakdown in: *Psych-Analytic Explorations,* 88-95 ed. Winnicot, C., Shephered, R. & Davis, M. London: Karnac 1989

CHAPTER FOURTEEN

Multi-Two-Dimensional Thinking and the Absence of Nothing in Autistic Patients

Marganit Ofer

Dedication: Two evenings a month, after working hours, at least twenty tired – but persistent – people come together to study Freud at Shmuel's. "Are you coming to Freud tonight?" literally means "are you coming to Shmuel's class? We're studying Freud", but for us, within us, the two have become inseparable.

The group is tired but Shmuel is not. He starts reading and, all at once, translating, elucidating, explaining and elaborating. There is room for questions and associations as well, but there is a lead actor. The roles are clear – a teacher and his students. And then the magic happens and each of us, sitting in our chairs, feels their mind growing.

And my mind, as is apparent in the following paper, has grown in rather unexpected areas and fields. And in the pages of the Standard Edition, with such vitality, with an understanding of complexity through Shmuel's simple words, I find resonance and inspiration for my thinking about autistic children.

My psychoanalytic thinking informs and enriches my work with autistic children and adolescents, but it is also challenged by it. It constitutes an attempt to understand modes of experiencing, being and thinking that are essentially different from the normal course of development.

Psychoanalytic treatment with autistic children mostly relies on Kleinian and neo-Kleinian thinking. These approaches highlight processes of incorporation and expulsion, introjection and projection.

These processes are primarily physical and from the very beginning of life, their mental, interpersonal and intra-psychic aspects emerge and develop. For this reason, interpretations offered in the treatment of autistic children will often entail their physical experience, their profound anxiety and the search for reparation.

In autistic children, one can observe both mental and interpersonal difficulties. In some of my previous papers (Ofer, 2012, Ofer, 2013), I depicted extreme autism as a psychic existence which lack a container; a psychic life in which experience and understanding are devoid of three-dimensionality, in which introjection and projection processes are absent or greatly diminished. Therefore, any understanding of concepts is inevitably binary; right and wrong, good and bad, big and small, Right-side up and upside-down and even inside and outside.[1] These opposites lack both complexity and relativity. Relativity may exist along a single axis – for example, small-medium-big – while preserving the binary structure and adding no complexity. Nevertheless, relativity, in the sense that a certain action may be suitable in one situation or for one person, but unsuitable in another, is absent. Hence the difficulty in problem-solving, in understanding idioms or in symbolization.

The image that emerged in me was a collection of two-dimensional pallets of understanding or knowledge that are wholly unrelated to each other: **multi-two-dimension**.

While I will not elaborate on this, I will offer a brief illustration: Eyal, a young autistic patient, regularly comes to our sessions after eating with his parents at a nearby restaurant. In an attempt to add to his independent functioning, his parents teach him how to get form the restaurant to my office on his own. Just to be sure, they text me, saying that he will be arriving by himself today. It is time to start the session, but Eyal is nowhere in sight. I walk down to the footpath and see him walking briskly. He passes me by and heads to the consultation room. I stop him:

"Hello, Eyal! I see you're coming by yourself today".

"Yes, today I'm walking to the consultation room on my own!"

---

[1] There is a certain understanding of the inside and outside of spaces, of here and there, but little else.

"And who are you going to meet there?"

"You"

"And where am I?"

"Here"

Meeting me on the footpath did not stop him from pursuing his mission of getting to the consultation room.

The image of two-dimensional experience and understanding leaves us with various questions. Physically, even autistic children start incorporating and expelling substances into and from their bodies, as soon as they are born. We may witness certain developmental problems concerning breast-feeding, increased regurgitation, decreased variation in food preferences, avoidance of certain textures – but the child nevertheless eats, digests and eventually excretes. What is, therefore, his physical experience?

In depicting early developmental impairment, psychoanalytic literature describes small containers, perforated containers, a fear of leaking. The image I would like to present is one of having no container at all, a mental state whose experience is not one of leaking out or dissolving, but of having no place to put things – to put presence as well as absence, something as well as nothing. This is a state in which the experience of loss, a prerequisite to growth, is precluded. I am not referring to states in which one can identify an avoidance of feeling the pain, grief or anxiety which both result from and facilitate the process of growth. Such avoidance can be interpreted and worked-through and it is central to psychoanalytic work. I am referring to a state which exhibits an inability to feel nothingness and loss, meaning that one has not the need, the ability or the opportunity to avoid them.

The difference between a 'perforated container' and 'no container' is essential to understanding the psychic and physical experience and the kind of anxiety involved, and must thereby inform the kind of interpretation offered.

In this paper, I would like to discuss two phenomena manifested in the physicality of autistic children. The first is 'hand flapping', a phenomenon listed in the DSM V as a symptom of autism and, like all the other listed symptoms, is both descriptive and unexplained. The second phenomenon is the link between the (problematic) development of language and problems with bowel control. I noticed that when autistic children, even those already weaned from diapers and toilet trained, learned to use language – though irregularly and at a later age – they manifested bowel-related symptoms: constipation, encopresis and lack of control.

Both 'hand flapping' and the relation between language development and bowel control may be viewed as part of normal development. Healthy toddlers can express their excitement, joy and anxiety through physical motion, by clapping their hands or by jittery and fidgety movements, perhaps like a dog wagging its tail. As for the relation between language development and bowel control – these are parallel developmental stages which occur more or less at the same age.

These phenomena confront us with questions about spectrum: 1. The spectrum between normal and pathological; 2. What is broadly known today as the autistic 'spectrum'. Both Tustin and Margaret Mahler recanted their hypothesis that early life entails a stage of 'normal autism' (Tustin, 2008). We know today that autism is neither an 'early developmental dysfunction' nor the beginning of a normal course of development. In my opinion, 'the autistic spectrum' is a similarly broad definition which contributes little to our understanding of the autistic disorder. I will revisit this point later on.

The 'hand flapping' autistic child – is he flapping as an expression of excitement? of anxiety? Many autistic children, mostly after spending years in specially adapted educational institutions, 'testify' that they are excited while 'flapping'. When asked what it is that they are excited about, they answer something like "I am excited about the coming Passover", or the next holiday in line, if they happen to be asked a few days later. These replies are unrelated to whatever happened before the flapping began. It is likewise insufficiently accurate to use the word 'excited' when discussing the flapping. The therapist who is attentive to what is going on in the room will try to say something about anxiety or panic as she understands these at that moment. I often saw such interpretations elicit no resonance in the patient whatsoever. I sometimes conclude that I have misconstrued the anxiety the child is experiencing at that very moment or that I have not phrased it in a way that is compatible with his understanding. However, taking the notion of having no container a step further, this same experience might be described differently. At this point, I resort to Freud, to 'the pleasure principle and the reality principle':

> "[the reality principle] heightened the importance, too, of the sense-organs that are directed towards that external world, and of the consciousness attached to them. [...] A special function was instituted which had periodically to search the external world, in order that its data might be familiar already if an urgent internal need should arise—the function of *attention*. [...] At the same time, probably, a system of *notation* was introduced" (Freud, 1911, p. 220).

In other words: a certain tension is rising; the baby, and later the child and the adult, recognizes this tension as hunger, for example. It will now scan for a solution to this problem: crying, calling out, going to the refrigerator, cooking or ordering a pizza.

When the container is absent, tension rises and is often left undefined; even if it is defined, it is very hard to find a solution for it. Internal sensory causes can be frequently overwhelming and, in addition, they cannot be defined as a need, a problem or a lack and are simply felt as intolerable bodily tension. Even when they are partially defined, the 'solution-scanner' is 'broken' so that one cannot (find an object and) discharge the tension and restore a state of homeostasis. It is at this point that we see flapping, jumping around and even self-injury, as attempts to release, discharge, even hurt the tension.

What is felt is not "nothingness" but "the presence of intolerable bodily tension", which has neither form nor solution. Therefore, in these situations, these children are nothing like a dog wagging its tail but are rather very miserable (Freud, 1911).[2]

---

[2] In 'Formulations on the Two Principles of Mental Functioning', Freud noted that "Restraint upon motor discharge (upon action), which then became necessary, was

The interpretation will involve the same bodily experience of unsolvable tension and the attempt to expel it from the body, alongside the attempt to understand the origin of this tension and any available solutions.[3]

I will now return to the subject of 'language and poop'. When a child learns to speak, he will learn to answer the question "where's the light?" and to name various objects and images. Some of these images are 'like' things that he knows from real life and some will be no more than an image or a toy (such as a dinosaur). He will be able to associate 'bow-wow' with a dog, 'meow' with a cat and 'moo' with a cow, even before visiting a dairy barn. But these are very simple associations. As it develops, language comes to represent 'nothingness'. We speak of that which is not present before us; we tell of what once was, of what we wish he had, of our imaginations and eventually express ideas that are entirely abstract. The development of language is made possible by a certain understanding or experience of nothingness – and it enables us to tolerate it and even replace it.[4]

Klein (Klein, 1930) noted that, in normal development, the capacity to understand, feel and know nothingness is related to the development

---

provided by means of the process of *thinking*, which was developed from the presentation of ideas. Thinking was endowed with characteristics which made it possible for the mental apparatus to tolerate an increased tension of stimulus while the process of discharge was postponed" (221). For the autistic child, the hands flapping is a kind of a thoughtless discharge activity.

[3] In "Beyond the Pleasure Principle", Freud (1920, p. 12-13) depicts anxiety as a defense against a sudden fright, as if saying "Happy is the man that feareth always" (Proverbs, 28, 14). Freud writes: " 'Fright', 'fear' and 'anxiety' are improperly used as synonymous expressions; they are in fact capable of clear distinction in their relation to danger. 'Anxiety' describes a particular state of expecting the danger or preparing for it, even though it may be an unknown one. 'Fear' requires a definite object of which to be afraid. 'Fright', however, is the name we give to the state a person gets into when he has run into danger without being prepared for it; it emphasizes the factor of surprise. I do not believe anxiety can produce a traumatic neurosis. There is something about anxiety that protects its subject against fright and so against fright-neuroses. In this sense, the autistic patient is more frightened than anxious."

[4] A normal one year old, playing in the yard with his grandmother, sees his father arriving. He might say "dadda… mmma", signifying the present parent and the absent one as well.

of language. And vise-versa: as language and the concomitant ability for conceptualization develop, so does one's awareness of nothingness and one's experience of absence. To this I would add that one's awareness of nothingness and absence evokes an anxiety which is regulated and checked by the child's experience with his excretions. This manifests the opposite process: food goes into his mouth and, while inside his body, becomes a presence, a something. This something can be felt, kept, offered to one's parents as a gift. In normal development, as these two processes occur simultaneously, the child uses them to mutually regulate his joys and anxieties. Later on, he will be able to tolerate nothingness through language and thinking.

Vignette – Nathaniel, 'An Almost Normal Child'

Nathaniel came to therapy at the age of five. He has a twin brother and an older adopted sister. In early life, he was diagnosed as autistic, though this diagnosis was eventually overturned. He suffered from verbal and motor dyspraxia, hearing problems and severe ear infections, that were recently resolved through ear tube surgery; he also began suffering from epileptic seizures. He came to therapy shortly after undergoing ear tubes surgery and as his epilepsy medication started taking effect. The chief complaint made by his parents concerned the encopresis which emerged around the same time.

Undergoing ear tubes surgery, gaining control over his epileptic sei-zures and receiving devoted care at an adapted kindergarten recently facilitated an 'outburst' of language. The child I met was already talking. I am surprised by how fast his language is developing; it is growing more and more complex with every session. In our first session, Nathaniel often touches me, rubbing and leaning against me, and it is evident that touch enables his sense of being. He hides inside a large bean-bag, closes himself inside and says: "I'm the baby, now cry real hard because you won't see me ever again". His playing features the kidnapping of babies, but also of my character, Dolly Marganit (a regular at our sessions, for many months). He kills me over and over again, but I never die. He imprisons me, leaving me no way out. I am always there, weak and confined, but forever there and he is always strong. At the same time, he begins a profound, conscious and playful exploration of issues of absence – both with me and outside of therapy. Where are his sister's biological parents? If they took his sister from far away, where were he and his twin brother? Why didn't his sister also get into mommy's tummy? Sometimes he says that she did. How old am I? He tells me how old his grandparents are and he is preoccupied with the question of when people die and who will die first.

I believe that this notion of "what isn't there" was made possible through the development of language. In turn, this notion allowed a more in depth understanding of the very same question – adding to this the possible experience of his 'absence' during an epileptic seizure, his tinnitus and his being acutely limited in establishing the presence of the external world by auditory means – Nathaniel is now turning his attention to issues of nothingness and absence, but these issues overwhelm him. As a defense, he develops encopresis, which offers him the internal feeling of the presence of his feces and at times the presence of their smell surrounding him. In one of our sessions, a certain smell wafted about the room. I ask him about poop and farts. He answers: "It's not me. It's him, your friend from the other room, he's always farting on me!" I think about this person, whom Nathaniel knows about but has no connection to; this person who, one can imagine, is connected to me, when Nathaniel is not in the room; about how it is none other than him, this 'nothing', this 'something that isn't Nathaniel's', this possible object of envy, who is the source of the symptom... This example serves to demonstrate what may be developmentally normal relationship between language and poop, which may be developmentally normal. The development of language is enabled when one can understand and tolerate nothingness. Once language is established, one's understanding of nothingness deepens and becomes overwhelming. Then, encopresis may appear as a testimony to this pain and difficulty, as an attempt to master this pain, before the capacity to contain it is fully developed.

I am hardly the first to hypothesize the relationship between poop and containment. Meltzer notes that one's awareness of the existence of a container is involved with the feeling of feces in one's rectum, rather than with the process of eating (Meltzer, 1975; Weddell, 1975).

As mentioned before, I often encountered these two phenomena in close proximity: a weaned autistic child who starts speaking at a late age and this development is accompanied by the emergence of encopresis, which fades after a while.

I would like to use this phenomenon as a stepping stone in exploring yet another question which involves the absence of a psychic container in autistic children, which leads to two-dimensional thinking, to having 'no place' to put or work-through nothingness, which means that it cannot exist.

This notion has certain implications for the development of thinking in autistic children and adults as well as for the modality of our interpretations in therapy. What I would like to offer is an additional set of images: alongside the child or adult with a 'perforated container' and fears of leaking – a child with no container, who has nowhere and nothing to think with and must shake off his distress, rather than project it. This physical and psychic experience is unknown to us. This brings us back to the issue of the spectrum: is there an autistic spectrum and is there a spectrum ranging between autistic and normal? I would like to suggest a different kind of spectrum: a spectrum concerning the development of the psychic container and its qualities – its size, flexibility, durability, the extent of its perforation, etc. This model offers various images that capture our varying capacities to contain and work through loss, pain and conflict.

However, an 'absent container' is a unique and rare state, with its own attendant psychic and physical experiences. Pain and nothingness are not projected or rejected in an attempt to avoid the experience of pain; **psychic pain or loss are not avoided, they simply do not exist**. This does not mean that these children are happy, on the contrary, in addition to being frustrated, they dwell in a perpetual state of misunderstanding, which is either not experienced or shaken off. As there is nowhere to put 'nothing', there is also nowhere they can put 'something', meaning that joyful experiences fail to 'fill' them and they are constantly preoccupied with accumulating more and more – collections, notes, etc. – but are never full.

Vignette: Nir, An Autistic Adolescent with Two-Dimensional Thinking

Most of this conversation is written down as we speak; at the end of the session, the notes are bound into a book.

Nir: "I was at a graduation party. With David".

(David is his older brother, who came with him to the party because their parents are abroad). Nir's leg is all jittery, shaking off the absence of his parents – he has no idea what to do and where to put this experience.

Me: "Your parents weren't there and David came instead of them".

Nir: "Yes, I want to tell you what happened at the graduation party".

His leg stops bouncing. Nothingness has been shaken off and we are left with something. He will tell me what happened, that is, not his own experience but a list of events that he will also write because that means they 'exist' (are represented?)

Nir: "Ran is not graduating this year and also me not". (Lively autistic movements begin).

Me: "This year is over and then you have one more year and after that you won't be going to school anymore and your parents will find a new place for you".

Nir: "After that I'll go to some hostel".

(Nir visited a classmate who lives in a hostel and has been repeatedly asking to move into that hostel right away ever since. Not living at home evokes no anxiety, no sense of 'future nothingness', no lack or longing. He talked obsessively about his friend's hostel and his exhausted parents explained to him that after finishing school he will move into *some hostel* and that they are looking for one. The phrase 'I'll go to some hostel' plugs the hole of 'no more school' – there is nowhere to put this nothingness, meaning that Nir can neither think it or avoid thinking about it. As we are talking, he writes everything down; he goes over each letter twice so there are no empty spaces and stops listening so as not to create a 'misunderstanding' gap').

Me: "It puts your mind at ease to think that there would be something else after school". (His movements stop).

Nir: "You have permission to write five".

(We are writing books and adding page numbers. He insisted on adding the numbers himself. Once, while writing, I gently asked if I could write the page number. Ever since, whenever I happen to start a new page while writing, he states: 'you have permission to write').

I add the number, speak and write.

Nir: "There's a space in the five. Close it".

Me: "There, I'm closing it".

(There can be no 'nothing' between the different parts of the digit. I realize that he is not anxious about anything leaking or running out through that space; his psychic, graphic and physical experience is that spaces are impossible. Therefore, his autistic movements cause his jaw to lock and his folded fingers tap on his teeth, creating yet another circle).

Nir suffers from very severe autism and has been in therapy with me for many years. He is about to graduate from the educational institute in which he is enrolled and his parents must decide about his future. Because his thinking is two-dimensional, it is difficult for him to keep himself busy or 'full' and needs an external framework that could keep him busy. His two-dimensional thinking means that his judgment is virtually non-existent, so that his employment opportunities are limited. Anxious about his future, his parents make a last-minute decision: after fifteen years of psychoanalytic psychotherapy, they turn to a new attempt, a different 'promise'. The future therapist (who will not be conducting any kind of psychotherapy) stipulated that the current therapy be terminated. To my surprise, the parents follow through and rather hurriedly: I only have a handful of sessions to say goodbye to Nir.

Nir comes in and, as usual, talks about other things that have happened since our previous session. In fact, he is listing them. I tell him that his parents decided that we will not be meeting anymore, because he will start seeing Manny. Nir says: "I won't be coming anymore, I will go to see Manny". "How are you feeling?" I ask. "Good", he says. I say: "It's sad that we won't be meeting anymore". "Ohhh, not good", he replies, starting what he himself calls 'autistic movements' – shaking and tapping his fingers against his teeth. He seems to be in terrible distress, which he is unable to shake off. Nir has an equation in mind: out with Marganit, in with Manny. He is not preoccupied with whether he is happy or sad, with how to imagine Manny, who does not exist yet, or how would 'no Marganit' feel like. He thus has no interest in that bothersome question, 'why?' Everything was fine until we started talking. He is not sad about saying goodbye to Marganit, nor is he glad about seeing Manny. He simply understands that the former has ended and the latter is about to begin. When I mention sadness, he is not sad, but rather rightfully afraid that he gave the wrong answer. On his part, the answer to the question "how are you feeling?"[5] is not reporting or sharing his feelings. The possible answers are 'okay' and 'not okay', but how can he tell which is the right one? If I do not join in to the answer 'everything is okay', he realizes that he gave the wrong response… He is overwhelmed by the tension of not knowing and must shake it off, his leg jittering and trembling.

In the following session, Nir walks in and says:

"The watch has no cover" (The little plastic loop where one inserts the strap is broken) He starts his frantic movements.

"I didn't say everything twice". (He crams the pencil in the space between his fingers)

"The trip was postponed to November" (Many movements)

I notice what is lacking: the part of the watch strap that he calls 'a cover' for some reason, meaning that he is feeling that its surface is exposed; the trip that will not happen anytime soon. All these lacks are shaken off by distressed movements, by persevering repetition, or by

---

[5] Nir often walks up to people and says, "Hello, how are you? How are you feeling?", even though he is indifferent about the answer.

reporting that he 'didn't say everything twice', as his environment often 'rebukes' him for being repetitive. Yet another physical response to lack, to nothingness, is cramming his pencil into the space between his fingers. Recently, Nir has been preoccupied with the little stretch of skin between his fingers. There is a space between the fingers and it fills that space. He notices that there are squares on his skin – not intersecting lines which form squares, as it naturally seems, but squares that are overlain on a surface. That surface is in a space and thus somewhat able to cancel that space. I say: "pretty soon we will stop meeting each other". "I'll still go to see Manny", he replies.

I wonder about his use of the word 'still' – a rare and exceptional word for him. It is seldom featured in his syntax and when it does, it merely plugs certain syntactical sequences, in a way that is unrelated to its conventional meaning. Is he now using its accepted meaning? Could the experience underlying his words be: "despite of what I somehow gather is happening in you and despite of your insistence that I should not erase you and replace you with Manny, despite of the nothingness and the sadness it entails, I will still go to see Manny".

I look at him. I have known him for many years and have grown very attached to him. I have seen his tensions, his dismantling and his relative joy at being able to understand. With senseless laughter that seemed to come from somewhere inside, I saw him indifferent, I saw him miserable, I saw him failing to understand, but now, for the first time, he seemed demented; like a person suffering from dementia.

I believe that not letting the absence of nothingness exist, that my insistence on saying – "nothingness is here! Let's put it right here in the room, let's talk about it" – made him resort to dementia. He seemed to be stupid or crazy, rather than indifferent.

I come to our last session with profound sadness. Nir informs me that he will start seeing Manny after the summer and that he will come visit. His distress movements exhibit intense shaking off. I start crying. I say: "Not meeting means no Marganit, it means no sessions, it means not coming to the office. It feels like a really big tension inside the body and the tension wants to come out, it comes out through the movements. The tension wants to come out, it wants to stop".

He looks at me for a moment. Crying, I say to him: "for you, tension comes out in movements and for me, it comes out in tears".

He stops his movements and says: "I am making autistic movements and you are crying."

In conclusion, we designate a key place for characterizing and understanding physical and psychic movements and their relationship in our work – inside and outside, incorporating and expelling, milk, urine and feces, regurgitation and vomiting, a physical container and a psychic container, introjection and projection. We ourselves are also the outside – the holding outside; the mother holds her baby, therapists hold the setting – containing means using our container to work through and transform. The images are too numerous to mention, from Bion's Container (1962) to Meltzer's Claustrum (1990) and Steiner's Psychic Retreat (1993) and many more. Every image offers us another perspective, another way of understanding the inside and the outside and interplay of material between them.

I would like to offer the notion of having 'no container', as tantamount to two-dimensional thinking. I propose this as a model rather than an example of a particular child. Even the most acute autistic patient eats and voids himself. A person can be very autistic and still speak and remember. This implies that there is a primary container that had either failed to develop for some reason or had become 'glued', like the lungs of premature babies, which may collapse without surfactant, or like intrauterine adhesions that make pregnancy impossible.[6]

Durban (2014) offers the term 'pipelike child': a child for whom psychic material goes in and comes right out. Durban is not necessarily referring to autistic children, but he does mention autism as a possible pathology underlying this 'pipelike' state. I find this to be yet another interesting way of thinking about a state in which introjection does not exist and projection appears like a process of voiding without any target container. Nevertheless, it still implies, as mentioned before, that the utter absence of a container is not possible. Durban elaborates on the psychoanalytic sources on which he

---

[6] Anzieu (1995) depicts a ball that has been deflated and reduces to two-dimensions.

drew in coining this pictorial term. He mentions a Shaman who told him that a good therapist is a 'half-full' therapist: if she is too full, she has no room to admit the other; if she is empty, the admitted material has nothing to latch on to. The surfactant in our lungs works the same way, by keeping lung vesicles from sticking when we exhale. Premature babies lack this substance, which enables vesicles to stay partially open during exhalation, so that oxygen can enter during inhalation.

I find that the 'no container' model offers significant lines of thinking, which help understand experiences that lie beyond the familiar spectrum, **phenomena that are not more or less like us, but are of a different variety**. Something that has nowhere to enter and nowhere to exit to. There is simply no room; there is no room for presence and thus the world never feels full; but there is also no room for nothingness. **Therefore, the experience is not one of avoiding psychic pain – pain simply cannot exist**. Things are not projected into the other but rather regurgitated, shaken off. **Our tendency as therapists to view regurgitation and shaking off as projection is not always accurate**. It is not always an instance of communicative projective identification; sometimes it is uncommunicative and therein lies the tragedy of autism. This understanding offers us a more profound familiarity with the autistic experience. It allows us to take this material upon ourselves **as if** it were given to us and try – while keeping in mind that we are working with a child with two-dimensional understanding – to simplify his distress and offer solutions. On rare occasions, given the secure holding provided by a long and intensive course of therapy, we may try to **offer him pain**.

Psychic growth always involves pain. With all our patients, we are constantly offering ways to tolerate this pain. When we offer pain to the autistic child, we might be offering something that he will experience as alien, that will slide right off his 'Teflon envelope'; but on those rare occasions, when the patient is carefully held and contained, pain will be accepted. Pain may be so great at that moment, that it might resemble the pain caused by a knife trying to separate an inner container that has been glued to itself. When this works, it is quite the optimistic moment.

The diagnosis of autism has been so widespread and supposedly inclusive of vast differences between individual patients, but it ended up negating the differences between people. Today, some adults who have been diagnosed with autism have no desire to be cured. They have sufficient clarity and communication skills to fight for this goal. They describe themselves as 'differently wired', asking that we let them live out their lives without 'fixing' or changing them. Could it be that such 'differently wired' people are not on the same 'spectrum' as autistic patients with two-dimensional thinking?

We know today that normal autism does not exist; but is everything we call autism is truly autism? Is it really a spectrum? Perhaps what had seemed, until recently, as our ability to correct and amend old misunderstandings about the relationship between autism and intellectual disability or the confusion of autism with childhood psychosis is, in fact, a new misunderstanding?

Autism is a severe disorder which is eventually manifest in impaired thinking, judgment and reality-testing (thus, in many ways, autistic thinking is quite similar to Freud's notion of the unconscious).

Contemporary neuroscientists will also argue that the old notion of the connection between autism and childhood psychosis is not an un-politically correct hypothesis but rather a phenomenon that is being substantiated by new evidence from brain imaging. The same holds true for the connection between autism and intellectual disability.

The 'multi-two-dimensional' model takes us back to the extreme nature of this disorder and to its physical and psychic experience. We are required to accept the autistic patient as a different person, rather than an extreme version of a familiar disorder. He is a different human being and if we are able to accept his difference, to see him as he is rather than project our preexisting understanding onto him, we could try and help him with the arduous task of reinstating nothingness as something that can be perceived. We could keep him from bursting with repetitive speech and movement, from being blocked and empty.

When there is nowhere to put nothingness, when it is nowhere, it is nothing and the autistic patient, through his inability to experience nothingness (which is a painful somethingness), may end up living in a world devoid of meaning.

References

Anzieu, D. (1995). *Le Moi-Peau*. Dundo, Paris.

Bion, W.R. (1962). A psychoanalytic study of thinking. *Int. J. Psycho-Anal.* 43:306-310

Durban, J. (2014). Despair and hope: on some varieties of countertransference and enactment in the psychoanalysis of ASD (Autistic Spectrum Disorder) children. *Journal of Child Psychotherapy*, vol. 40, n. 2, 187-200.

Freud, S. (1911). Formulations on the Two Principles of Mental Functioning. S.E., 12: 213-226. London: Hogarth

Freud, S. (1920). Beyond the Pleasure Principle. S.E., 18: 1-64. London: Hogarth

Klein, M. (1930). The importance of symbol-formation in the development of the ego. In: *Love, Guilt and Reparation*, The Free Press, 1975.

Meltzer, D. (1975). Adhesive identification. *Contemp. Psychoanal.*, 11:289-310.

Meltzer, D. (1990). *The Claustrum: An Investigation of Claustrophobic Phenomena*. Karnac Books Ltd..

Ofer, M. (2012). Multi-two-dimension: on autistic thinking. Lecture presented at the psychoanalytic society, December 2012.

Ofer, M. (2013). When the glue does not hold: on adhesive identification, multi-two- dimension, and dismantling. Lecture presented for the publishing event of "The Meltzer Reader" in Hebrew. Bookworm Publishing house.

Steiner, J. (1993). *Psychic Retreats: Pathological Organizations in Psychotic, Neurotic and Borderline Patients*. Karnac Books Ltd.. Tustin, F. (2008). Autistic Barriers in Neurotic Patients. (In epilogue of the Hebrew version, Bookworm, Tel-Aviv, 2008) Weddell, D. (1975). Disturbed geography of the life-space in autism – Barry. In: Meltzer et al. (Eds) *Explorations in Autism*. Clunie Press.

IV. Psychoanalysis and Social Reality

CHAPTER FIFTEEN

Psychoanalysis and Culture[1]

Cláudio Laks Eizirik

1. Introduction

Psychoanalysis is a branch of science developed by Sigmund Freud (1856-1939) and his followers, devoted to the study of human psychology. It is usually considered to have three areas of application: 1.a systematized body of knowledge about human behavior (psychoanalytic theory); 2.a method of investigating the mind; 3. A modality of therapy for emotional illnesses or psychic suffering (psychoanalytic treatment).

Psychoanalysis has as basic principles the notion that our mind is predominantly unconscious and that all our current actions, feelings and thoughts are associated with or derive from previous meaningful experiences, mainly the ones that happened during our childhood. (Moore and Fine, 1990).

The complex relationship between psychoanalysis and culture can be illustrated when we consider that it appeared in the end of XIX century, in Vienna, a cultural milieu in which the "intelligentsia" was developing innovations in many areas simultaneously. The Viennese cultural elite had a rare combination of provincialism and cosmopolitism, tradition and modernity, which produced a sort of cohesion greater than in other cities at that time.

According to many authors (Gay, 1989; Mezan, 1996) Vienna offered a stimulus for the emergence of psychoanalysis, and this consisted

---

[1] A different version was given as a Lecture at Beijing Unuiversity, 2010 and was published in: Psychoanalysis in Asia, ed by Alf Gerlach, Maria teresa Hooke and Sverre Varvin, karnac, 2013.

in the presence of professors such as Brücke and others at the university, in a school system that provided the students with the best of western, especially German, culture, and in the complex relations between Viennese Jews and their environment, characterized by a combination of mutual attraction, hate and contempt. But the decisive element can only be found in Freud's own singularity and in the many influences he suffered throughout his personal and intellectual development. (Perestrello, 1996; Eizirik, 1997).

2. Freud's ideas about culture

Despite the fact that Freud devoted his efforts mainly to develop psychoanalytic theory and treatment, he also reflected on the trends of the culture of his time in several works, in which he also examined the roots of human behavior from a psychoanalytic perspective.

In Totem and Taboo (1913) Freud studied the resemblances between the mental life of savages and neurotics. Among other ideas, he explained that like neurotic, primitive peoples feel ambivalent about most people in their lives, but will not admit this consciously to themselves. They will not admit that as much as they love their mother, or their father, there are things about them they hate. The suppressed parte of this ambivalence (the hate parts) are projected onto others. In the case of natives, the hateful aspects are projected onto the totem, so they can think: I do not want my mother to die, the totem wanted her to die. This ambivalence can also include the relationship of citizens to their ruler or figures of authority. Another important idea of this book is about animism. The animistic mode of thinking is governed by what Freud called the omnipotence of thoughts, a projection of inner mental life onto the external world. This imaginary construction of reality can be seen not only in primitive people but also in neurotic and mainly delusional or psychotic disorders. As we will see this can also be found in religions, as well as in situations in which a social group or nation consider another group or nation as enemy, without any objective evidence.

In The Future of an Illusion (1927) Freud attempts to turn our attention to the future that awaits human culture. By human culture, he means all those areas in which human life has lifted itself above the animal condition and in which it differs from the life of beasts. In this sense, human culture includes, on the one hand, all the knowledge and power that men have accumulated in order to master the forces of nature, and on the other all the necessary arrangements whereby men's relations to each other may be regulated. Freud maintains that the essence of culture lies not in man's conquest of nature for the means of supporting life, but in the psychological realm, in every person's curbing his/her predatory drives. One of the drives restrainers that men has devised to perpetuate culture is religion. Freud defines religion as an illusion, consisting of certain dogmas, assertions about facts and conditions of external and internal reality which tell one something that one has not oneself discovered, and which claim that one should give them credence. Religious concepts are transmitted in three ways and thereby claim our belief: because our primal ancestors already believed them; because we possess proofs which have been handed down to us from antiquity and because it is forbidden to raise the question of their authenticity at all. Psychologically these beliefs present the phenomena of fulfillment of wishes that are the oldest, strongest and most urgent of mankind, among them the necessity to cling to the existence of the father, as the figure of God, the prolongation of earthy existence by a future life and the immortality of human soul.

So, according to Freud's view, religion represents man's helplessness in the world, having to face the ultimate fate of death, the struggles of civilization and the forces of nature. He sees God as a manifestation of a child-like longing for a father, and any sort of God retain a threefold task: they must exorcize the terrors of nature, they must reconcile men to the cruelty of Fate and they must compensate them for the sufferings and privations which a civilized life in common has imposed on them.

That is why Freud suggests that any kind of religion is an illusion and that eventually the scientific thinking would prevail over this kind of magic way of facing men's fears.

We can see today that Freud's analysis of religion was possibly accurate, but his view of the future was too optimistic. The current reality shows that all sorts of religion still prevail in many areas of the world, and that even radical expressions of it, known as fundamentalism, are seen under different names, but retains basically what I just described as an imaginary construction of reality.

In Civilization and Its Discontents (1930), he enumerates the fundamental tensions between civilization and the individual. The primary friction stems from the individual's quest for instinctual freedom and civilization's contrary demand for conformity and instinctual repression. Many of mankind's primitive instincts (for instance, the desire to kill and the insatiable craving for sexual gratification) are clearly harmful to the well-being of a human community. As a result, civilization creates laws that prohibit killing, rape, and adultery, and it implements severe punishments if such rules are broken. This process, argues Freud, is an inherent quality of civilization that instills perpetual feelings of discontent in its citizens. As human beings are governed by the pleasure principle, and this principle is satisfied by the instincts, it is understandable that such a feeling of discontent emerges as well as aggressive feelings towards authoritative figures and towards sexual competitors, which both obstruct the gratification of a person's instincts.

These ideas can be seen nowadays at different levels, for instance in the relation of each one of us with our parents, family, school and the society at large; the great challenge that each one faces is how to obtain a reasonable balance between the pleasure principle- the fulfillment of our unconscious wishes- and the reality principle- what each one can obtain in his/her relations with the others, without producing harm or ignoring the rights of the others.

3. Contemporary psychoanalytic views on culture

Now I will turn to more recent attempts to describe our culture and our globalizing world from a psychoanalytical perspective. Several authors, both analysts and thinkers from other fields have tried to offer insights on our complex and changing world (Eizirik, 2007). I would now like to summarize some of these views.

Van der Leeuw (1980) characterized our Zeitgeist as constituted by (1) a great flood of information, quantification and massive growth that leads to superficiality, hampers independent thinking and is accompanied by a leveling process, as a consequence of which silence, solitude and privacy become endangered, and congestion disturbs man's consciousness of space and the experience of space he needs for his life; (2) changes in the role of family as the basis of society, motherhood being increasingly neglected; (3) the dominant role of seductive advertising, encouraging immediate gratification and creating the illusion that total gratification is possible; (4) the increasing search for excitement, stimulation, brief and often violent explosions of emotions and the urge for rapid recharge, instead of the cultivation of warm, tender feelings, in particular where children are concerned.

From a wider perspective, Lasch (1978) coined for our era the expression "culture of narcissism", resulting from the breakdown of the family and the accentuation of instinctive gratification. As social pressures have invaded the ego, it has become harder to grow up and acquire maturity. This leads to a failure of normal superego development. So in a world dominated by images, individual progress can only come from projected images and erroneous impressions produced by insecure egos. In this world it is difficult to discriminate reality from fantasy, and what we really are from what the products we consume suggest that we are. The "culture of narcissism" has abolished collective discipline and concentrated work, in favor of a world of impressions, appearances and disguises.

Kernberg (1989) explored the nature of the appeal of mass culture, particularly as it is communicated by the mass media. He examined the regressive effects of group processes on the recipients of mass culture, and the striking correspondence between the conventional aspects of mass culture and the psychological characteristics of latency. Among others, he stressed the following trends in contemporary culture: the simultaneity of communication; the illusion of being a member of the crowd connected with a central figure who communicates what is important and what one should think about it; the denial of complexities; the predominance of conventional assumptions over individual thinking; the stimulation of a narcissistic dimension in the receiver, and also a paranoid one, in the form of justified suspicion or indignation; the application of a simplistic morality to social and political matters in the form of clichés (for instance, that good people together will solve problems). In his view, conventionality may be the price of social stability, in spite of the danger of more severe group regression. More recently, Kernberg (1998) described a striking tendency in large groups to project superego functions onto the group as a whole in an effort to prevent violence and protect ego identity by means of a shared ideology.

The postmodern condition, a term coined by Lyotard (1979), has become an essential part of any discussion of our culture. In spite of the controversial acceptance of this concept, several trends in our era are often described as typical of the so-called crisis of the culture. Taking into account several different descriptions of our time, we find references to these trends: complexity, skepticism, challenges to all meta-narratives which were a central part of the project of Enlightenment, acculturation through images in more and more virtual realities, claims to the right to difference and to follow alternative lifestyles, the social demands for participation and for the rights of women, pacifists, homosexuals and other minorities, the growing presence of the so-called pathologies of immediate gratification, the idealization of ambiguity, an era of simultaneity and immediate accomplishment of ideas, wishes and purposes (Arditi, 1988; Baladier, 1995; Castoriadis, 1996; Ahumada, 1997; Eizirik, 1997; Carlisky and Eskenazi, 2000).

In the late 1980s and early 1990s Zygmunt Bauman published a number of books that dealt with the relationship between modernity, bureaucracy, rationality and social exclusion. Bauman, following Freud, came to view European modernity as a trade off; European society, he argued, had agreed to forego a level of freedom in order to receive the benefits of increased individual security. Bauman argued that modernity, in what he later came to term its 'solid' form, involved removing unknowns and uncertainties; it involved control over nature, hierarchical bureaucracy, rules and regulations, control and categorization — all of which attempted to gradually remove personal insecurities, making the chaotic aspects of human life appear well-ordered and familiar. However, Bauman began to develop the position that such order-making efforts never manage to achieve the desired results. When life becomes organized into familiar and manageable categories, he argued, there are always social groups who cannot be administered, who cannot be separated out and controlled. In his book *Modernity and Ambivalence* (1991) Bauman began to theorize such indeterminate persons by introducing the allegorical figure of 'the stranger.' Drawing upon the sociology of Georg Simmel and the philosophy of Jacques Derrida, Bauman came to write of the stranger as the person who is present yet unfamiliar, societies *undecideable*.

In *Modernity and Ambivalence* (1991) Bauman attempted to give an account of the different approaches modern society adopts toward the stranger. He argued that, on the one hand, in a consumer-oriented economy the strange and the unfamiliar are always enticing; in different styles of food, different fashions and in tourism it is possible to experience the allure of what is unfamiliar. Yet this strangeness also has a more negative side. The stranger, because he cannot be controlled and ordered, is always the object of fear; he is the potential mugger, the person outside of society's borders who is constantly threatening. Bauman's book, *Modernity and the Holocaust* (1989) is an attempt to give a full account of the dangers of these kinds of fears. Drawing upon Hannah Arendt and Theodor Adorno's books on totalitarianism and the Enlightenment, Bauman developed the argument that the Holocaust should not simply be considered to be an event in Jewish history, nor a regression to pre-modern barbarism. Rather, he argued, the Holocaust should be seen as deeply connected to modernity and its order-making efforts. Bauman argued that procedural rationality, the division of labor into smaller and smaller tasks, the taxonomic categorization of different species, and the tendency to view rule-following as morally all-good, played their role in the Holocaust coming to pass. And he argued that for this reason modern societies have not fully taken on board the lessons of the Holocaust; it is generally viewed – to use Bauman's metaphor – like a picture hanging on a wall, offering few lessons. In Bauman's analysis the Jews became 'strangers' *par excellence* in Europe; the Final Solution was pictured by him as an extreme example of the attempts made by societies to excise the uncomfortable and indeterminate elements existing within them. Bauman, contended that the same processes of exclusion that were at work in the Holocaust could, and to an extent do, still come into play today.

In the mid and late 1990s Bauman's books began to look at two different but interrelated subjects: postmodernity and consumerism. Bauman began to develop the position that a shift had taken place in modern society in the latter half of the 20th century – it had altered from being a society of producers to a society of *consumers.*

This switch, he argued, reversed Freud's 'modern' trade-off: this time security was given up in order to enjoy increased freedom, freedom to purchase, to consume, and to enjoy life. In his books in the 1990s Bauman wrote of this shift as being a shift from 'modernity' to 'post-modernity'. Since the turn of the millennium, his books have tried to avoid the confusion surrounding the term 'postmodernity' by using the metaphors of 'liquid' and 'solid' modernity (2000) .In his books on modern consumerism Bauman still writes of the same uncertainties that he portrayed in his writings on 'solid' modernity; but in these books he writes of these fears being more diffuse and harder to pin down. Indeed they are, to use the title of one of his books, 'liquid fears' (2005). According to Bauman, at the dawn of the twenty-first century, we live again in a time of fear. Whether it is the fear of natural disasters, the fear of environmental catastrophes or the fear of indiscriminate terrorist attacks, we live today in a state of constant anxiety about the dangers that could strike unannounced and at any moment. Fear is the name we give to our uncertainty in the face of the dangers that characterize our liquid modern age, to our ignorance of what the threat is and our incapacity to determine what can and can't be done to counter it.

This new culture that presents permanent change and complexity, produces increasing perplexity, anxieties, losses of models and values which are felt as a threat to the integrity of the self, and to psychic identity. And yet, at the same time, poses the challenge of learning to live in and to share with the others this brave new world. (Huxley, 1932).

4. And what about each person and his/her identity?

It is widely recognized that an individual's capacity to remain himself during periods of change is fundamental to his sense of identity, which he experiences emotionally. Establishing a sense of identity means maintaining stability in the face of changing circumstances and the successive stages of life cycle. But how much change can an individual tolerate before it works irreparable harm on his identity?

Grinberg and Grinberg (1989) suggested that the establishment of a sense of identity depends most importantly on the internalization of relations with meaningful persons and their assimilation by the ego. The ego assimilates objects by means of authentic introjective identification, not by manic projective identification, which creates false identities and a false self.

In their book on migration and exile, the Grinbergs report that events such as migration, which causes drastic change in a person's life, can pose threats to the sense of identity. Victor Tausk, who introduced the term *identity* in psychoanalytic literature (1919), maintained that just as a child discovers objects and his own self, so an adult in his struggle for self-preservation frequently repeats the experience of "finding himself" and "feeling like himself". The immigrant in his struggle for self-preservation needs to hold onto various elements of his native environment (familiar objects, music, memories, and dreams representing different aspects of his native land) in order to be able to feel like himself.

It is interesting to note that in all his writings, Freud only once used the term *identity* (1926), and he gave it a psychosocial connotation. In a speech in which he tried to explain his connection to Judaism, he spoke of "obscure emotional forces" that were "all the more powerful the less easily articulate they were" and of "the clear consciousness of an *inner identity* based not on race or religion but on an *aptitude common to a group* to live in opposition to and free of the prejudices that undermine the use of the intellect". Thus, Freud refers to something in one's core, one's interior that is crucial to the internal cohesion of a group.

Erikson, commenting on Freud's statement (1956), deduced that the term identity expresses "the relation between an individual and his group", suggesting a certain consistent sameness and shared character traits.

In *Identity and Change* (1971), the Grinbergs introduced the notion that one's sense of identity is born of the continuous interaction among spatial, temporal and social integration links. They have had ample opportunity to study these links as they appear in the patient-analyst relation. What follows is a synthesis of the complex permutations that set the stage for the acquisition of a sense of identity in the psychoanalytic process; from these we may infer the ways in which identity comes to be formed and how its disorders affect individual development, the relation between the individual and society, and, most important, the individual's experiences of change.

One should take into account that a patient generally comes into analysis with conflicts that to some degree affect his sense of identity and his conscious or unconscious motive for seeking analysis is the need to consolidate his sense of identity.

The sense of identity expresses, preconsciously and consciously, a series of unconscious fantasies which, once integrated, constitute what could be called the unconscious fantasy of the self.

The process leading to the acquisition or maturation of one's sense of identity can be developed, in fact, with the psychoanalytic process, for the analytic framework itself provides a "container" to hold and keep within bounds the projections made by "pieces of the self". The container, at the same time, becomes the crucible in which complex operations are performed on these pieces before they can become integrated in a whole.

The Grinbergs use the expression "pieces of the self" as a metaphor describing the unconscious fantasies of certain patients. The fantasies underlie the absence of relationship between various levels of ego repression; the pieces are dissociated parts of the ego, particular roles or identifications with certain objects that function independently of one another, as if they were islands cut off from one another.

Although this image describes the characteristics of diffuse identity, typically schizoid, the container notion is just as applicable to other kinds of identity disorders that afflict patients with clinical neurosis or psychosis.

Another image that helps to illustrate the analytic process and the framework as boundary and container can be found in the notion of the analyst as the arms or, more regressively, the skin that holds together the parts of the baby/patient.

Inspired by the contributions of Melanie Klein and Wilfred Bion, the

Grinbergs suggest that object relations and identification mechanisms at work in the analytic process and manifested in the relationship with the analyst are worthy of attention. The analyst's container function, together with his interpretive role, allows the patient to work through and consolidate his sense of identity. In this process, the patient accepts the infantile parts of the self and detaches from those regressive aspects of the self that block the path to the firm establishment of an adult self.

5. *Psychoanalysis in a globalizing world*

Contemporary clinical practice makes psychoanalysis suitable for different kinds of patients, with varying degrees of psychic suffering or different forms of personality disorders, but also, as has been amply described, presents a specific sort of patient – showing more severe conditions with the growing presence of pathologies of immediate gratification or, as Kristeva (1993) puts it, *the new diseases of the soul*. Living within a culture of narcissism (Lasch, 1978) or of immediacy, or 'liquid modernity' (Bauman, 2000), patients are offered the promise of faster methods, whose effectiveness is proven and guaranteed by the so-called evidence-based psychiatry. Widespread socio-economic crisis and unarguable problems such as that of distances in the urban centres might render it difficult to put to practice the psychoanalytic method in its full scope. Taking into account what was previously described, one can expect that an unavoidable tension might be present in the analytic process or in the analytic field (Baranger and Baranger, 1961) considering that these somehow more stable psychic elements like identity will get in touch with the changing world of our time.

Current patients, living in a globalizing world, might feel it difficult to adapt to the analytic setting, where silence, intimacy and a long joint work through emotions and memories might be seen as strange or old fashioned. Usual analytic procedures like the couch and several sessions a week might also be seen as different to what is more widely publicized about other methods.

Despite the long clinical experience of more than a century and a lot of effectiveness studies that show the strength of the analytic method, one cannot forget that scepticism and challenges to meta-narratives are common trends of our culture.

Ricoeur (1970) mentioned that Freud, Marx and Nietzsche were masters of suspicion, in the sense that they did not accept well established truths.

As I tried to show, several psychoanalytic insights are useful to understand the globalizing world we live in.

But, in any case, there are still questions about what is the relevance of psychoanalysis itself, with all its complexities and requirements in a world dominated by "liquid modernity" (Bauman, 2000), in which human relations seem to be so provisional and very often meaningless? Or in which some recent examples of the demonic power of the compulsion to repeat, so well described by Freud, something that, according to Green (2002) assassinates time, can be found in the different expressions of fundamentalism, as well as in brutal social and economic differences that keep millions of people condemned to famine, diseases and early death; or in which systematic attacks on the environment threaten our shared world? But for the other hand, we can witness new and fascinating possibilities that have changed forever our methods of communication, information systems, science and the humanities and new methods of expression or language are created in the arts, and new meanings are found to symbolize and deepen our understanding of the human mind and body. (Eizirik, 2008).

In this changing world, psychoanalysis responds to change with change. Not only are our different theoretical schools in full development, but we are also more than ever in a position in which we are able to work analytically in closer emotional contact with our patients , as well as more equipped to analyze patients with severe conditions.

We face the main challenges of analytic education acknowledging the existence of different methods of analytic education, and developing studies on how to obtain analytic competence. As for our relation with the outside world, we can see that in each society, country or region new and stimulating initiatives show that, after a period of a sort of "splendid isolation", psychoanalysis is again, as in Freud ´s time, in the forefront of the international struggle for the freedom of critical and independent thinking.

At the same time, as I hope I have shown in this lecture, psychoanalytic ideas are an important instrument to understand the current state of affairs of our culture, and in which ways it affects psychic identity. Among Freud's many contributions to the understanding of the human mind and behavior, I would like particularly to stress again his insights on the continuous internal conflict between love and aggression and the ways this tension produces powerful unconscious mental mechanisms that can lead to different expressions of hatred, violence and war. This internal struggle is significantly influenced by the way early upbringing contributes to fostering aggression or, alternatively, to developing and enhancing the capacity for love and consideration for others.

This means that a lifelong process of mental growth begins with the quality of the mother-child relationship, together with the presence of a father figure (or some equivalent), essential in supporting in the development of the reality principle. The family and the community then holds, stimulates and assists in the capacity for the individual to think independently and to transform primitive feelings into the expression of civilized relations with others.

This process of development of subjectivity needs, ideally, optimum or at least adequate internal and external conditions. When open social structures are lacking, significant damage may occur.

Analytic treatment of victims of the holocaust, dictatorships, situations of abuse or different expressions of violence demonstrates how these traumatic events are psychically integrated and represented. Often there is unresolved mourning and the inability to symbolize. These deficits in mental processes can be and often are passed on across the generations, only to reemerge in subsequent later generations.

The contributions offered by Shmuel Erlich and his co-workers (2009) are wonderful examples of how psychoanalysis can be extremely helpful to individuals and groups in order to face past traumatic situations and to build together new ways of understanding and creating better ways of communication.

An important distinction has been demonstrated between intergenerational and transgenerational psychic transmission. Intergenerational transmission refers to the conscious transmission of mental content and processes such as identification and fantasies, which are organized into family history and inherited by the next generation, resulting in a structuring effect on the mental apparatus. Transgenerational transmission occurs unconsciously and is transmitted to future generations. It involves mental contents which are dissociated and not symbolized through words or stories. Thus primitive and unintegrated affects resulting from trauma, pain and loss are not worked through and are not mastered. This kind of transmission remains encapsulated and acts as a violent intrusion into the individual's sense of self as well as being transmitted to future generations.

When lies and misdemeanors are perceived as sanctioned social values within a culture, for instance the different forms of prejudice manifested through racism, a lack of respect for minorities, women, the elderly and immigrants, this can produce transgenerational transmission. When it is the father figure who provides the lie, it becomes impossible to develop the mental apparatus and the notion of subjectivity and to establish appropriate social values.

The current situation in the world, with areas dominated by grinding poverty, ethnic wars, religious fundamentalism, urban violence and other similar situations, produces trauma and violence which can only contribute to the transmission of more hatred and violence to future generations.

So what do we do to prevent this negative transmission of hatred? In my view, prevention requires urgent action, particularly action directed towards children and their families, where this hateful and violent transmission manifests itself. If left unattended it might eventually produce the terrorist perpetrators of tomorrow. Improving basic conditions of life, health, and education through massive investment in the poor areas of the world is a concrete and essential way of preventing the development of hatred, war and violence.

It is similarly important to address and deal with the massive and destructive trade in arms, and to regulate and contain the worst excesses of market economies in order to encourage mutually respectful and collaborative cultures, which can develop harmoniously and, above all, peacefully towards one another.

Informed by analytic knowledge, we know that establishing ways of reducing social division and the projection of hatred are also important mechanisms for social cohesion. This requires finding ways to implement the difficult task of listening to others, be it the stranger, or even the enemy. It was Freud who discussed how this "stranger" is in fact someone who represents a hidden and unwanted part of ourselves. A good example of listening to the other was recently established at the Baremboim-Said Foundation, where, through music, Israeli and Palestinian children learn how to listen to each other and to play together.

From a psychoanalytic perspective, we understand the need to produce and play new sounds, the sounds that can only be heard when collaborative efforts put together different people with differing values and prejudices in order to build tolerance and new ways of working together.

The psychoanalytic contribution to the prevention of hatred, war and violence thus occurs in two ways. First by treating patients whose psychic transformation will also produce positive changes in their subsequent generations and, and second by taking part in joint activities or initiatives where we can show how much open listening can correct distorted perceptions and increase the ability to tolerate and identify with the others.

This is naturally not an easy task. It is also an intergenerational one. We share Freud's conviction that, despite many challenges, the voice of reason is soft, but never gives up the attempt to be heard.

Despite so many differences, concerning our culture and our language, we all share the unique experience of working with words. The most important Brazilian poet, Carlos Drummond de Andrade once wrote in a poem: Come closer and stare at the words/Each one has a thousand secret faces hidden under the neutral one/and asks, without caring about the poor or terrible answer you were supposed to give: /Have you brought the key?

The psychoanalytic key was used to open many doors, but there are still a thousand others waiting for us. I cordially invite you all to come closer and try to know more about psychoanalysis and its many faces, that can help us understand our uncertain, unpredictable and at the same time fascinating world.

References

Ahumada, J. (1997). Crise da cultura e crise da psicanálise. *Rev. Psicanál.* Porto Alegre, **4**: 51-96.

Arditi, B. (1988). La posmodernidad como coreografia de la complejidad. XVIII Congreso Latinoamericano de Sociologia, Montevideo.

Baladier, G. (1995). Le presént de la surmodernité. *Sciences Humaines,* **5**: 22-24.

Baranger, M. and Baranger, C. (1961) – La Situación Analítica como campo dinâmico. In *Problemas del Campo Psicoanalítico. Buenos Aires*: Ed. Kargieman, 1969.

Bauman, Z. (1991). Modernity and Ambivalence. *The American Journal of Sociology,* Vol. 97, No. 5 (Mar., 1992), pp. 1519 -1521

Bauman, Z. (2000). *Liquid Modernity.* Cambridge: Polity Press.

Bauman, Z. (2001*). Modernity and the Holocaust.* Cornell University Press.

Bauman, Z. (2005) *Liquid fear .* Cambridge: Polity.

Carlisky, N. And Eskenazi, C. (2000). *Resignación o Desafio: un enfoque transdisciplinario cobre la Sociedad actual.* Buenos Aires – México: Grupo Editorial Lumen.

Castoriadis, C. (1996). La crisis actual del processo identificatório. *Zona Erogena,* 31: 37-41.

Eizirik, C.L. (1997). Psychoanalysis and Culture: Some Contemporary Challenges. *Int. J. Psycho-Anal* 78: 789-800.

Eizirik, C.L. (2008). Psychoanalysis in a changing world. *Int. J. Psycho-anal* 89: 11-14.

Erikson, E. (1956). The problem of Ego identity. *J. Am. Psychoanal. Ass* 4.

Erlich, H. S.; Erlich-Ginor, M.;Beland, H.(2009) *Fed with tears, poisoned with milk.* Giessen:Psychosozial-Verlag.

Grinberg, L. and Grinberg, R. (1989). *Psychoanalytic Perspectives on Migration and Exile.* Yale University.

Green, A. (2002). *Idées directrices pour une psychanalyse contemporaine,* Paris, PUF.

Grinberg, L. and Grinberg, R. (1971). *Identidad Y Cambio.* Buenos Aires, Kargieman; Barcelona, Paidos-Ibérica, 3d ed.

Hartmann, H., Kris, E. & Loewenstein, R. M. (1946). Commentson the formation of psychic structure. PSOC, 2: 11-38.

Huxley, A. (1932). *Admirável Mundo Novo*, Porto Alegre, Editora Globo.

Kernberg, O. (1989). The temptations of conventionality. *Int J. Psycho-Anal.*, **16**: 191-205.

Kernberg, O. (1998). *Ideology, Conflict and Leadership in Groups and Organizations.* New Haven and London: Yale University Press.

Kristeva, J. (1993). *Les Nouvelles Maladies de L´ame.* Paris: Libraire Artheme Fayard.

Lasch, C. (1978). *The Culture of Narcissism.* New York: Norton.

Lyotard, J.F. (1979). *La Condición Posmoderna.* Barcelona: Anagrama, 1986 [The postmodern condition].

Moore, B. and Fine, B. (1990). *Psychoanalytic Terms & Concepts.* Yale University Press.

Nagera, H. (1967). The concepts of structure and structuralization. PSOC, 22: 77-102.

Rapaport, D. (1959). *The structure of psychoanalytic theory.* Psychol. Issues, monogr. 6, New York: Ont. Univ. Press.

Ricoeur, P. (1970*). Freud and Philosophy: An Essay on Interpretation.* New Haven, CT: Yale Univ. Press.

Tausk, V. (1919). On the Origin of the Influence Machine in Schizophrenia. *Psychoanal. Quartely* 2.

Van der Leeuw, P.J. (1980). 'Modern Times' and the psychoanalysts today. *Int. J. Psycho-Anal.* 7: 137-145

The one way road, an additional piece in the puzzle of German analysts post WWII

Ludger M. Hermanns, Berlin

Fifty-three members of the German Psychoanalytical Society (DPG) were forced to leave Nazi Germany after 1933. Nearly all of them were Jews and some were persecuted as socialists and communists. Karl Landauer and August Watermann were murdered in the concentration camps of Bergen Belsen and Auschwitz and Salomea Kempner died in January 1943 in the Warshaw Ghetto. Clara Happel and Max Levy-Suhl committed suicide, Clara Happel under the stress of emigration in the USA, whereas Max Levy-Suhl, who had survived the underground in Holland, was not stable enough to cope in the postwar period. Many of the emigrants lost close relatives in German concentration camps, and suffered years of hardship and privation after emigrating and during the first years of adapting to their new environment. Nevertheless, many were able to find some sort of surrogate home in psychoanalytic institutes in foreign countries, in which they could plant the seeds they had brought with them, as Martin Grotjahn once put it (in Peters, 1992, p. 19). Henry Lowenfeld wrote of how well the emigré psychoanalysts did both professionally and financially (in Peters, ibid., p. 37). Surprisingly, psychoanalysts were perhaps among the most successful groups of emigrants who, with their training in Berlin, Vienna, or Budapest, were often better trained and more experienced than their colleagues in the countries they emigrated to. By gaining respect, or sometimes even positions of power, they were able to regain some of their self-respect that had been smothered by having been persecuted and expelled. An important factor in this success story was if they were still young and adaptable, or already older. It was easier to get gradually rooted in the new country and its culture by founding new families and having children.

Who among the psychoanalytical emigrants had been able to return to Germany after 1945? Most of the "pillars" of the original Berlin Psychoanalytic Institute had not survived emigration for long. Max Eitingon was the first to die in 1943, then came Otto Fenichel in 1946, Ernst Simmel and Hanns Sachs in 1947, Karen Horney in 1952, and Siegfried Bernfeld in 1953. Almost none of them lived to celebrate their 70th birthday; only Franz Alexander and Sandor Radó, who died at the age of 73 (in 1964) and 82 (in 1972) respectively, lived longer.

Younger emigrants had already established a livelihood. Some of them had fought as soldiers in the US or British armies against Nazi Germany, and had become American or British citizens, so that a return to Germany was unthinkable. There are many examples of how difficult it was for them to reapproach their former home country. When Martin Wangh returned to Germany for the first time in 1959, for example, he had to run away again after only one day because, as he realized later in self-analysis, his "old secret German patriotism" came into unendurable conflict with the feelings of hatred he had developed (Wangh, 1995, p. 377f.). 27 years after Ernest Wolf had left Germany, he panicked at the border when re-entering the country, had to give over the steering wheel of the car to his wife, and had to flee the country the next day (Wolf, 1998, p. 417 f.). In 1955, Alexander Mitscherlich, together with Max Horkheimer and Theodor Adorno – the most prominent among the remigrants, who had been able to refound their former *Institut für Sozialforschung* [Institute for Social Research] at Frankfurt University – intensely campaigned for inviting international psychoanalysts to give guest lectures at the universities of Frankfurt and Heidelberg, on the occasion of Freud's 100th birthday in 1956. Many declined the invitation (Cf. Berger, 1996). Erik Erikson agreed to come only under the condition that young people made up at least half of the audience (Funke, 1989, p. 303).

Viewed in this light, it seems a rather absurd question to ask why emigrated psychoanalysts did not return to Germany after the collapse of the Hitler dictatorship and its military defeat in 1945. Why should they? Why should they voluntarily return to a country that had expelled them, and persecuted and murdered their relatives? As Léon and Rebecca Grinberg concluded at the end of their remarkable book on the psychoanalysis of emigration and exile: "One thing is for sure: One never returns, one always just goes away" (Grinberg & Grinberg, 1990, p. 267).

At first, only the socialist and communist colleagues among Jewish psychoanalysts had to fear for their lives after 1933, such as Wilhelm Reich, Ernst Simmel and later Edith Jacobson, to name only the most prominent ones, who could save their lives by fleeing the country. Soon afterwards, Jewish doctors lost their licenses for offering treatments covered by public health insurance, Jewish hospital doctors lost their jobs, and so-called "foreign Jews" were no longer allowed to work at the polyclinic of the Berlin Psychoanalytic Institute (BPI).

Even if all this was mainly the result of the anti-Semitic persecution by the national socialist state, another quite different factor came also into play: the conduct of non-Jewish, so-called "Aryan" colleagues vis-à-vis this life-threatening situation. During the three years between the establishment of the Nazi regime in 1933 and the dissolution of the Berlin Psychoanalytic Institute and its integration into a state-controlled, school-transcending psychotherapeutic institute in 1936, the members of the DPG and the BPI split – in accordance with the national socialist race doctrine – into a Jewish and an Aryan group, with the latter taking over all the leading positions. When the remaining Jewish members were forced, at a general meeting in December 1935 and in the presence of IPA president Ernest Jones, to "voluntarily" resign their membership in the DPG so as to make its further existence possible, a community of researchers and therapists that had been successful and flourishing for 25 years had reached its lowest point, on a human and moral level, and on a professional level. It was never to recover from the expulsion of its best and most creative members (cf. Brecht et al. 1993 for the details).

The lack of solidarity among colleagues, and the fact that those who remained in the country seamlessly took over the positions and functions of those who had been expelled, may have been a further reason that a smooth continuation, let alone a return, after the war was hardly imaginable.

Emigration specialists estimate that only some 30,000 out of 500,000 emigrés returned to Germany, and that most of these 30,000 had been political emigrants (Krauss, 2001). Thus, the question is not why someone did *not* return, but why some decided to return at all. According to Thomas Aichhorn (2006), three psychoanalysts returned to Vienna, at least for some time, to join the refounded Vienna Psychoanalytic Society (WPV). Not one former member of the DPG, however, returned to Germany to settle down as an analyst there. Nevertheless I could find seven emigrants who returned to Germany after 1945 who stayed there at least temporarily, and who practiced psychoanalysis there at least at some time or another: Klaus Fink, Ernest Freud, Fritz Friedmann, Erich Heilbrun, Walter Marseille, Erich Simenauer, and Frederick Wyatt.[1] I can single out only one of those who returned, and describe his return to Germany as an example:

Erich Simenauer (1901-1988) had been a surgeon and a prospective head physician, when he was arrested and hauled off in 1933 from his workplace at the Berlin *Urban* hospital. After his release, he emigrated, via Crete and Cyprus, to Tanganyika in East Africa, where he kept his head above water as a doctor for tropical diseases. In the 1920's, he had attended the courses at the old BPI, particularly those held by Radó, Fenichel, and Alexander. In the isolation of his African emigration, he further developed his analytical skills in writing about the life and work of Rainer Maria Rilke, resulting in a monography in 1953. After 1945 he established contacts through repeated talks and visits in Switzerland and England, and also at IPA congresses, where there was a lively scientific exchange particularly with other emigrants. When he had to leave the African tropical climate for health reasons, he decided to return to Berlin in 1957. Here he quickly made use of his regular analytical training, and soon became a member and training analyst. As we know from extant documents in the papers he left, in particular correspondence

---

[1] Walter Hollitscher originally from Vienna returned from England to GDR and gave philosophical lectures at the university but did no longer practice as psychoanalyst.

with other emigrants, he felt scientifically isolated in the "generation of the desert" which surrounded him. He often despaired in his loneliness, as he wrote for instance to an American colleague in 1962: "I should never have come back here, [it is] now mostly the patients who keep me here, I am … almost as isolated as in darkest Africa …" He complained to Berlin's Senator for Cultural Affairs, who had called on emigrants to return; he threatened to emigrate again, and closely watched for any signs of emerging anti-Semitism. It was only when he succeeded in putting his psychoanalytic experiences with children of victims of persecution and of persecutors to scientific use, and presenting his findings at national and international congresses, that he won attention and then also due recognition, which also found formal expression in the honorary professorship offered by the Berlin Senate, and honorary membership in the German and British Psychoanalytic Societies (cf. Hermanns, 1993, p. 615 ff.).

Let us now have a look at the analysts who had remained in the country. Did they welcome the return of psychoanalytic emigrants at all? From the extant letters of the postwar period we know that Carl Müller-Braunschweig, in particular, was anxious and hesitant in his attempts to re-establish contact with his former colleagues at the Institute and with the IPA leadership, plagued by the fear of being rebuffed because of his policy of collaboration during the Nazi regime. It was easier to re-establish relations with a representative of realpolitik such as Ernest Jones or with Anna Freud, who had been involved in his failed "mission" in Vienna, than with the former board member Ernst Simmel, for instance, with whom he failed to make contact before Simmel's death.

Affectionate letters were exchanged, however, between Müller-Braunschweig and his emigrated training analysands, or between Gerhart Scheunert and his training analyst Therese Benedek in Chicago. In most cases those letters were accompanied by care packages for the hungry and freezing Berlin analysts. The Rickman Report offers a heart-wrenching snapshot, particularly of the complacency and egocentricity of the two leading DPG officers, Boehm and Müller-Braunschweig (cf. King, 1989). While Müller-Braunschweig did succeed in having the newly founded German Analytic Association (DPV) admitted into the

IPA, a lively contact and exchange with international psychoanalysis set in only after his death in 1958.

In contrast to this, Alexander Mitscherlich, who as a neurologist had become acquainted with psychoanalysis in Zurich, America, and London, and who had been in jail for his anti-Hitlerism, wanted from the beginning to realize his plans to re-establish psychoanalysis in Frankfurt am Main deliberately with the help of emigrants. Thus we read in an application at the national foundation for research (DFG) in 1959 that, in order to reach the international standard of development, it would be "necessary, at least at the beginning, to engage teachers from abroad for a longer time period" (Berger, 1989, p. 279). Despite the excellent reputation he had gained for his anti-Hitler stance, and for his reporting from the Nuremberg Trials against physicians, he did not succeed in persuading even one of those emigrants closest to him, such as Henry Lowenfeld or William Niederland, to become director or collaborator at his newly founded Sigmund Freud Institute. But although the emigrants did not return for good, they more and more came as teachers and supervisors for short weekend visits, "sojourners," as they are called in the literature (Berry, 1990). The eminent contributions of Paula Heimann and Willi Hoffer found attention recently (Holmes 2013; Hermanns 2013). And with them, the theory and the institutional regulations returned, too. Here we have to distinguish again between the two poles of Berlin and Frankfurt. In Berlin there was no need to change anything in the organization of the work; the continuity was there, although the link to the past was very thin, and was represented by only a few people, pieces of furniture, plaques, and books. The former institutional model was faithfully reconstructed with very little means, while the polyclinic and the technical seminar could only be gradually re-established as regular institutions. But the Berliners were aware of their modest personal resources, as is testified in a critical report by Käte Dräger (written in the fifties, published 2013).

At the psychosomatic clinic in Heidelberg and at the Frankfurt Institute, there was special emphasis on modern research principles, going back to Franz Alexander's work at the Chicago Institute, and to the organization of the British Psychoanalytical Institute and the Tavistock

Institute – which had been visited by various members in the 1950's and early 1960's – that were taken over and applied in a creative way. With London in particular, close contacts regarding supervisory work were established, for instance, with Michael Balint, Willi Hoffer, and Paula Heimann, to name only a few.

To counteract the inexperience in modern therapeutic technique, international workshops were organized in Hamburg in 1957 and 1958, followed by similar ones in Frankfurt. From 1959 onward, Central European Meetings, held in German, with participants from Holland, Switzerland, Austria and Germany, served a similar purpose (Bruns, 2003). In contrast to the early 1950s, the orientation toward American analysis clearly decreased (Schröter, 1999), also because dozens of German analysts sought to get additional training in England, Holland, and Switzerland. This tendency is also shown by the "importing" of foreign textbooks, beginning with first translations in the postwar period: Franz Alexander's *Our Age of Unreason: A Study of the Irrational Forces in Social Life* (1942/1946), as well as his *Psychosomatic Medicine* (1950/1951), and two books of Karen Horney, *The Neurotic Personality of Our Time* (1937/1951), and *New Ways in Psychoanalysis* (1939/1951). This also holds true for the journals *Psyche* (since 1947) and *Jahrbuch der Psychoanalyse* [*Yearbook of Psychoanalysis*] (since 1960), which satisfied the great need to catch up with international developments by publishing translations and by reprinting older original works.

While Müller-Braunschweig, in his book *Streifzüge* [*Forays*] (1948), returned to what had been tried and tested before 1933, and Felix Schottlaender, for instance, advocated rather synoptic concepts (echoing existential analysis, philosophical anthropology, and encounter psychology), Gerhart Scheunert from Berlin (later in Hamburg) was one of the most open-minded analysts among the older generation. He gave some important talks about the latest developments in libido theory, in ego psychology, and regarding the concepts of transference and countertransference, and thus introduced these concepts into the German discourse (see Bohleber, 2010a and 2010b). By no means, however, was one of the foreign schools favoured over another; rather, attempts were made to view cases in light of various theoretical and technical concepts, including those of the

Kleinian school. Scheunert further pursued the line taken by his training analyst Therese Benedek, who lived in Chicago, with whom he led a lively exchange by correspondence, and some of whose articles he himself translated and had published in journals.

Generally speaking, it can be stated that the transfer of theory and technique from the countries of emigration back to Frankfurt and Berlin was comprehensive and successful. The reception of theory, too, occurred in two phases, with the reception of the Kleinian English school, in particular, coming much later than that of the theory brought over from America.[2]

In 1968 Theodor W. Adorno complained in a radio broadcast that in Germany, due to the interruption of the reception of psychoanalysis during the Third Reich, whole disciplines had not recuperated from what had happened (Sender Freies Berlin, 1968, p.67). We may ask ourselves if this situation has fundamentally changed today, 50 years later. We may hope so, but we are still not always sure of it. *A sign of hope may be that after 1977 when the repudiation of an invitation to an IPA congress in Berlin was challenging it was possible to have such congresses in Hamburg 1985 and even Berlin 2007 who were frequently visited.* The German Psychoanalytical Association (DPV) recently awarded Peter Loewenberg (Los Angeles) and Shmuel Erlich (Jerusalem) two well known psychoanalysts with early German roots and with an eminent record of bringing authentic psychoanalysis back to this country, with an honorary membership, and I am very pleased to include this short study for Shmuel to congratulate him on his birthday.

References

Aichhorn, Th. (2006). Zurück nach Wien? Die Rückkehr von Psychoanalytikern aus dem Exil. In: *Vom Weggehen. Zum Exil von Kunst und Wissenschaft*. Wiesinger-Stock, S.,Weinzierl, E., Kaiser, K. (Hg.). Wien (Mandelbaum), 261-276.

---

[2] The actual issue of the German journal for the history of psychoanalysis LUZIFER-AMOR (No. 58 October 2016) is dealing with the early American influences in German postwar psychoanalysis.

Alexander, F. (1946). *Irrationale Kräfte unserer Zeit. Eine Studie über das Unbewußte in Politik und Geschichte.* Stuttgart (Klett).

Alexander, F. (1951). *Psychosomatische Medizin. Grundlagen und Anwendungsgebiete.* Berlin (de Gruyter).

Berger, F. (1996). „Das Tragen eines Smokings wäre ein Fauxpas." Die Veranstaltungen zum 100. Geburtstag Sigmund Freuds im Jahre 1956. In: *Psychoanalyse in Frankfurt am Main.* Zerstörte Anfänge, Wiederannäherung, Entwicklungen. Hg. von T. Plänkers et al. Tübingen (edition diskord), 335-348.

Berry, J. W. (1990). Psychology of Acculturation. In: *Cross-Cultural Perspectives, Proceedings of the Nebraska Symposium on Motivation,* 1989, John J. Berman (Ed.), 201-234.

Bohleber, W. (2010a). Die Entwicklung der Psychoanalyse in Deutschland nach 1950. *Psyche* 64: 1243-1267.

Bohleber, W. (2010b). Psychoanalyse als naturwissenschaftliche Erfahrungswissenschaft. Gerhart Scheunerts Hinwendung zur Ich-Psychologie. *Jahrbuch der Psychoanalyse* 61:39-55.

Brecht, K./Friedrich, V./Hermanns,L.M./Juelich, D.J./Kaminer, I (Ed.)(1993): *„Here life goes on in a most peculiar way".* *Psychoanalysis before and after 1933.* English edition by H. Ehlers. London/Hamburg (Goethe Institut/Kellner Verlag).

Bruns, G. (2003). Die langsame Rückgewinnung der Mitte. Unvollständige Bemerkungen zur Geschichte der Arbeitstagungen der Mitteleuropäischen Vereinigungen. *Zeitschr. Psychoanal. Theor. Prax.* 18: 255-263.

Dräger, K. (2013). Fundstücke aus Psychoanalytischen Archiven (IV): "Daß es sich bei der Gründung des Berliner Psychoanalytischen Institutes 1950/51 ... um eine Pioniersituation handelte." Karl-Abraham-Institut (Hg.): Semesterjournal, 61–66.

Funke, H. (1989). Die andere Erinnerung. Gespräche mit jüdischen Wissenschaftlern im Exil. Frankfurt a.M. (Fischer Taschenbuch).

Grinberg, L. u. Grinberg, R. (1990). Psychoanalyse der Migration und des Exils. München-Wien (Internationale Psychoanalyse).

Hermanns, Ludger M. (2013). „Ein äußerst angenehmer Wiener" als "Schirmherr" für die DPV: Über Willi Hoffer und seine Rolle beim

Wiederaufbau der Psychoanalyse im Nachkriegsdeutschland. Jahrbuch der Psychoanalyse 67: 31–53.

Holmes, M. (2013). Die Emigration von Paula Heimann nach London und ihr Beitrag zur Wiederbelebung der Psychoanalyse in der BRD nach 1945. In: Hermanns, L.M./Henningsen, F. u.Togay J. C. (Hg.). Psychoanalyse und Emigration aus Budapest und Berlin. Frankfurt a.M. (Brandes & Apsel), 157-172.

Horney, K. (1951). Neue Wege in der Psychoanalyse. Stuttgart (Gustav Kilpper).

Horney, K. (1951). Der neurotische Mensch unserer Zeit. Stuttgart (Gustav Kilpper).

King, P. (1989). Activities of British psychoanalysts during the Second World War and the influence of their inter-disciplinary collaboration on the development of psychoanalysis in Great-Britain. Int. Rev. Psycho-Anal. 16: 15-33.

Krauss, M. (2001). Heimkehr in ein fremdes Land. Geschichte der Remigration nach 1945. München (Beck).

Müller-Braunschweig, C. (1948). Streifzüge durch die Psychoanalyse. Reinbek (Parus).

Peters, U.H.(1992). Psychiatrie im Exil. Die Emigration der Dynamischen Psychiatrie aus Deutschland 1933-1939. Düsseldorf (Kupka).

Schröter,M. (1999). Die Internationalisierung der deutschen Psychoanalyse nach dem Zweiten Weltkrieg. In: Westbindungen. Amerika in der Bundesrepublik. Hg. von H. Bude u. B. Greiner, Hamburg (Hamburger Edition), 93-118.

Sender Freies Berlin(Hg.)(1968). *Um uns die Fremde. Die Vertreibung des Geistes* 1933-1945. Berlin (Haude & Spenersche Verlagsbuchhandlung. Cf. Th. W. Adorno, p. 67-68.

Simenauer, E. (1953). Rainer Maria Rilke. Legende und Mythos. Bern (Haupt).

Simenauer, E. (1993). Wanderungen zwischen Kontinenten. Gesammelte Schriften zur Psychoanalyse. Hg. von L.M.Hermanns, Stuttgart-Bad Cannstatt(frommann-holzboog).

Wangh, M. (1995). Ein psychoanalytisches Selbstbildnis. In: Psychoanalyse in Selbstdarstellungen, Bd. 3, hg. von L.M.Hermanns, Tübingen
(edition diskord), 331-418.

Wolf, E.S. (1998). Gegen den Strom schwimmen. Umwandlungen und
Wiederbelebung. In: Psychoanalyse in Selbstdarstellungen, Bd. 4, hg.
von L.M. Hermanns, Tübingen (edition diskord), 369-430.

CHAPTER SEVENTEEN

Psychoanalytic Group Work with Transgenerational Residues of Historic Traumatization: The Case of the German-Israeli Conferences[1]

Mira Erlich-Ginor

To Shmuel, partner in initiating and carrying through meaningful social projects

I am about to present a project that started with hesitant steps 21 years ago, in Nazareth, under the title: "German and Jews, the past in the Present", and underwent, and is still undergoing, transformations. It is a project in which psychoanalytic understanding is applied to a weighty social issue.

Speaking of the Holocaust Today, Yes/No? Why?

The Holocaust – the systematic annihilation of European Jews by Nazi Germany as its programmed "Final Solution" of the "Jewish problem" – is one of the most horrendous destructive acts ever witnessed. It is the systematic annihilation of one people by another, by means of the most advanced technological and industrial achievements of 20th century civilization. The Holocaust is an essentially European phenomenon: it took place exclusively on European soil, and it was perpetrated by one of

---

[1] Based on a lecture delivered in December 2015 in Krakow

the most advanced and culturally leading European nation – Nazi Germany. Its roots are implanted in the European history of the struggle between Judaism and Christianity and the deeply embedded anti-Semitism that grew out of it over many centuries.

The immediate question that must be answered is: Horrendous as it was, what is the point of speaking about the Holocaust today? Is it relevant in some way to the experience of the new generations that grew up well after it took place? Would it not be better and perhaps even wiser to let it come to rest as a paragraph or a marginal reference in a history textbook? Isn't it better to let bygones be bygones?

My answer to these questions and objections is a definite "No!"

When I present this work to you, you are in my mind not as an audience of neutral observers to whom I tell a story about someone else, but as participants and "shareholders" in this collective story.

As we know, artists often serve as social barometers, as mirrors of societal processes. Two Polish artistic productions came up in the last few years and deal with the relationship between Poles and Jews and Poles and Poles, against the background of the Holocaust. The first is "Nasza Klasa", a play by Tadeusz Słobodzianek (first performed in Warsaw in the theater Na Woli in 2010). The second, two years later – the movie Pokłosie (Aftermath) by Wladyslaw Pasikowski (2012). Both received international prizes and are performed in many countries. As far as I could learn, the two productions aroused mixed feelings in Poland. It is important and interesting to think: what made it possible for these two productions to take place in the last years? Is the time ripe to deal with the aftermath of the Holocaust? Are the artists ahead of the rest of society? Are they leading it? Will they be ignored?

Reading about Tadeusz Słobodzianek, I learned that he has been writing for the past 30 years. It appears that he needed all this time to be able to write Nasza Klasa.

These Polish attempts show that even if the subject is unpopular, and although it took place more than 70 years ago, the shadow of the Holocaust and its radioactive fallout continues to poison the lives of descendants of both perpetrators and victims in the most palpable ways (Bohleber, 2007). It is a poignant example of the profound way in which historical trauma continues to affect the lives, the minds and the psychical well-being of future generations, even though they did not directly experience it (Moses, 1992). It is a poignant and painful illustration of the extent of the inhuman – or perhaps, on the contrary, very much human – atrocities of which individuals, large groups, and modern states are capable.

Although the Holocaust is an essentially European phenomenon, unparalleled and unique in human history, the perpetration of extreme atrocities has many parallels across other continents as well. The past and present history of Asia, Africa, the Americas and even Australia is not exempt from this. We are all familiar with the atrocities of the Japanese, the Khmer Rouge, and the Chinese Cultural Revolution, the genocides of the Armenians by the Turks and in Rwanda, Congo and Sudan, the fate of the American Indians and Australian aborigines, to name just the most prominent. The present murderous atrocities going on in the Middle East – in Syria and by the Islamic Republic – are current examples, and I must also mention the criticism leveled against Israel, from within and without, about its recent war against the Hamas in Gaza.

As mental health professionals and people who are social minded we must do our best to understand the roots of such human cruelty and our seemingly unlimited capacity for destructiveness.

Can psychoanalysis help in any way to deal with the aftermath of such destructiveness? Does it have anything to offer? Perhaps an even wider, more fundamental question would be: Can psychoanalysis play a role on the political scene?

The answer to these questions would take up a paper in itself. I will only say that while I do not believe that *psychoanalysis as a science* can or should take political positions, I believe that as a *method of intervention* based on its specialized understanding of the human mind it has much to offer. In particular, it can contribute to working with people who are affected by the residues of trauma. I therefore think that the approach and method we have developed for working with the aftereffects of atrocities deserve your attention and reflection, and you may find it applicable to situations and circumstances with which you are familiar.

An accompanying aspect of the need to work on the residual effects of such atrocities is the powerful tendency to deny their existence, and thus to get rid of the associated guilt and aggression. Holocaust denial, only 70 years afterwards and while survivors are still alive, is gaining strength, and is an outright attack on the possibility to mourn and to move on internally.

It took many years and crossing huge psychological distances for the experience of the Holocaust to be put into words and become available for internal work. Yet 70 calendar years are not a long time on the intra-psychic timescale.

For the past 20 years we have initiated and conducted, together with colleagues from Germany, Israel, England and elsewhere, a series of Group Relations Conferences designed originally to work with the residual effects of the Holocaust on the lives of German and Israeli psychoanalysts, psychotherapists and mental health professionals. In time, these conferences developed to include Diaspora Jews, affected others, and Palestinians. The venues included Israel (Nazareth), Germany (Bad Segeberg) and Cyprus. Recently the focus has shifted to European victims and perpetrators, and the venue to Poland. Our forthcoming conference in 2016 bears the title: "*A House Divided against Itself? Identities and Cultures in Violent Conflict.*" It is clearly related to the current traumas, fears and violence Europe is experiencing, with which you are all familiar.

Participants came to the conference with trepidations: the days ahead of them will not be easy, as the decision to come to this conference was not easy.

It is not easy to participate in these conferences as member or as staff. Participants come to do an important internal work in the presence of their own kind and the "Others". Painful moments are the order of the day, so are moments of deep sorrow and compassion.

In what follows I will briefly describe the Group Relations approach, and illustrate the processes that take place in these conferences with a few selected examples. Finally, I will discuss certain aspects of the work and the themes that have emerged from it.

The Group Relations Approach

Group Relations Conferences are a unique adaptation of psychoanalytic exploration and understanding combined with an Open Systems approach. The psychoanalytic basis for this work is firmly grounded in the drive and object relations concepts of Melanie Klein (1946) (e.g., splitting, projection and projective identification, good and bad internal object, destructiveness, guilt and reparation) and Wilfred Bion (1961) (e.g., group-as-a-whole transference, the dynamics of Basic Assumption groups vs. Work group) as well as later developments (e.g., Turquet (1975) on Large Group dynamics). Open Systems Theory (von Bertalanffy, 1976) has contributed important structural concepts and insights that affect the life of social entities, organizations and institutions, such as role, boundary and primary task, and the place and function of leadership. The GR methodology, based on the combination and integration of both approaches, was developed by the Tavistock Institute of Human Relations in 1957 and has since spread globally. Typically, Group Relations working conferences have centered on aspects of *authority and leadership*. They are geared towards *learning from one's own experience* in the various group settings provided – Small and Large Study Groups, Review and Application Groups, Plenaries, and an Intergroup or Organizational/System Event. The learning is entirely individual and evolves in both here-and-now and more action oriented settings.

The Theory in a Nutshell

Group Relations conferences are designed to be a safe container. This is achieved by providing a combination of strong and clear *boundaries* and *interpretations*. The most evident boundaries are those of *time, space* and *task*: every event starts and ends at a precise time and in a specified territory; staff members stay in role. These strong boundaries provide the necessary conditions for a certain regression that takes place once one's habitual roles are unclear or irrelevant, defences are diminished and the experience is of being in a new and unknown psychic space. It is a challenging state of mind, anxiety provoking, yet pregnant with the potential for discovery and creativity.

The *staff* in these conferences have a complex task: They act as *consultants* to the various events, and also form the *management* that maintains the boundaries in which the events are held and unfold. They are available for projections and interpret them. The interpretations usually pertain to the here-and-now and are built on counter-transference and identifying processes of projective identification. Each staff member works with several group configurations. The staff also works as a group in which the task is to decipher and understand what happens in the conference as a whole. The fact that there are typically 9-12 staff members provides opportunities for differential projections. To work as staff can be very meaningful and highly emotional.

Developing the Nazareth Conferences Design

Our work initially centered on the two nationality groups involved in the trauma of the Holocaust – Germans and Israelis – and has gradually expanded to include affected Others, and more recently Palestinians and Europeans. The usual format of a Group Relations conference, which is based on *individuals* signing up, had to be adapted for working with two recognized and identified nationality groups in the early conferences. All of this is fully described in our book that provides an account of the first three conferences – "*Fed with Tears, Poisoned with Milk*" (Erlich et al., 2009).

My presentation here will include brief excerpts from these proceedings as illustrations. The most essential point in this work is that *each national or ethnic group needs the actual presence of the other one in order to be able to do its own internal work*, whether on bereavement, aggression, guilt, revenge, victimization or deprivation. We are convinced by our experience that this method provides a valuable approach to working with ethnic, religious and nationalistic atrocities and their transgenerational residues.

"I am so disappointed – why are there so few Israelis here?" This question of a German analyst opened the first conference. An immediate answer came from an elderly Israeli woman: "If you had not killed so many of us, there would have been more here." This painful dramatic exchange launched a series of working conferences in which German analysts met with their Israeli counterparts. These conferences gradually evolved to have a life of their own: they have a historical past, an intense and absorbing present that is different for each one, and an as yet unknown future. There were nine conferences so far: in 1994 and 1996 in Nazareth, in 2000 in Bad Segeberg, four in Cyprus and three more in Poland. I will try to provide a picture of what transpired and surfaced in these meetings, but it should be made clear that this effort, sincere and serious as it may be in trying to communicate, cannot be wholly successful. It is highly experiential and personal: just as in an analysis, it has to do with learning through and from one's own personal experience. In a very deep sense, each conference participant had her/his own, different and unique conference. It is therefore nearly impossible, and to some extent misleading, to describe it and to generalize about it.

Let us now zoom in on some of the events to illustrate the emotional and unconscious themes and materials that come up. These examples are taken from the only conference held in Germany.

Zoom In on the Plenaries

All participants – members and staff – take part in the Plenaries. In the Opening Plenary, which is the entry point into the conference, an Israeli woman asked herself why she came to Germany: it did not seem to make sense now that she was here. A German woman spoke about her wish-fear to attend the conference. She had planned her coming for four years. In anticipation, she asked her parents for the first time what they did during the war. Their response was to sever their relationship with her. She felt devastated and cried bitterly. Another German woman, in a flat, affectless voice, stated: "I am the daughter of an ordinary Nazi mother." This phrase had an immensely compelling force. It immediately became the *leitmotif* and title for many subsequent contributions.

In another Plenary towards the end, an Israeli man related his telephone conversation with his mother. He told her that after the conference he planned to travel to Berlin with his new German friends.

His mother said to him: "Don't go with them – they killed your grand-parents!"

The theme of mothers – "ordinary Nazi" and otherwise – and what they passed on to their sons and daughters emerged as central in this conference. It was elaborated and extended to include "ordinary Jewish" mothers as well as "Jewish Nazi mothers." It found expression in the poignant image of an Israeli woman consultant: "I was *milked* with tears." This was immediately followed by a German woman who said: "And I was milked with poison." This was a powerful, nearly palpable image, of being suckled at the breast and taking in with one's 'mother's milk' the poison that came with it, whether depression or murderous-ness. This peculiar verbal construction ("milked") made immediate sense and was taken up as quite natural. It evoked the underlying double meaning in which mothers were experienced as giving suckle, milk, and at the same time as "milking" and draining their children.

Zoom In on the Small Study Group

SSGs are composed of 9-12 members of different nationality groups meeting with a consultant. Language and its powerful, preconscious way of surfacing unconscious and buried issues became an immediate focus. "Innocent" words on the building floor-plan were loaded with meaning: *Lager* (concentration camp), and *Gruppenraum*, which connected with *Lebensraum*. The German environment was suffused with its cultural symbols and overtones. For some Israelis it was painfully connected with smells and tastes of food and cooking, trees and plants, and aspects of the physical surroundings – the sharp, unexpected surfacing of deeply missed childhood smells and tastes.

The immediacy of so many forgotten, forbidden and repressed memories made it difficult at first to speak in the Small Group. People spoke in hushed tones, in almost inaudible whispers – as in a house of mourning. No names were given or asked for. This changed suddenly when an Israeli woman said: "I am named Sara, after my grandmother." She and the group experienced this simple, "ordinary" statement as if a bomb was dropped in the room.

Another scene: All the women are dressed in black. The members are all mixed, surrounded by each other's nationality. Death and mourning are in the air, as well as the wish to let go of the burden of one's national identity. The manifest theme is *poison* and *paranoia:* being betrayed by one's parents; the world as a sick, cancerous place. The real danger, however, is – shifts and changes in one's identity. The discussion turns to snow and winter. The consultant offers the association of Schubert's song "*Gefrorene Tränen*." Dead parts of selves are buried under the snow, perhaps still alive. The question is posed, "Were the Israelis brought to Germany to thaw out the frozen German parts"?

In the last small group session, members sit in same-nationality pairs. Again, they talk in hushed voices, as if in the presence of the dead. It is as if the deceased parents are present, encircling the group circle. Beside the mourning and veneration, there is the fear of invading the space of the other. The work of re-finding one's lost parts must proceed cautiously, so as not to violate the space and identity of the other, who is now so very precious.

Zoom In on the System Event

Perhaps the most telling and central event in the conference is the System Event. The two nationality groups start separately, in different locations, with the option of forming groups in different locations, as well as the potential for meeting the other nationality group(s). The staff group is located in its own territory and participates in two ways: it carries on its work as usual, but in full public view, so that members can observe it and interact with it. The staff is also available to provide consultation to the members' groups. The staff intervenes in the developing process by issuing working hypotheses – interpretations – which express its view of what is happening in the event at that moment. The atmosphere in the System Event is typically quite intense and charged. It may, however, sway from euphoric excitement and manic feelings of being powerful and "accomplishing something" to utter confusion, depressive passivity and dangerous resignation.

In the first two Nazareth conferences, the German group was seen as efficient, active and powerful, while the Israelis seemed passive, helpless and resigned. An intervention by a consultant in the first Nazareth conference was that "while the Germans were marching, the Jews sat and debated what to do." In the conference in Germany, the Israeli group – quite unlike the previous conferences – became extremely active. There was a leadership struggle in it, resulting in a powerful group taking over, with a sense of mission and purpose, of knowing how to play the game and "get it right." This created resentment and disunity among the Israelis. Some of them experienced it as a Fascist takeover, with which they could not identify. Several Israelis left the big group, to create or join other groups. The first to leave was an Israeli man of the pre-war generation, who wanted to create a group together with Germans to investigate events in Germany from 1933 to 1945. For a while he was a singleton, a group of one, wandering around in disarray, like a refugee in flight, carrying plastic bags with his belongings. Seven or eight Germans, who provided him with shelter and protection, later joined him. The name adopted by this group was "The German Catastrophe." An Israeli woman came to the Staff in a stormy, highly charged emotional state. She wondered if the staff knew what was actually going on. She felt confused, angry and disoriented. She could not see what all this had to do with her grandparents who were murdered in Auschwitz.

The German group, which in the previous conferences was quite active, was more passive and subdued this time. Acting in an orderly and democratic fashion, it became beset and plagued by procedural debates. The group stayed in paralysis until it asked for and received consultation which freed it up. It then formed several subgroups, which were joined by Israeli members. The titles these groups took were instructive: "On Violence and Sentimentality" (all women); "Lack of Safety"; "The Murdered and the Murderers"; and "The German Catastrophe" already mentioned.

Throughout this conference in Germany, in sharp contradistinction to Nazareth I and II, there were repeated defensive enactments, at first totally unconscious, of German incompetence. This took on a number of faces: The Germans idealized the competence of the Israelis, and unjustly downgraded their own. There was evidence (e.g., in the SSG) of the Germans "lobotomizing" themselves, cutting off their heads and brains, their capacity to think and feel. They often complained of their inability to think and to use their intellect, an experience bordering on madness. This was linked to an observed German tendency to carry on as inadequate, incompetent and tongue-tied in international meetings. It was accompanied by a tremendous amount of shame and guilt. It was also evident that the Germans longed for their Jewish colleagues and counterparts. They felt deprived, severely handicapped and lacking without them. They longed desperately for the taste of the Jewish breast and milk, of which they had ridded themselves.

Discussion

Many have expressed doubts and reservations about these conferences. Some Jewish colleagues who live in Germany felt offended: Why could not their German colleagues have these discussions with them? Why "import" Israeli Jews? Strong objections were also raised in Israel. Some Israeli colleagues regard attending these conferences as an act of exoneration and forgiveness, which they meet with resistance and refusal. There is great difficulty on both sides of the fence with the underlying principle and the main lesson of these conferences: *The presence of the other is a necessary condition for being able to do your own internal work.*

Normal intrapsychic capacities shrink under the impact of ordinary trauma, but they are severely incapacitated by the impact of the horrendous nature of the Holocaust. It seriously limits the capacity to work on one's internal state in isolation. The line that divides Germans and Israelis also joins them as distinct and unmistakably different partners in these traumatic historical events and their aftermath. As patients in analysis, we require the presence of the other in order to do our own work, although, or because, this other has no connection with our own history. In the attempt to deal with what happened in the aftermath of the Holocaust *within* both Germans and Jews, however, we must also deal with what transpired *between* them. It makes all the difference in the world whether this work takes place entirely at the internal fantasy level, or in the actual presence of the other. And it is especially telling when this other actually represents the psychic and historical reality in question. This work is therefore not about forgiveness, pious absolution or false exoneration. It is rather about one's *personal and national identity* and relationships – with parents and grandparents, friends and neighbors, culture and history.

Identity was indeed an essential and central theme in this conference as in most of them. The "ordinary Nazi mother" is an image of a poisonous breast, exuding venom and death, of which the child is the victim. It was impressive to see the tremendous significance of food in the relationship with parents and culture. A German man exclaimed in angry disbelief, "My relationship with my mother was all about 'fresh potatoes!'" Food, smell and touch are some of the elements out of which the earliest sense of self and identity, of psychosomatic existence and of being firmly rooted in a cultural soil, are constructed. But identity, the lifelong sense of our own self and "me-ness," is also defined by the image of the other, the "not-me," which it includes and uses. The German identity was burdened with shame and guilt, and was experienced as handicapped and incapacitating. In the German identity, the Jew is an 'Other' who occupies a special place. He or she is ambivalently regarded as possessing aliveness and wisdom, making him an object of both desire and envious attack. Within the German identity, there seems to be embedded an elemental Jewish component as an idealized/envied/hated other.

In the Israeli/Jewish identity, on the other hand, different issues were apparent. The part of the other is not necessarily German. The other, for the Israelis, can take on many different faces – European, Arab or the catchall non-Jewish/Gentile. It is indeed part of Jewish identity that *anyone* may take the role of the stranger and persecutor. In this conference, however, for the Israelis the 'Other' became the "non-Israeli" Diaspora Jew. Feared and resented, the anger of the group focused on him and threatened to scapegoat him. To an extent, this had to do with the greater affinity of the Diaspora Jew to the Germans. In another respect, it represented the Israeli hate for the Diaspora Jew who is experienced as the negative of and a threat to the newly won "Israeli" identity.

These issues around identity become even more painful when identity is undergoing change. The changed image of the other causes a shift in the perception of oneself. The other is an invaluable determinant of one's own identity, and therefore as the image of the other changes, it causes the personal and collective group identity to change with it. This change is experienced as a serious threat on all psychic levels: it destabilizes one's sense of the world as an organized, coherent, meaningful place. It obscures the clear delineation of good and bad objects and self-images, upsetting habitual patterns of projection and creating havoc with ambivalent splits of love and hate. It upsets the primitive schizo-paranoid order, and hinders progressive movement to a depressive integration. Worst of all, however, it undermines one's ties and roots in psychic and social reality. The changed perception of the other militates against the view of the world that was part of the emotional ties with one's parents and family. It is an assault on the family ego (Klein & Erlich, 1976).

In the System Event, such threats to identity clearly emerged as a result of Germans and Israelis coming in close contact. Because the conference has shaken deeply established identity patterns by changing one's view of oneself and the other, it produced the disarray, tension and upset described. It is difficult to give up familiar roles, such as the role of the perpetrator for the Germans, and that of the victim for the Israelis. The overriding fear that blocks change is the danger of *betrayal* – of parents, relatives and culture – and the associated shame and guilt.

I want to close this brief and almost impossible account on a personal note. It cannot be emphasized enough how unique and different it was to work in these conferences. It feels entirely different than any other Group Relations conference we have worked in, and the modes of taking up the professional role and responsibilities are colored by these differences. I and my colleagues felt a sense of mission, of contributing and being part of an endeavor of historical and social significance that reaches far beyond the immediate. There is also a strong feeling of camaraderie and identification with the members, and envy of *their* being in the member's role. This identification with members, who often are professional colleagues and friends, makes it difficult to work with them without being either too close or too distant. The Small Study Groups consultants reviewed the way they took up their role in this conference, which felt very different from the usual mode. We found that our preferred stance was on the boundary between a 'Group Relations' and a 'facilitation' mode, at times even on the boundary of 'group psychotherapy.' We accepted the working definition of our role to be: *Partners in Search of Understanding.*

Perhaps I did not make it sufficiently clear that GR conferences are not therapeutic – it is not group analysis or group psychotherapy, where we strive to alleviate personal suffering associated with psychopathology. The primary aim of these conferences is *learning* – about oneself, about hatred and prejudice, about the strain and difficulty around relationships, identity and the meaning and burden of belonging to a social, ethnic or national group with a given traumatogenic history. One learns – or better said: one *may* learn – about the residual effects of such historical traumata and their living manifestations in one's psyche and life. We believe, and our experience supports it, that such learning can bring about significant internal change. But we must leave it to the individual participants and to you to reflect on whether such change can or should be called therapeutic.

References

Bertalanffy, von L. (1976). *General Systems Theory: Foundations, Development, Applications.* Publisher: George Braziller.

Bion, W. R. (1961). *Experiences in Groups.* New York: Basic Books.

Bohleber, W. (2007): Remembrance, trauma and collective memory. *Int. J. Psycho-anal.* 2007, Nr. 88, p. 329- 52.

Erlich, H. S. (2013). *The Couch in the Marketplace: Psychoanalysis and Social Reality.* London: Karnac.

Erlich, H. S., Erlich-Ginor, M. & Beland, H. *Fed with Tears – Poisoned with Milk. The "Nazareth" Group-Relations-Conferences: Germans and Israelis: The Past in the Present.* Psychosozial Verlag: Gießen, 2009.

Freud, S. (1915). Thoughts for the times on war and death. S.E., 14:273-300. London: Hogarth

Freud, S. (1933). Why war? S.E., 22:195-216. London: Hogarth

Klein, H. & Erlich, H. S. (1976). Some psychoanalytic structural aspects of family
function and growth. *Adolescent Psychiatry*, 6:171-194.

Moses, R. (1992) *The Meaning of the Holocaust to Those Not Directly Affected.* New York: International Universities Press.

Turquet, P. M. (1975). Threats to identity in the large group. In: L. Kreeger (Ed.), *The Large Group: Dynamics and Therapy.* London: Constable.

CHAPTER EIGHTEEN

Being German In a Conference The Past in the Present"[1]

Dorothee C. von Tippelskirch-Eissing

It is a great honour for me to be included in the list of the contributors to this Festschrift for my highly estimated colleague who has become a dear, truthful and reliable friend over many years of cooperation in different areas, for H. Shmuel Erlich. This text seemed to be appropriate for this occasion, as in giving an example of my experience in the conference "Shaping the Future by Confronting the Past: Germans, Jews and Affected Others" in 2004, I am speaking of the conference where Shmuel and Mira and myself met for the first time, working together. Thus this year has become the beginning of a very fruitful encounter, that has opened the path for an immense learning and development, personally and professionally, in terms of my psychoanalytic path, my work in different institutional contexts and last but nor least in the world of Group relations Work. I am deeply grateful for the enormous support I have received from both, Mira and Shmuel, and I am hoping for a remaining long way ahead of us walking together in actually very unstable worlds.

"The Past in the Present" is a concept very familiar to Psychoanalysts, since it belongs to one of Freud's early descriptions of neurosis: the neurotic person is suffering from "reminiscences", from a past that cannot become transformed into "past", but is activated in the presence. Maybe you recall the image of the person who

---

[1] Based on a lecture delivered at the IPAC in Boston 2015 as part of a PCCA panel: "Working through Collective Atrocities With Psychoanalytic Tools".

sees the memorial of the black death and starts crying as if death had carried away its victims not centuries ago, but only yesterday.

The material I am going to present to you, is this kind of experience. This is precisely one of the reasons why this work is necessary – to make us able to live in the present and prepare for a future life, and not remain imprisoned in his or her version of the past.

At the same time, it is what Group Relations conferences offer to the participants: learning from the experience, that we do act in the "Here and Now" as if we were meeting "Then and There" – in the case of these particular conferences – as Jews and Germans in the 1940th, maybe in a German town, where Jews are persecuted and deported, maybe in a camp.

The German way to the conferences

Different Processes in the German and in the Israeli Psychoanalytic communities had led to the idea of the necessity of this work.

Let me give you some elements for the German way to these conferences:

It is possible to describe three different phases in German Society concerning the attitude towards the Holocaust, as the historian Jörn Rüsen has suggested:[2]

1) The period right after the war, characterised by silence, "concealing knowledge and extra-territorialisation";
2) "Moral distancing" from the parents' generation in the second generation;
3) Third phase (after 1989): signs of a process of "historization and acknowledgement" of the Holocaust, the beginning of German integration of identity: "We were the perpetrators".

---

[2] In the following I refer to H. Beland, The Stages of the German Psychoanalysts on Their Way to the First Nazareth Conference, in: Fed with Tears – Poisoned with Milk, ed. by H. Shmuel Erlich, Mira Erlich-Ginor and H. Beland (2009), where he quotes J. Rüsen, p. 21.

Two aspects should be mentioned concerning the German Psycho-analytic community: The "inability to mourn" and the history of the German Psychoanalytic Groups and their split, after the war.

The "inability to mourn", was diagnosed and conceptualized by A. and M. Mitscherlich in post-war German Society. The painful acknowl-edgement had to be realized: this "inability to mourn" was applicable also to German Psychoanalysts as a group. As group members, the Psychoanalysts shared the "collective paralysis", the collective "inability to feel the own entanglement in the expulsion, dehumanization, and killing of the Jewish population"[3], of their own Jewish members who once had been so important for the founding of our Psychoanalytic Society and Institute (See Ludger Hermann's chapter 17: The one way road, an additional piece in the puzzle of German analysts post WWII).

The preparation for the first "Nazareth Conference" was marked therefore by the "strange experience that the individual process is always dependent on collectively held unconscious defensive attitudes."[4]

After the war the collective of the German Psychoanalysts had split into two groups: it is clear in retrospect that both groups were suffering from unconscious feelings of guilt and denied "an incredible depression, marked by the imputations of having betrayed Freud and having adapted to Nazi ideology during the twelve years of dictatorship".[5]

The split, and the recognition of one of the two Societies, the Associ-ation (DPV), by the IPA in 1951,- which I am a member of – and the non-recognition of the DPG, the original society, (which became a component society of the IPA only in 2009), allowed the illusion of the DPV being on the "side of persecuted psychoanalysis, and therefore almost belonging to the persecuted ones".[6]

This illusion collapsed when at the IPA congress in Jerusalem in 1977 the German invitation to the IPA to come to Berlin was rejected. The first congress of the IPA held in Germany took place in 1985 in Hamburg. For

---

[3] Ibid., p.22.
[4] Ibid.
[5] Ibid.
[6] Ibid., p.23.

this conference an exposition was prepared showing the history of the Psychoanalytic Society in Germany under Hitler – the shared past of our two psychoanalytic groups. The Nazareth Conference (and a Group Relations Conference of the two groups, in 1996, Seeon, Director: Ross Lazar) became an important element in the very slowly rapprochement of the two German psychoanalytic societies. The acknowledgement of the shared past and the process of assuming responsibility have been central for this move. In the Nazareth conferences, members of the two groups have cooperated from the beginning in the staff and membership for the first time, paving the way to work between them.

Experiences / Vignette and Comment

The group relation approach that we apply in our work, has several working hypotheses. I want to mention two of those:

- Everybody present in the conference is part of the field of experience and dynamic, no one remains outside; this is valuable for members and staff alike.
- Everybody brings in his / her personal factors, such as his / her history, identity, and his / her formal and informal, manifest and latent roles.

Working on a paper like the one I am presenting to you, I realise how difficult my German legacy makes it for me to express myself freely. Building on his experience of the Nazareth conferences, Hermann Beland, one of the co-founders of the project, has described this difficulty on the part of German psychoanalysts in taking up Freud's heritage – to speak and contribute to an exchange of thoughts and ideas in an international context. He suggests that this expresses a "typical German, paranoid complex of guilt" that is a legacy of the Holocaust. It is such phenomena that we try to grapple with in the Nazareth Conferences.

However, being involved with the work of such conferences also carries such destructive loadings that one might well wish to be elsewhere.

I will give you some examples of my own conference experiences. Specifically my experience as a member in the conference in 2004.

Being a member (2004) – here and now?

When I attended the conference "Shaping the future by confronting the past: Germans, Jews and affected Others" in Cyprus in 2004, I found myself sitting in a group of "Germans" at the beginning of the System Event (SE).[7] The System Event had started the second day, after we had already worked together in the Small Study Groups (SSG) and in the Large Study Group (LSG). Now the SE started in three sub-groups, as Germans – Israelis – and Others with the task to explore our "German-ness", "Israeli-ness" and "Other-ness", and to get in contact with the other groups.

After a short while an Israeli colleague entered our "German group", she wanted to join and to explore her "German-ness".

This session became a formative experience for me and was crucial to my ongoing involvement in this kind of work.

I became a member of a group of Germans, in which a discussion about two questions went on for endless 40 Minutes:

- The first question had to do with her presence: whether "she" could stay in our group or whether "she" would have to leave, since "she" was not German;
- The second question had to do with the language. The conference language was to be English, unless everybody in the room shares another language, the situation was formally clear: as long as we were all Germans, we could speak German, the moment a non German speaking person entered the room, the

---

[7] For the explanation of the different elements of the setting, such as the System Event, Large Group and Small Group etc. see the description of the structure and design of the conferences, as Mira Erlich-Ginor describes it in the chapter 18: "Psychoanalytic Group Work with Transgenerational Residues of Historic Traumatization: The Case of the German-Israeli Conferences" in this book.

language should switch into English. The question was whether we would have to speak English, "only because of 'her'".

In the quite chaotic, extremely excited situation no argument could be heard, no thinking was possible, and I felt more and more helpless. I felt I could not make an impact on the further development nor could I end the absurd discussion.

The situation ended, when the Israeli colleague, who had remained silent observing us, finally got up and said: "By the way I have a name, my name is …" Then she left crying, returning to "her" group, the Israeli colleagues.

After this had happened I could not remember the name of any of the conference **members** any more. I went around, asking people for their name, even of one of the **Israeli women**, which I had discovered on the first day of the conference that we had the same name, her name being the Hebrew version of my Greek rooted name, Dorothee.

Only when I realized this, could I make the connection to the group-event that had caused such confusion within me. As if I had become a member within a National-Socialist German group with no place for Jews and where my own identity had dissolved.

The language issue continued to be present in the conference; it turned to be a problem without solution.

Some German colleagues had the feeling that the Israeli colleagues were attacking the German group by sending members who could not speak German, while they could have send another colleague who could have spoken German.

In the next session a group of Israeli colleagues had asked for an Inter-Group meeting. The Israelis entered the room designated for this purpose in quite an excited state of mind. I felt their extreme anxiety.

This meeting was not helpful in clarifying the situation between the German and the Israeli group members. The meeting ended with the leaving of the Israeli delegation. I had the feeling that they had left in a horror, as if expelled from the German country – as if the difference in time and space collapsed. Some of my German colleagues believed, that they heard the Israeli colleagues laugh outside – immediately came the interpretation: "they" had laughed at "us".

That evening I was in a state of despair: the German-Jewish misery seemed to be in endless repetition without a way out.

You may ask, why and how such an experience can be important, what is it good for?

Comment

This was quite a frightening experience, but an experience that within the conference could be contained and borne with the help of the other members and the consultants. In the containing conference setting an event like this does not lead to the catastrophe of expulsion or annihilation, it does not lead to a raw, where people have to separate and leave one another.

In the safe environment of the conference it is possible to stay together and accept that each member of the group is a necessary part of the effort to understand what has happened to the group as a whole. It is a very painful process but one that can lead to further integration of the person's own history, the realization and acknowledgement that we are who we are, and that history has been as it has been, the facts cannot be changed, but they can be acknowledged and don't have to be denied.

I think, this kind of experience demonstrates how the position of the knowing subject can be suspended. The conference opens a possibility to another kind of understanding, to a process of social understanding, to which all group members belong. Each one has his / her part in it.

Sometimes a person may say something horrible, but in the context of the conference, there is the possibility to understand that even the "worst" and most painful contribution is made on behalf of the group. It does not help the process of understanding if the individual is excluded or punished or condemned, but it furthers our understanding if we try to understand that this group member has expressed an unconscious attitude that is present in the group, and that this element is important and a challenge for each one who is present to own.

For me this kind of experience has become the ground for my understanding of Bion's concept of the 'group mentality', where he also mentions the concept of collective guilt:

> Germans are told that they are responsible for the behaviour of all; of the Nazi government; silence, it is said, gives consent. Nobody is very happy about insisting on collective responsibility in this way, but I shall assume nevertheless, that unless a group activity disavows its leader it is, in fact, following him. In short, I shall insist that I am quite justified in saying that the group feels such and such when, in fact, perhaps only one or two people would seem to provide by their behaviour warrant for such a statement, if, at the time of behaving like this, the group show no outward sign of repudiating the lead they are given.[8]

I think it is important to keep this question open, keeping in mind that Bion is struggling here with the technical – and may be the ethical – question of an interpretation given to a group.

In Cyprus I could learn how this attitude can strengthen tolerance and liberate from feelings of envy: Strengthen Tolerance, because it can be experienced how the terrible things said by another person, belong to the group and its members, and thus also to myself. The valency of that other might have put him in the situation not to withhold an unconscious thought or attitude or phantasy anymore, and to give it an expression, so that it is out there. But it belongs to the group, to "us", it is not a "not me".

Liberation from feelings of envy, when it comes to the moment, where you can feel, that the desire to be the most bright participant, bringing the most significant expressions or important insights is lowered by the experience that it is not so important who says what – that it is definitely a social process that opens towards the possibility that an unconscious content finds an expression, no matter through whom, but

---

[8] W. Bion, Experiences in Groups (1948), in: Experiences in Groups and other papers, London (1961), reprint 2001, p58.

as a result of a group process. Equally it is possible to make the experience that a consultant gives an interpretation to one of the group members that I do not need to hear with an envious feeling as the interpretation is at the same time given to everybody present in the group and inviting further processing.

In short: the method incorporates the condition for the possibility to make the very important experience of being part in a learning process, in which many contribute and each one is a significant part that cannot be removed or replaced.

References

Bion, W. R. (1961). *Experiences in Groups And Other Papers.* London: Tavistock Publications Limited.

Erlich, H. S. Erlich-Ginor, M. & Beland, H. *Fed with Tears – Poisoned with Milk. The "Nazareth" Group-Relations-Conferences: Germans and Israelis: The Past in the Present.* Psychosozial Verlag: Gießen, 2009.